DAVID MATTHEWS

Essays, Tributes and Criticism

David Matthews (Clive Barda)

Poetics of Music

General Editor: Christopher Wintle

DAVID MATTHEWS
Essays, Tributes and Criticism

edited by

Thomas Hyde

Plumbago Books

2014

Plumbago Books and Arts
26 Iveley Road,
London SW4 0EW

plumbago@btinternet.com
www. plumbago.co.uk

Distribution and Sales:
Boydell & Brewer Ltd.
PO Box 9
Woodbridge
Suffolk IP12 3DF

trading@boydell.co.uk
tel. 01394 610 600
www.boydellandbrewer.com

Boydell and Brewer Inc.
668 Mount Hope Avenue
Rochester
NY 14620, USA

David Matthews. Essays, Tributes and Criticism
Edited by Thomas Hyde (1978-)
Poetics of Music, General Editor: Christopher Wintle (1945-)

First published 2014

ISBN: 978-0-9566007-6-9 (hardback), 978-0-9566007-8-3 (softback)

Typeset in Adobe Minion Pro by Julian Littlewood

Printed by ShortRun, Exeter

Contents

Part Two: Tributes

Part Three: Criticism

Above: Peter Pears with David Matthews in The Maltings, Snape (Nigel Luckhurst)
Below: Simon Rattle (left, holding a cup), Olivia Kilmartin, Arthur Campbell
and David Matthews (right) at Dartington, August 1978

Editor's Preface

In the preface to a collection of essays by the composer Hugh Wood, also published by Plumbago, Bayan Northcott points out that 'there are no autobiographical pieces … what we learn of Wood's musical life is incidental …' David Matthews's writings are in many respects the opposite. Put simply, Matthews is not a composer *and* writer on music: he is a composer who writes. And though, like Wood, he avoids analysing his own finished pieces, and only seldom provides detailed explanations of his compositional processes, he rarely discusses a topic without mentioning his own experience: an extended essay on the fugue ends with him 'declaring an interest'; the two pieces on Mahler reproduced here contain much biographical material on his involvement in the performing version of the Tenth Symphony; a discussion of Sibelius's symphonic thinking, so important to his own symphonic cycle, begins 'When I was ten years old, I went to my first symphony concert …' and a review of a book of twentieth-century musical sketches states 'in the past two days I have composed the draft of a short piece … its thirty-eight bars are written in pencil on both sides of a single sheet of paper'.

Fortunately, his skills as a writer ensure that this potentially self-promoting approach instead casts unique light on a topic. There is much to be gained from this; and it would perhaps be surprising to expect anything else from this particular composer. The approach gives Matthews's writing, at its best, a sense of urgent commitment: the reader knows that commentary and judgement are coming from an insider. And it is this quality, the happy overspill of Matthews's life as a composer into every other activity he undertakes, that has shaped this book. In the second chapter, 'Renewing the Past', Matthews describes how he became a composer and recalls the important figures in his development. Here, and in his subsequent writings, I have used endnotes to amplify the biographical elements. These notes include extracts from letters and private journals that explore further his working relationships with Benjamin Britten, Michael Tippett, Deryck Cooke, Hans Keller and others. Thus, a musical biography of the man, loosely chronological, is counterpointed with the man's writings.

As the bibliography indicates, the quantity of published words by David Matthews is almost as staggering as the quantity of his musical compositions. This volume therefore includes just a selection of his writings, grouped under three headings to form Part One. First, a set of essays surveys the compositional scene in a broadly historical fashion; a second set addresses the Western symphonic tradition, in particular Mahler and Sibelius; and finally a number of book reviews, mostly for the *Times Literary Supplement*, focus on individual composers. The aim has been to include texts that have particular relevance to Matthews's creative life or illumine his artistic approach. Needless to say, much has had to be excluded, not least on his love of the visual arts and poetry. But it is hoped this volume will lead the reader not only to Matthews's music, but also to his other writings.

Part Two contains a number of tributes from a few of his many collaborators, friends and composers reflecting the esteem in which he is held by so many. Two extended memoirs, by composer Peter Sculthorpe and philosopher Roger Scruton, chronicle friendships in which both the man and his music have proved inspirational. The essays of Part Three focus on aspects of the music itself, beginning with an overview of Matthews's output by Malcolm MacDonald. The symphonic cycle receives complementary readings by two analysts, Arnold Whittall and Edward Venn. Hugh Wood writes on a selection of the string quartets, while Geraint Lewis discusses some of the symphonic poems and concertos. The present writer reflects on Matthews's musical voice, and Frank Ward provides a light-hearted envoi.

Published to celebrate the composer's seventieth birthday in 2013, this volume reflects David Matthews's growing reputation in Britain and abroad. In recent years a large number of commercial recordings have ensured that more music lovers than ever now have access to his works. Music is composed to be performed and heard. I hope that this volume will encourage readers to discover, or return to, David Matthews's music with curiosity and enthusiasm.

Thomas Hyde
London, June 2013

Acknowledgements

My first thanks must go to David Matthews himself, who has supported this project from start to finish. His extensive personal archive has made research and assembly much easier than it would otherwise have been. Though, understandably, he has refrained from interfering with the overall content, he has been meticulous in reading drafts and revising his own writings. His permission to reproduce extracts from his private journals has allowed me to add a personal flavour to the first part of the book.

Christopher Wintle has been essential to the process, both as general editor and founding director of Plumbago Books. His vast academic and editorial experience has proved vital in leading this novice through the various tangles that appear in a project of this complexity. Thanks, too, to his staff, especially to Kate Hopkins for proof-reading and Julian Littlewood for typesetting.

Faber Music have been publishers of David Matthews's music since the 1980s and have been nothing but supportive. I am particularly grateful to Sally Cavender for general co-ordination and dispatch of scores to the contributors. Her continued advocacy of David's music over the years has been of unrivalled importance.

Various individuals and organisations have contributed financially to this book. These include Anthony Bolton, Justin Broackes, Carl Davis, Virginia Grace, Robbie Lamming, Robin Leanse, Sir Paul McCartney and the Lucille Graham Trust. My thanks to them all, as also to Edward Clark, the composer's personal manager, who led the fundraising and helped ensure targets were met, and Ninfea Cruttwell-Reade, my former student who carefully prepared the musical examples. Jenifer Wakelyn, David Matthews's wife, proved a crucial supporter of the project from the outset and a scrupulous proof-reader of several drafts. Dr Nick Attfield (Brunel University, London), Dr Rachel Moore (Junior Research Fellow at Worcester College, Oxford) and Dr Ben Winters (Open University) all read drafts and made valuable comments. I also gratefully acknowledge Antony Bye (editor of the *Musical Times*), Roger Scruton (Claridge Press and *Salisbury Review*), Robert Matthew-Walker (editor of *Musical Opinion*), the *London Review of Books*, the *Times Literary Supplement*, Boydell & Brewer Ltd. and Cambridge University Press.

Finally, my thanks to all the contributors. This project was very much a collaborative effort, and has been all the more enjoyable for it. Any outstanding errors are my responsibility.

~

I gratefully acknowledge publishers' permission to reproduce extracts from the following scores:

Benjamin Britten: *Death in Venice*, Op. 88, 1977; String Quartet No. 3, Op. 94, 1977: Faber Music Ltd.

David Matthews: Symphony No. 1, Op. 9, (1975-78, rev. 2007) 2010; Symphony No. 3, Op. 37, 1987; Chaconne, Op. 43, 1988; Symphony No. 6, Op. 100, 2007; *Journeying Songs* Op. 95, 2008; Symphony No. 7, Op. 109, 2010; *Dark Pastoral*, Op. 112, 2010; String Quartet No. 12, Op. 114, 2011: Faber Music Ltd. *September Music*, Op. 24, 1982: Boosey & Hawkes Ltd.

John McCabe: *April Sonatina*, 2013: Novello & Company Ltd, all rights reserved, international copyright secured.

Judith Weir: Partita for solo viola, 2013: Chester Music Ltd, all rights reserved, international copyright secured.

TH

Publisher's Note

We always aim to use photographs by permission. However, it is not always possible to identify or contact the owners, and we invite interested parties to come forward with reasonable and substantiated claims.

The cover portrait, like the frontispiece, is by Clive Barda.

CW

Part One

David Matthews:
Selected Essays

The young David Matthews (Maurice Foxall)

Surveying the Scene

1   At 70: A Report on Progress

Approaching 70, I feel I still have much to learn about the craft of composition, which would take more than a lifetime to master. I was not taught harmony or counterpoint formally, but learned both gradually through composing. Counterpoint has always seemed to me to be central to composition, so I am glad now to be able to use it with some confidence.

My music is closely related to my own life, and to my feelings and emotions. This is Romantic, but I try to objectify my feelings through the use of classical forms. My first concern has always been with the symphony and allied forms such as the string quartet: the comprehensive, large-scale instrumental piece that has a relation to classical symphonic form, and is developed using procedures related to classical tonality. I have always been a tonal composer, but I feel more relaxed now about using tonality than I did when I started to compose.

I find it natural to use traditional forms, and think it important to try to uphold them. I don't do this unselfconsciously; I am aware of the course of musical history of the last century. But a period dominated by narrow ideas of modernism is over, and we are rediscovering links with the past, among which the symphonic tradition seems to me one of the most important.

I have recently begun to use birdsong quite extensively in my music, both of the birds I hear singing from my garden, and also of Australian birds, which interest me particularly because of their distinctly melodious songs. Using birdsong brings me closer to nature, which is one of the main inspirations for my music.

I am happy to think of myself as an English composer, because I believe that all good music has local roots. At the same time, English composers have always been eclectics, taking from elsewhere what interested them most. My strongest affinities are still probably with the central European composers who were my first heroes: Beethoven, Wagner and Mahler – and above all Sibelius, whose transformation of his symphonic inheritance, and whose personal development from Romanticism to Classicism, has always seemed to me a paradigm of what a post-Romantic composer can achieve.

Notes

Source: Unpublished manuscript. David Matthews was born on 9 March 1943 in Walthamstow, London, and brought up in nearby Leytonstone. His parents were from lower-middle and working-class backgrounds. Not having had higher education themselves, they were anxious that David and his younger brother Colin (b. 1946) should. After attending the local primary school they both won scholarships at the age of eleven to a minor public school, Bancroft's School in Woodford. Both boys had piano lessons, though both gave up (David at the age of thirteen) and spent the next few years listening only to the new rock and roll music. At sixteen David rediscovered classical music through radio broadcasts and, having bought a recording of Beethoven's Ninth Symphony at Christmas 1959, began to compose his own symphony. Since music was not taught at their school, David could not consider reading music at university, so read Classics at Nottingham University from 1962 until 1965. Following graduation, David considered working as a music critic and gained freelance work with help from Deryck Cooke. During this period, he also undertook private composition studies with Anthony Milner and in 1967 received his first professional performance when a string quartet (since withdrawn) was premiered by the Dartington Quartet. His first orchestral performance took place in January 1970 when two orchestral songs were premiered by Jane Manning with the London Philharmonic conducted by Norman Del Mar under the auspices of the Society for the Promotion of New Music.

2   Renewing the Past: Some Personal Thoughts

An individual composer cannot predict the course of musical history, nor can he or she tell others how they are to compose. But since composers are no longer the natural inheritors of a tradition and of a musical language they can unthinkingly adopt, they must choose their own particular language themselves and also work out their relation with the past, and in doing so, they will inevitably acquire an overall view of what music, from their perspective, should be. My own view is founded on a few central principles, which were unfashionable at the time I began to write music in the mid-1960s but which now, at the start of the twenty-first century, have come to seem quite legitimate, except to those diminishing few who attempt to hold on to the rigid prescriptions and proscriptions of modernism. These are: that tonality is not outmoded but a living force; that the vernacular is an essential part of musical language; and that the great forms of the past, such as the symphony, are still valid. The remainder of this essay will attempt to elaborate and justify these three propositions.

It hardly needs to be said now that the proclaimed dogma of the post-Second World War avant-garde that tonality was dead was mistaken. Tonality flourishes again everywhere, and by no means only in the simplistic form adopted by the minimalists. My own attitude to tonality, in one sense, is straightforward: I hear music tonally, so it would seem perverse to resist what I hear. Although many passages in my music move away into regions where a sense of tonality is lost, I am always compelled eventually to bring the music back to a tonal centre. I am conscious of a balance to be preserved between stability and instability. When I listen to non-tonal music, it is very difficult for me to hear it except in relation to tonality: non-tonal music seems fundamentally unstable. This seems quite reasonable if one hears music as an expressive language, as I do. The alternative is to hear it as pure sound, which my ears will not allow me to do.

The temporary eclipse of tonality began with Schoenberg, who obsessively pursued the advanced chromaticism of *Tristan* and *Parsifal* to its logical conclusion, where extreme emotional states could be expressed by means of a totally chromatic musical language, free from any sense of tonal stability. His Mosaic, law-giver's personality led him to codify this Expressionist language, which had been an ideal vehicle for the nightmare worlds of *Erwartung* and *Pierrot lunaire*, and to propose his new method of composition based on the equality of all twelve notes of the scale as a wholesale replacement for the tonal system. Schoenberg's authority was such that he and his successors have had an enormous influence on the music of the second half of the twentieth century. This is a curious phenomenon: as Deryck Cooke remarked, it was 'as though the whole main modern movement in literature had taken Joyce's *Finnegans*

Wake as its starting point.'[1] Schoenberg's belief in the comprehensiveness of his system ('every expression and characterisation can be produced with the style of free dissonance')[2] was, however, mistaken: the musical modernism that stemmed from him is almost invariably limited to a narrow range of expression, which stays at a pitch of high tension, and cannot naturally evoke states of joy, gaiety, exuberance.

This might be called the common sense view of Schoenberg, but I think it is nevertheless true. It is, of course, a simplification, ignoring, for instance, the deep attachment Schoenberg retained to tonality which means that none of his serial works – the late ones especially – are entirely free from tonal references. He did not go as far as Berg, the modernist composer whom everyone loves, who reconciled serial technique with tonality by deliberately choosing twelve-note rows with tonal implications and using these rows with great freedom, and who was thus able to combine Expressionism with late-Romantic eroticism and tenderness. The purist Webern, on the other hand, abolished all sense of tonality, and his serial works really do breathe the air from other planets. Other, later classics of serial modernism such as Boulez's *Le Marteau sans maître*, Stockhausen's *Gruppen* and Stravinsky's *Aldous Huxley Variations* inhabit a world of intellect and refined sensation, but one remote from human feeling. It was a path that, pursued further, could only lead to sterility; and it is interesting that Boulez (for instance in *Rituel*) and Stockhausen (in *Inori*) have both made some accommodation with tonality, and Stravinsky in his final work *Requiem Canticles* partly reverted to the harmonic world of his earlier music.

Modernism in all the arts has often mirrored the isolated, anguished state that the twentieth-century artist found himself in. While a sense of isolation is almost inevitable, given the breakdown of a common culture, does it follow that all serious artists must also be afflicted with existential angst? There is a genuine art to be made out of existential despair (for instance the early works of Peter Maxwell Davies), but composers should beware of the self-indulgent use of an extreme language, which should not be an easy option. On the other hand, it seems particularly difficult nowadays to take an opposite standpoint. In writing tonal music and trying through it to express the sheer joy and exuberance I often feel at the fact of being alive, was I simply being naive, out of touch with the modern world? I was encouraged in what I was attempting to do by hearing the music of Michael Tippett and reading his writings on music. Tippett in the 1930s opted to be a tonal composer of a strongly conservative kind, using melodies derived from folksong and aiming at a classicism modelled ultimately on Beethoven. In an article in 1938 he had written:

> An artist can certainly be in opposition to the external 'spirit of the
> age' and in tune with some inner need, as, for instance, Blake was. A

composer's intuitions of what his age is really searching for may be, and probably will be, not in the least such obvious things as the portrayal of stress and uncertainty by grim and acid harmonies. The important thing ... is that he should be in some living contact with the age.[3]

Tippett associated tonal stability with psychological wholeness, which he himself achieved through a rigorous course of Jungian self-analysis. The split psyche associated with modern man, on the other hand, found its most appropriate means of expression in atonality. What Tippett said, and the music he wrote that demonstrated his beliefs, such as *The Midsummer Marriage*, made perfect sense to me, though ironically in the late 1960s he seemed to be betraying his ideals in a quest for novelty. It is significant that he later regretted some of his more extreme experiments, and in old age reverted to a much more stable kind of music, culminating in his last piece, the serenely beautiful *The Rose Lake*.

~

Although as a young composer I had no wish to follow Boulez or Stockhausen, I was, as a romantic adolescent, immersed in the early works of Schoenberg, Berg and Webern, in Scriabin and Szymanowski, in Strauss's *Salome* and *Elektra*, and above all in the symphonies of Mahler, who was the most important influence on the music I began to compose. My music became highly chromatic and had a strong flavour of pre-war Vienna. I sensed the need to purify this language with a strong dose of classicism, but I was not clear how it was to be done. In the early 1970s I reached a compositional crisis and for several years was unable to finish a work that satisfied me. Around that time I met the Australian composer Peter Sculthorpe and became his composing assistant for several years. In 1974 he invited me to come and stay in his house in Sydney.[4] Living there for several months, as far away from Europe as it was possible to get, had a profound effect on me: I was able to look at Europe with a detachment never before possible. From Australia, with its relaxed way of life, its burgeoning new culture and its strong belief in itself, the contemporary culture of Europe seemed exaggeratedly neurotic. Hearing European modernist music in Australia, it sounded bizarre: why all this tension and agitation? I was not so laid-back as to imagine that music could do without tension altogether, but a certain redressing of the balance seemed necessary. Peter's own music, which combined European and Asian influences, achieved an equilibrium of Romantic expressiveness and Classical poise. Peter reminded me that contemporary European music was an exception to the rest of the world, where a stable, tonal basis to music had never been called into question. Although the particular manner of his music has always seemed an ocean's distance from my own, Peter has been one of the strongest influences on my subsequent development, and I hold his compositions in the highest regard.

D. H. Lawrence's perception of Australia as an untouched land where life 'had never entered in' but was 'just sprinkled over' remains largely true, and the real subject of all Australian art is the extraordinary Australian landscape.[5] But the European artist cannot free himself entirely either from history – of which our man-made and man-ravaged landscapes speak eloquently – or from musical history. Minimalism, a born-again tonal language that disregards the past, is not really suited to Europe: though a product of New York, it seems most at home in California where the sun shines and the burden of history weighs lightly. Minimalism is a secular, hedonistic music: the so-called 'holy minimalism' we have in Europe, in the music of Pärt, Górecki and Tavener, is different in essence; but these composers have also tried to escape the past, or at least the past since the Renaissance, reverting to medieval Christian ideals much as the Pre-Raphaelites tried to do in the nineteenth century. Like Pre-Raphaelitism, theirs is a somewhat artificial stance, though the strength of all three composers' religious convictions gives a depth to their music, which might otherwise sound dangerously thin. I recognise the value of traditional religious faith to provide a foundation for art: those who have such faith are enviably secure, and their art will reflect this (in music, Messiaen is the best recent example). Speaking for myself, however, I cannot ignore either the Renaissance or Romanticism, both of which represented huge and irreversible strides away from Christianity and its central doctrine of man's reliance on God and the Church for salvation, and towards a conception of man on his own, self-reliant, though able to discover the divine element that is within us. This was already inherent in the humanism of the Renaissance, and became the philosophy of Romanticism. Because of its over-optimistic idealisation of human potential, Romanticism failed to bring about the wholesale transformation of mankind that many of its proponents hoped for, but that does not mean that there is any other real substitute for its essential beliefs.

Beethoven still seems to me the ideal of the modern composer. He won through his personal anguish towards a profound spirituality in the *Missa Solemnis* and the late sonatas and string quartets that is the equal of the unselfconscious spirituality of medieval music, but which he achieved by himself. His dramatic use of tonality within sonata form, whose parameters he expanded enormously in his late works, made his spiritual quest in music possible. Wagner attempted a similar path, expanding Beethoven's forms still further into music drama. His great achievement was the comprehensiveness of his musical language: he developed chromaticism to an unprecedented level of expressive power, so that, for the first time, the overwhelming force of sexuality finds its full musical equivalent; but alongside this precarious chromaticism is a stable, elemental diatonicism. In *Parsifal* the struggle between eroticism and spirituality is finally resolved in the latter's favour, in a sublimated A♭ major. Whether Wagner achieved true spirituality in *Parsifal* is still a controversial topic, which it is impossible to pursue here; but the immense yearning for transcendence in the work cannot be denied. The same conflict between body and spirit, between disruptive chromaticism and stabilising diatonicism, is found in Mahler, Wagner's truest successor; but Mahler was less in thrall to sensuality than Wagner and there is a more natural spiritual quality to his music. Mahler's attitude to tonality, as a drama mirroring the drama of life, is, like Wagner's, indebted to Beethoven. The drama is eventually resolved: triumphantly, as in the majority of the symphonies; tragically, as in the Sixth; or transcendentally, as in *Das Lied von der Erde* or the Ninth. This dramatic approach still seems to me to be valid, even if one chooses not to work on such a large scale as Mahler – which is wise advice for most composers.

What I suggest (once again to compress a huge topic into a few sentences) is that, if tonality is to regain its full power, it must be used dynamically again. Most contemporary tonal music is static; but stasis, it seems to me, is ideally a condition to be achieved – as, for instance, in Beethoven's last piano sonata, where the static, contemplative slow movement is heard as a consequence of the dynamic drama of the first movement. The dynamic use of tonality will involve both modulation and the rediscovery of dissonance as a disruptive force. Although one can no longer easily define the difference between consonance and dissonance, it is still possible to conceive of harmony as either stable or unstable. Unless there are real harmonic contrasts in a piece it cannot have dynamic movement. Perhaps because our most frequent experience of movement nowadays is as passengers in cars, trains or planes, observing the landscape speeding by while we ourselves remain still, most fast movement in contemporary music, whether tonal or atonal, is merely rapid motion without any involvement of physical energy. Fast music in the past was related to the movement of the body, walking, running or dancing. The fundamental importance of dance to music is something I shall return to later.

It was Schoenberg who also brought about the other revolutionary change in twentieth-century Western music when he renounced the use of the musical vernacular. Throughout its history, European art music maintained a close contact with folk music, on which its modal and diatonic melodies were based, and there was no unbridgeable gap between serious music and popular, right up to the beginning of the twentieth century. Schoenberg himself had used diatonic melody naturally and skilfully in his early works, notably in *Gurrelieder*. In the scherzo of his Second String Quartet, the work in which he brought tonality to its breaking point, Schoenberg quotes the well-known Viennese popular song 'O, du lieber Augustin' and makes a point of repeating its refrain 'Alles ist hin' ('it's all over'). For Schoenberg now, the use of the diatonic vernacular was indeed over: he banished it from his subsequent, non-tonal music, except once or twice as a ghostly, poignant memory (as in *Pierrot lunaire*). Schoenberg still based his music on melody, but on the chromatic melodies he derived from his note rows (it is impossible to believe they are not in some way synthetic). Webern, once again, went further than Schoenberg in virtually excluding recognisable melody from his serial music, and the post-war Darmstadt composers, under the influence of Adorno, turned Webern's composing principles into a creed. Adorno's neo-Marxist argument was that 'mass culture', which includes popular culture, based on tonal clichés, is another bourgeois-imposed opiate, a device for keeping the masses in subjection; serious composers therefore should have nothing to do with this corrupt musical language and so must embrace its opposite, serialism, an esoteric high art music for the elite.[6]

This was a drastic over-simplification: tonal clichés and bad popular music are one thing, to reject all post-Mahlerian tonal music including Sibelius and the neoclassical Stravinsky, as Adorno did, is quite another. Just as with the arguments against tonality, we can now see that these ideas, which for a time sustained modernism at least as a valid musical style, are, as general principles, simply erroneous. Jazz and popular music are an integral part of twentieth-century art and Gershwin and Ellington, for instance, are two of the century's most significant composers. Tippett, who was the last major British composer to use folksong as a foundation for his music, was also one of the first in this country to realise that blues and jazz – and later, rock – could be a viable alternative vernacular to folksong. This idea had already been adopted by the *Neue Sachlichkeit* composers of Weimar Germany. By the time Tippett began to compose, folksong had died out as a living force, except in the remotest parts of Britain. But it did not simply disappear into the museum culture of the Cecil Sharp Society and Morris dancing. In the 1950s and 1960s young, mostly urban people began to revive folk music at the same time as they began to listen to and to play rock, the new popular music derived from black American blues and white Country and Western music. Blues, rock and folksong from Britain and North America united into a new vernacular language. It is a true vernacular, for its music has largely been written by the musicians who sing and play it, unlike the popular music of the first half of the century, which was for the most part the product of non-executant composers.

Tippett's use of the blues as a vernacular, for instance in *A Child of Our Time* and the Third Symphony, is successful because he grew up with the blues as a natural language. He was less happy with rock, because he did not grow up with it, and I find his introduction of the electric guitar into his opera *The Knot Garden* faintly embarrassing, even if I warm to his intentions. My own generation, those born during and immediately after the Second World War, encountered the beginnings of rock as we were emerging from childhood into adolescence, and for many of us it was a crucial event. Some of my earliest genuine musical experiences were of hearing mid-1950s rock – Elvis Presley and Little Richard: the effect on me of this wildly orgiastic music, so different from anything I had encountered in my cosy suburban childhood, was overwhelming. The Beatles were hearing and absorbing this music at the same time, as well as older types of popular music, and they seem to have inherited the folksong tradition instinctively (Paul McCartney has told me that he did not remember hearing any folksongs while he was growing up).[7] One of the earliest recorded Beatles' songs, 'I saw her standing there', is, as Wilfrid Mellers has remarked, pure folk monody: an utterly simple four-note melody with prominent flattened sevenths.[8] It was through hearing songs like this that my generation was reintroduced to the folk tradition.

In listening to rock music, I rediscovered the elemental power of tonality. Rock musicians, ignorant of musical history, used the triad as Monteverdi had used it at the start of *L'Orfeo*, as if it were a freshly-minted sound. Taking their cue from rock music, the minimalists too used the triad in this way. Both showed that even the most over-exploited musical cliché can be renewed from a state of innocence. The majority of composers, myself included, are not innocent in this way, yet any language handled with real confidence can have validity: conviction can overcome self-consciousness. I agree with Alfred Schnittke when he writes: 'Contemporary reality will make it necessary to experience all the musics one has heard since childhood, including rock and jazz and classical and all other forms, combining them into a synthesis … The synthesis must arise as a natural longing, or through necessity.'[9] Schnittke's own work went a long way in putting these ideas into practice. Many others are thinking along similar lines. The vernacular has indeed been rehabilitated, and if all is again open to us, then the renewal of melody, which is contemporary music's most serious need, may be possible. For the loss of accessible, singable melody in the music of Schoenberg and his successors was a devastating blow to its comprehensibility. The masterpieces of European music in the past all had an immediately accessible surface layer, which was primarily the melodic line. The fact that the majority of the musical public are as likely to miss the deeper, structural level in Beethoven as they are in Boulez is not an argument against the desirability of an accessible surface, for Beethoven's melodies are the keys that give access to the deeper levels of his music.

The contemporary Western vernacular may not be much help here, for contemporary rock music demonstrates an increasing impoverishment of melody (as Roger Scruton has convincingly argued in *The Aesthetics of Music*),[10] and indeed of rhythm and harmony, so that it now offers meagre rewards to anyone who wants to make use of it. My own generation was more fortunate. It may be that the necessary renewal of melody will come from outside Western culture, from parts of the world where a living folk tradition still flourishes, one that has not yet been exploited and corrupted by commercialism. Whatever way, it must happen, for unless our musical culture is once again founded on melody, it is moribund.

Postmodernism, then, permits a return to music of all the elements that modernism proclaimed were done with forever. But if we are all postmodernists now, we should not be superficial in our attitude to the past, parading styles like dressing up in old clothes. Much postmodernist art ransacks the past indiscriminately, with little sense of history. A more responsible attitude is to attempt to integrate the present with the past by re-establishing a continuity with those of its forms that contain the greatest accumulation of historical meaning. I have been much concerned throughout my composing life with two of these forms, the symphony and the string quartet. The first is a public form, the second private, but they share the same Classical archetype, which is so well-known that almost everyone who listens to music will have some notion of what a symphony or string quartet should be. According to Hans Keller's useful theory, the richest kind of musical experience is provided by 'the meaningful contradiction of expectation'.[11] This assumes that the listener will have some idea of what to expect, so he will be pleasurably surprised by the contradictions that an inventive composer will provide. If on the other hand you attempt to be wholly new, then no real surprises are possible. To write a movement in sonata form is somewhat daunting, as you are competing with – and almost inevitably failing to equal – the many supreme examples of such movements from the past. But it gives you access to a world where meaningful contradiction has been practised for two-and-a-half centuries. Although many of the devices of confounding expectation have been over-exploited and have themselves become clichés, it is not impossible to renew them by inner conviction; and there are still new games to play.

One game nineteenth-century composers played was with the repeat of the exposition. Up to Beethoven's time, this was a formality. Beethoven was the first to dispense with it, for instance in the first 'Rasumovsky' Quartet, Op. 59, No. 1. In the opening movement, he pretends to repeat the opening of the exposition; then, just when we have accepted this, the music sheers off into the development.[12] Throughout the nineteenth century composers either continued to use the repeat convention, which, because it was no longer taken for granted, could itself become a surprise, as in Mahler's First Symphony, or else devised cunning ways of disguising their intention not to repeat – an outstanding example is in the first movement of Dvořák's Eighth Symphony. In the finale of my own Fourth Symphony, a modified sonata movement, I have taken the game a stage further. The exposition begins to repeat, but after three bars it goes off into what sounds like the development. After less than three bars of this, however, there is a pause and the exposition material begins again, though not exactly as before, so there is still a little confusion. After six bars, following this triple bluff, we are finally launched into a proper repeat – except that it is a quadruple bluff: for this repeat is not quite an exact one either!

My Fourth Symphony contains two scherzos in its five-movement scheme, both of which have connections with the contemporary vernacular. The first, in a hard-driving tempo, is based on fragments of melody that could be from rock music, while the second is a tango, which I thought of as a contemporary substitute for the Classical minuet. The tango has been used by composers (including Stravinsky and Martinů) since the 1920s, and it seems to me to be an ideal type, with the infectious rhythms and erotic overtones that the waltz and the minuet once possessed, but which have been dulled by time. What is crucial is that dance rhythms must find their way back into contemporary music. Dance was another of post-war modernism's puritanical exclusions, because of its supposed tainted association with popularism. But music began with song and dance, and however sophisticated it becomes, it must never lose touch with these essential human activities. The Classical symphony achieved an equilibrium between mind and body by following an initial sonata allegro, where the intellect was dominant, with two movements, a song and a dance; the finale was then often a movement of play, with the body's energy enhanced by the intellect's games.

Because the Classical style produced nothing of great value in this country and our own symphonic tradition only truly began with Elgar, today it may be easier to write symphonies and string quartets in Britain than in Germany or Austria. The symphonies of Vaughan Williams and Tippett, and the string quartets of Tippett and Britten, represent outstanding innovatory attitudes towards these forms. It is not fully appreciated just how rich a quartet culture there is currently in Britain, with many young ensembles of the highest quality keen to include new works within their repertoire. The typical concert in which a contemporary string quartet is played alongside works by Haydn, Mozart, Beethoven or Schubert is, to my mind, a most rewarding experience: the new work often gains in juxtaposition with the old, through the stimulating contrasts in style and technique within the same medium. The string quartet, perhaps even more than the symphony, seems infinitely capable of renewal, and I should be content to write nothing but string quartets for the rest of my life, the possibilities for variation within this most satisfyingly balanced of ensembles being so rich. In my Ninth String Quartet, a tango is succeeded by a 'moto perpetuo' which ends with a reference to the style of the Irish reel, a folk form that is still exuberantly alive.

Composers can never know how their audiences will hear their music; they can be certain that it will not be as they hear it. Although I do not think of the audience when I am composing, but only of the notes I'm writing, and sometimes of the players I'm writing them for, I do seek a creative dialogue with my audience, and hope for some kind of appreciative understanding of what I am trying to do. The deliberate refusal of some modernist composers to engage with an audience, and the consequent unintelligibility of their music is, I think, a sad feature of contemporary musical life. It has never been the attitude of more than a small minority, but it has done great damage in making the very notion of 'contemporary music' a frightening prospect for many listeners. Repairing the damage has always been one of my chief concerns, and I dream of a time when, as in the past, contemporary music will once again be the focus of interest for the majority of concert audiences. It is probably a fanciful dream, but its only chance of fulfilment is in the hands of composers.

Notes

Source: *Reviving the Muse: Essays on Music after Modernism*, ed. Peter Davison, Brinkworth, Claridge Press, 2001, pp. 199-212.

1   Deryck Cooke, *Vindications: Essays on Romantic Music*, London, Faber and Faber, 1986, p. 195.

2   Arnold Schoenberg, *Style and Idea: Selected Writings of Arnold Schoenberg*, ed. Leonard Stein, London, Faber and Faber, 1975, p. 245.

3   'Music and Life' in: Michael Tippett, *Music of the Angels*, London, Eulenberg Books, 1980, p. 33.

4   Matthews first met Peter Sculthorpe (b. 1929) in 1972 when Sculthorpe was Visiting Professor at Sussex University and Matthews was living nearby in Burwash, Sussex. The first work Matthews assisted on was Sculthorpe's theatre piece *Rites of Passage*, commissioned for the opening of the Sydney Opera House. Matthews writes:

> Peter Sculthorpe came in the morning, and we had a session on his music, which I am editing. He is somatatonic but quietly spoken, open and friendly, but also quite nervous. His music seems to be exactly true to his temperament: the Australian landscape, sea, stars, hot wide plains, *lento e calmo*, but in the middle a brooding, solitary man, *angoscioso*. I like this music; it is a genuine expression, and the kind of language he uses is right for what he wants to say. We had a good lunch on the lawn (at last it was warm enough) on my home-made bread and cheese. (*Journal*, 1 June 1972)

> We talked about his Sydney Opera House work *Rites of Passage*. He is rather unsure about what instruments to use. I advised him not to give up using brass as he was thinking of doing: strings & percussion wouldn't seem to be a weighty enough accompaniment for such an epic piece as he plans. His ideas about the nature of the work are absolutely right for an Australian opera. He says, correctly, 'Australia has no tragic heroes, only solitude'. And so impersonal ritual rather than personal drama. (*Journal*, 9 June 1972)

5   D. H. Lawrence, letter to Else Jaffe, 13 June 1922, in: *The Collected Letters of D. H. Lawrence*, ed. Harry T. Moore, London, Heinemann, 1962, Vol. 2, p. 707.

6   Roger Scruton, *The Aesthetics of Music*, Oxford, Oxford University Press 1997, pp. 468-72.

7   Matthews assisted Paul McCartney (b. 1942) on several projects, most notably the choral-orchestral work *Standing Stone*. Matthews later contributed a choral work, *The Doorway of the Dawn*, Op. 76, to *A Garland for Linda* in memory of Linda McCartney. Matthews writes:

> Horrid rainy day. Went down to E. Sussex to see Paul McCartney at his studio farm near Icklesham. He was affable & very open & we talked easily for nearly 2 hours. He is writing a symphonic piece of some kind (he was quite vague about it & I don't think he knows yet what kind of piece it's going to be) for the Hallé [later the London Symphony Orchestra], & I'd been asked to go to see him with a view to being its orchestrator ... He showed me round the studio he has built, very well equipped – & his collection of instruments, among them the bass played by Bill Black for the Elvis Presley songs. He picked it up & played & sang 'Heartbreak Hotel' on it – that was rather a treat. (*Journal*, 17 January 1995)

> Another session with Paul McC, who played me 'Yesterday' and 'When I'm 64' on the piano during our session, & talked about his recent reunion of the other 2 surviving Beatles to fill out one of John Lennon's last demo tapes – he confessed to being worried about the propriety of doing that, but said how enjoyable it had been to be a Beatle again – I can imagine. He will never find a substitute. (*Journal*, 27 February 1995)

> Session at Hog Hill with Paul. In one of his asides he told me that the line 'The movement you need is on your shoulder' in 'Hey Jude' was a makeshift which he intended to replace, but John told him to keep it as that was the best line in the song – so he did. (*Journal*, 13 December 1996)

> To Hog Hill via Hastings, where met Steven Isserlis, who had come to play my arrangement of Paul's song 'Here Today' with me. We practised it and 4 other Beatles songs which Steven had brought with him, arrangements by his sister. Then Paul arrived & we played then through to him, & he joined in on 'Got to get you into my life' on drums – his replica of Ringo's drumkit. Rather a good moment. Steven, who is a much more knowledgeable fan than me, got a lot of 1st-hand Beatles anecdotes & was obviously thrilled – I felt v. pleased at being able to do this. (*Journal*, 7 December 1998)

8   Wilfrid Mellers, *Twilight of the Gods*, London, Faber and Faber, 1973, pp. 34-5.

9   Alfred Schnittke, *Tempo* 151, December 1984, p. 11.

10   Roger Scruton, *op.cit.*, pp. 500-06.

11   A full explanation of the theory can be found in: Hans Keller, *1975 (1984 minus 9)*, Dennis Dobson, 1977, pp. 136-39. Matthews became acquainted with Hans Keller (1919-85) through Deryck Cooke, and dedicated his Piano Trio No. 1, Op. 34 (1983) to him. In his diaries he writes:

> Lunch with Deryck Cooke. Hans Keller joined us & discussed the prospects of betting on England drawing tonight's international (they did) – he is several hundred pounds up since he started putting his football knowledge to practical uses a few seasons ago. We had an argument about Schoenberg:

to my contention that in later (12-note) Schoenberg there are not exhibited those qualities of greatness which are apparent (albeit in somewhat embryo form) in the early works & at least are not entirely absent from the middle-period pieces, HK replied: "if someone were to tell you that Beethoven's Op. 18 quartets were superior to the late ones you wouldn't bother to argue" – after which my side of the argument lost much of its vigour. He admits to having the same experience from late Schoenberg as from late Beethoven. I cannot even see an analogy between the spiritual worlds of Schoenberg & Beethoven … but leaving this aside, how is it possible to make objective judgements on music as controversial as Schoenberg's at present? The answer is it is not. Naturally I think my judgements objective as well as subjective – at least I can hardly help myself thinking so – but HK's are equally valid, as is presumably his verdict on Sibelius: "a master but he means nothing to me". Now why does Sibelius mean nothing to him when I find him immensely affecting? Why don't all musicians (at least!) have the same responses? (*Journal*, 15 January 1969)

Lunch with Deryck Cooke and Colin [Matthews]. Another discussion on Schoenberg … Enter Hans, who directed the conversation to soccer where it remained while he did. It is hard to say whom he admires most, Schoenberg or Jimmy Greaves, but these would appear to be the twin poles of his life. (*Journal*, 29 January 1969)

12   Keller describes this procedure and its relation to later composers in: Hans Keller, *Essays on Music*, ed. Christopher Wintle, Cambridge, Cambridge University Press, 1994, pp. 185.

3   'The Rest is Noise'
(book review)

The premiere of Arnold Schoenberg's *Gurrelieder* at the Musikverein in Vienna on 23 February 1913 was a triumph. Schoenberg's two-hour work for soloists, chorus and the largest orchestra anyone had ever used took him over ten years to complete: he had begun the composition in 1900, but the orchestration was not finished until 1911. Meanwhile his music had changed from opulent late-Romanticism to the Expressionist atonality of *Erwartung* and *Pierrot lunaire*. Public performances of the orchestral tone-poem *Pelleas und Melisande* and the First and Second String Quartets had been greeted with bewilderment and some hostility. But this evening was different: as the music reached its sumptuous C major conclusion, the audience burst into ecstatic applause and rose to their feet, their cheers mingling with shouts of "Schoenberg! Schoenberg!" The composer, however, was nowhere to be seen. Eventually he walked to the podium and bowed to the orchestra. But he turned his back on the audience, refusing to acknowledge them. As his friend the violinist Francis Aranyi said, it was "the strangest thing that a man in front of that kind of a hysterical, worshipping mob has ever done".

It was, nonetheless, a calculated response. A month later, a concert in the same Musikverein including Schoenberg's First Chamber Symphony of 1906 and recent works by his pupils Alban Berg and Anton Webern was brought to a halt by a near-riot during the attempted premiere of Berg's *Altenberg Lieder*. The police had to be called and a lawsuit ensued. Schoenberg soon decided he had had enough. He had bared his soul in his early music, which is full of intense emotion, expressed with prodigious technical skill; yet audiences had continually rejected it. 'If it is art, it is not for all,' he was later to write, 'and if it is for all, it is not art.'[1] He formed a Society for Private Performances, to which only paying members were invited, and critics excluded. A rift between the composer and his public had been formalised. Schoenberg's later twelve-note works make few concessions to accessibility: however much they are admired by a few, they have never been accepted by the general listener and are never likely to, though Schoenberg himself still sometimes imagined they would. As he wrote to Hans Rosbaud in 1947:

> But there is nothing I long for more intensely (if for anything) than to be taken for a better sort of Tchaikovsky – for heaven's sake: a bit better, but really that's all. Or if anything more, then that people should know my tunes and whistle them.[2]

A forlorn hope; yet it shows that, despite everything he had said and done, Schoenberg had not renounced the ideal of wider communication. Certainly he never went as far as his American disciple Milton Babbitt, who wrote in 1958:

> I dare suggest that the composer would do himself and his music an immediate and eventual service by total, resolute and voluntary withdrawal from the public world to one of private performance and electronic media, with its very real possibility of complete elimination of the public and social aspects of musical composition.[3]

The role of the composer within society is naturally enough one of the chief themes of Alex Ross's compelling book *The Rest is Noise*, which sweeps through the turbulent history of twentieth-century music, pins down many of its main creative figures in deft portraits, and gives concise and intelligent accounts of their most important works. Particular societies and places are vividly evoked and the role of music within them acutely examined: Paris and Berlin in the 1920s, Stalin's Russia, Hitler's Germany, the Darmstadt school after the Second World War. There is, however, a serious drawback to Ross's approach. He admits at the start that 'there is no attempt to be comprehensive' and that 'much great music is left on the cutting-room floor'. What this means in effect is that someone like Shostakovich – or Strauss – who was caught up in the political drama of the twentieth century will generally get more attention than a composer who may have written superlative music but who lived an uninteresting life (Ross makes a notable exception with Messiaen). A prime case is Carl Nielsen, who is allotted one sentence (a complimentary one, admittedly) in the chapter on Sibelius. I'm not alone in judging Nielsen's Fifth Symphony to be one of the greatest of twentieth-century works, the equal of Sibelius's Fifth; but Nielsen is an outsider to the main currents of the century, had no significant influence on posterity, and so has been sidelined.

A slightly different approach might also, for instance, have assigned more space to Busoni and Scriabin, both of whom did in fact attract much attention during their lives but are still at a tangent to the mainstream on which Ross tends to concentrate. It could be claimed that eventually both composers will be seen to have been as important figures as Schoenberg. Busoni's theories, which are concerned with expanding harmonic language while preserving the laws of tonality, may well appear more significant for the future of music in the long run than Schoenberg's dogmatic rejection of tonality and his attempt to replace it with a new system of his own devising. Busoni's masterpiece, his opera *Doktor Faust*, is surprisingly ignored by Ross, who throughout the book makes copious references to the Faust legend and in particular to its treatment in Thomas Mann's story of Adrian Leverkühn. Scriabin invented a harmonic system almost as revolutionary as Schoenberg's but staying just within the bounds of tonality, which had a profound influence on Stravinsky (though he later denied it) and also on Messiaen; his late sonatas are masterpieces by any reckoning. Scriabin's monomaniacal plan for a cosmic piece that would transform the universe, unrealised at his death, is the ultimate Faustian gesture, and looks forward to the similarly grandiose ambition of Stockhausen's opera sequence *Licht*.

Ross is music critic of *The New Yorker* and understandably writes from an American perspective. So American composers are given proportionately more coverage than those from other countries. Certainly the American contribution to twentieth-century music cannot be undervalued. It could be claimed that Charles Ives virtually invented modernism single-handed; Gershwin, Ellington and Copland were all important in countering the idea that the composer should not court popularity; John Cage, whatever the intrinsic value of his anti-compositions (I happen to find almost all of them extremely tedious), had a huge influence during his lifetime by the sheer force of his personality; while the Minimalists – Steve Reich, Philip Glass, John Adams – not only overthrew the hegemony of the post-war European avant-garde but have affected much of the music that is being written today in all parts of the world, both serious and popular. But Ross also provides a comprehensive history of twentieth-century American music that includes accounts of obscure black composers from the early years of the century, as well as of eccentric experimentalists such as Harry Partch and Henry Cowell.

A British reader will find it hard not to feel that the music of this country has been undervalued. Britten deservedly has a chapter of his own, but otherwise Elgar is allotted a few sentences in Ross's opening chapter on Mahler and Strauss, Holst and Vaughan Williams are merely examples of 'folkish composers', Walton is mentioned in a list of symphonists and the name of Delius does not appear at all. I'm aware that Britten is the only one of these composers whose music is played worldwide and whose acceptance outside this country is unproblematic. Elgar's Cello Concerto is a repertoire piece in most countries, yet Germans for instance still find his symphonies baffling (exactly why is hard to fathom, since to my ears Elgar has much in common with both Strauss and Mahler). Vaughan Williams's symphonies, which I would rate alongside Shostakovich's, are, it seems, incomprehensible to much of the rest of Europe, as is Tippett's opera *The Midsummer Marriage*, which, while not wholly as successful dramatically as *Peter Grimes*, could be claimed to be musically superior to anything that Britten wrote. I don't think these are merely the views of a biased nationalist, and time may justify them; after all it took over 350 years for the great Tudor music of Tallis and Byrd to become known outside this country. It is probably impossible not to be biased towards one's national music: a French reader (this English one too) will regret that Dutilleux is not singled out as one of the foremost living composers, while a Romanian will lament the omission of Enescu. Ross does not set out to be all-inclusive or objective, so it is perhaps unfair to go on criticising him for omissions. Suffice it to say that in a hundred years' time the relative significance of twentieth-century composers will, I expect, look markedly different to how they appear in *The Rest is Noise*.

In American music, as in European, there is a division between those who have been concerned to speak to an audience and those who, like Ives, Cage, Babbitt and Carter, have accepted or even courted alienation. The former are in the majority: alienation has largely been a European phenomenon, with Boulez as its high priest (Boulez's absurd hostility towards his contemporaries in the 1940s and 1950s is amusingly chronicled by Ross). Ross tends not to take sides but I sense he sympathises with the communicators. His heroes are Sibelius, Strauss, Stravinsky, Copland, Shostakovich and Britten, all of whom had a significant role within society. A few twentieth-century composers achieved extraordinary fame: the fiftieth birthday of Sibelius in 1915 was front page news in the Finnish newspapers, his portrait was displayed in most of the Helsinki shops; and at an evening concert where the first version of his Fifth Symphony had its premiere, he was presented with a civic address bearing fifteen thousand signatures and given a Steinway grand piano (Sibelius did comment in his diary 'It is difficult to take this seriously'). It is inconceivable that anything like this would ever happen to a composer of classical music today. At best, he or she can only hope to create a mild ripple in the mass media pond: the last work whose premiere was a major public event was probably Britten's *War Requiem* in 1962. The great communicators today are in the world of rock music.

Ross briefly touches on rock. He is interested, for instance, in the links between the Minimalists and groups such as The Velvet Underground, and in Stockhausen's influence on The Beatles; but he doesn't really deal with the fact that for the majority of educated Westerners today, who read contemporary novels and look at contemporary art, their main experience of new music is through rock. If they are interested in classical music, it is likely to be in the music of the past. Rock music, with its direct appeal to the emotions, seems to stand at the opposite extreme from contemporary classical music, which is held by most people to be 'difficult' and remote from ordinary life. But rock music, however good – and I'm as big a fan of Bob Dylan as anyone – is limited in its expressive range and by its avoidance of musical complexity: it cannot plumb the depths of our experience.[4] Classical music can do that, but contemporary classical music, it seems to most people, does not (minimalism, some of which is genuinely popular, has the same limitations as rock). While the levelling-down of society in the last fifty years has tended to marginalise serious and complex music, composers themselves are partly to blame for their failure to communicate directly on an emotional level, leaving the field open for rock music to take over.

Ross also chooses not to discuss melody, which has become perhaps the chief problem in the music of today. The popular music of the mid twentieth-century – Kern, Berlin, Porter, Gershwin – was exceptionally rich in memorable melody. Rock music, with a few exceptions (outstandingly, The Beatles) relies less on melody and more on striking short motifs, like the opening guitar riffs of such Rolling Stones' songs as 'Satisfaction' and 'Jumpin' Jack Flash', or simple but memorable chord progressions, as in most Dylan songs. In classical music, it is now possible for a composer to reach a position of considerable eminence without having written any memorable melodic ideas, which is curious. Some composers would no doubt claim that the invention of melody is no longer their concern; yet how can music survive into the future as a communicative language if it denies its origins in song? The best music is singable; we remember it by singing it to ourselves, either in our heads, or aloud. Which brings us back to Schoenberg and his desire for his tunes to be whistled. Schoenberg began as a gifted melodist, as in *Gurrelieder*, or *Pelleas und Melisande*, whose gorgeous love theme I sometimes whistle myself. But his twelve-note melodies are almost impossible to remember, not just because of his self-imposed rule that the twelve notes of the scale must be traversed without repetition on the way, but also because of the underlying non-tonal harmony, which makes it very hard to pitch the notes accurately. It is possible to invent a memorable melody containing all twelve notes of the scale, for example the B minor fugue theme from Book I of Bach's *Well-tempered Clavier*; but Bach's tune repeats a few significant notes, and one can always sense the tonal background in B minor, which makes all the difference.

Since hardly anyone writes twelve-note music these days, the particular melodic problem associated with it should no longer apply. Yet somehow memorable melody faded out of classical music in the last part of the twentieth century. It seems to be fast disappearing from popular music too. Ross, who seems unaware or unconcerned about the problem, is optimistic about twenty-first-century composition: 'In a decentered culture, it has a chance to play a kind of godfather role, able to assimilate anything new because it has assimilated everything in the past ... in the freedom of their solitude, [composers] can communicate experiences of singular intensity.' Maybe, but freedom and solitude are also likely to foster isolation. I can see a few more things that stand in the way of a wealth of meaningful music in the future. One is academicism, represented at its most extreme by the attitude of Milton Babbitt: this inevitably leads towards sterility. Then there is the widespread self-consciousness that makes composers afraid to express emotions.

Music must be from the heart, to the heart, as Beethoven said, not just from the brain. True music comes into being in a mysterious interaction between the unconscious and the intellect, but it begins in the unconscious, and unless composers trust in their feelings and in unconscious sources of inspiration they will not bring their music fully to life.

Notes

Source: Review of *The Rest is Noise: Listening to the Twentieth Century* by Alex Ross in: *Musical Opinion*, Vol. 132, No. 1471, July-August 2009, pp. 12-14.

1   Arnold Schoenberg, *Style and Idea. Selected Writings of Arnold Schoenberg*, ed. Leonard Stein, London, Faber and Faber, 1975, p. 124.

2   Arnold Schoenberg, *Letters*, ed. Erwin Stein, London, Faber and Faber, 1964, p. 243.

3   From Milton Babbitt, 'Who Cares If You Listen?' in: *The American Composer Speaks*, ed. Gilbert Chase, Louisiana State University Press, 1966, p. 242.

4   David Matthews is a long-standing Bob Dylan fan:

> Bob Dylan concert at Earl's Court … At last the lights went off again, shadowy figures were seen coming on stage; lights up to cheers, & Dylan & his band started off with 'You gotta serve somebody'. Three guitarists & drums & Dylan himself (in dark glasses), were added to the black quintet – a good solid sound, rather like Eric Clapton – the musicians were excellent, especially the lead guitar & the sound quality was vastly superior to most rock concerts I've attended, not too loud, & varying dynamics – what sophistication! About half the songs he sang were new (the song about Lenny Bruce was particularly good) & half were new versions of old songs, including a hard driving rock'n'roll version of 'Like a Rolling Stone' which rather took away its edge. In this & in 'Mr Tambourine Man' and later in 'Blowing in the Wind' he changed the original vocal lines to a kind of gospel descant. He sang (with a few interruptions from the girl singers) for over 2 hours, then said goodnight, but returned for 3 encores: 'Blowing in the Wind' with gospel choruses, 'It's alright Ma' with just acoustic guitar (exactly as on *Before the Flood*) & a reggae version of 'Knocking on Heaven's Door.' It was all very fine – whether as good as in the past I don't know; but his Christianity doesn't really seem, as yet, to have spoiled the music … As everybody says about Dylan, the music does have a meaning, & he communicates it quite superbly; & the songs, even at their most basic, have a strange power which is unaccountable except by reference to, I have to say, genius. (*Journal*, 1 July 1981)

4   *The Art of the Fugue*
(book review)

Counterpoint, the art of combining two or more independent melodic lines, is the prime distinguishing feature of Western music. Music began with monody – unaccompanied melody – and with rhythmic patterns beaten out on sticks and drums. The majority of the world's folk music is monodic. Often percussion underlines the rhythm, and sometimes a drone is added, an unchanging note in the bass, which keeps the tune in touch with the earth as it makes its aerial flights: this is a feature of some of the most sophisticated non-Western musics, for instance Classical Indian. Indonesian music uses heterophony – different versions of the same melodic line sounding together. Imitation is occasionally found in other non-Western musics. But European counterpoint is something else altogether. Counterpoint is a conversation; it acknowledges the presence and participation of the other. Two independent voices may be played by the same musician, on a keyboard for instance, but they are more often given to two players, who must listen to each other. It is significant that counterpoint grew to maturity in Europe where the concept of democracy was born.

By no means all European music is predominantly contrapuntal; much of it is melody with harmony, and this kind of music has the widest popular appeal. Even a complex piece such as a Beethoven symphony will almost always have a main melodic line that you can sing or whistle your way through. But try whistling a Bach fugue. After the first few bars where the main subject is announced unaccompanied, the music divides into two parts, then three, then possibly four, or even five or six. The contrapuntal discourse is continued throughout the duration of the piece. How can you hear all these lines at once? Most of us probably don't. The experience of listening to a fugue is stimulating yet at the same time forbidding. This is the most intellectual music that has been devised. But it is also capable of expressing emotion on the highest level, and where intellect and emotion are in perfect balance, the result can be sublime. To give three supreme examples: the B minor fugue in Book 1 of Bach's *Well-tempered Clavier* (the '48'), the six-part ricercare from the same composer's *Musical Offering*, and the opening fugue of Beethoven's C♯ minor Quartet, Op. 131.

In the preface to his new book on Bach's keyboard fugues, *The Art of Fugue*, Joseph Kerman quotes Charles Rosen's perceptive comments:

> The 'pure' fugue, the meditative fugue, is basically a keyboard work for Bach ... Only the performer at the keyboard is in a position to appreciate the movement of the voices, their blending and their separation, their interaction and their contrasts. A fugue of Bach can be fully understood

only by the one who plays it, not only heard but felt through the muscles and nerves.[1]

Rosen is surely right, and in the same way a string quartet is best understood by a player taking an active part in the instrumental conversation. Mere listeners, however, should not despair. It is possible, with practice, to learn to hear contrapuntal music, especially if you can read music and follow a score. Then you will see as well as hear how, for instance, in the first fugue of the '48' (one of the 16 fugues that Kerman analyses in some detail) the first seven notes of the subject are inverted – turned upside-down – in two overlapping sequences as the second voice comes in with the subject a fifth higher, as prescribed by the rules of fugue. This little piece of clever craftsmanship – one of many in the course of this fugue – is, on re-hearing and in contemplation, much more than that: it becomes a mystery, a demonstration of the uncanny power of counterpoint to suggest the unfathomable.

Fugue developed out of canon or round, music making strict use of the device of imitation and exhilarating to perform, as anyone who has sung 'Frère Jacques' or 'London's Burning' will know. Canon is a ubiquitous compositional resource: it can even be found in rock music – for instance in the Beatles' 'She Said She Said', and in the fade-out endings of a number of the Beach Boys' songs. Fugue is a freer form than canon, but there is a general scheme that most fugues adhere to. First, an exposition: the voices enter with the subject one by one (in any order). As the second voice enters the first voice continues with an accompanying 'countersubject', which must fit the subject whether it is played below it, or above. Additional countersubjects may be invented for further entries of the subject. Devising memorable countersubjects is a test of compositional prowess, one at which Bach especially excelled. A development follows where both themes appear in new keys (if it is a tonal fugue) and combinations. Then a return to the home key. Finally, there is a possibility for a 'stretto', where the subject entries overlap, typically over a sustained note in the bass emphasizing the main tonality.

Kerman's book, which usefully includes a CD containing scores of all the fugues discussed and recordings of some of these played on piano, harpsichord, clavichord and organ by Davitt Moroney and Karen Rosenak, concentrates on analytical detail and does not attempt to put Bach in the wider context of fugal writing throughout musical history. He assumes a fair amount of prior knowledge, including understanding the vocabulary of harmony; but musically literate readers will find their appreciation of these fugues greatly enhanced by the insights that Kerman brings from a lifetime's study as he examines the music with scrupulous care, bar by bar. His prose is technical but never dry. Reading his commentary on the B major fugue from Book II of the '48', for instance, made me think anew about the way the subject rises, falls and rises again to a higher note, and how this contour is mirrored in the progress of the fugue: the highest note, a B, occurs three times, but only on its third appearance is it entrusted to the subject, where it feels like the climax of great aspiration. It descends from this high point

> with the greatest dignity and calm. With no harmonic undercutting and no tumble of faster notes ... The soprano response feels like a slow, deep bow ... touched with something like regret, though feelings are blurred by another suspended note ... Even as the fugue quietly gives up aspirations for the heights, it moots confident new possibilities, even now, for breadth.[2]

Eloquently precise. Music like this attains such expressive perfection that I for one am reduced to bathos in attempting to describe my reactions to it. Kerman is undaunted. He concludes his book by asking himself what he has tried to do, questioning the very practice of writing about music, and gently justifying it:

> Talk mediates, differentiates, elucidates, and consoles; we use words, however imprecisely, to talk about love and death because talk, it seems, we must. We also use and surely must use words to talk about music.

The art of fugue had only been practised for a hundred years or so when Bach brought it to perfection, an achievement insufficiently appreciated by his contemporaries, some of whom thought the whole thing out of date. The new classical style that swept through Europe in the mid-eighteenth century, and whose first practitioners included Bach's sons, was one centred more on accompanied melody than polyphony. But fugue did not die out with Bach; there was soon to be a revival of interest, and in fact there has been virtually no major composer since Bach who has not written at least one notable example of a fugue. There are exceptions: Chopin's forms admitted Bachian counterpoint, but not the fugue, which must have seemed alien to his Romantic, poetic sensibility. (It had not appeared so to his more Classically-oriented contemporaries Mendelssohn and Schumann; Schumann's sparkling fugal conclusion to his Piano Quintet, for instance, comes as a delightful *bonne bouche*.) Chopin was the most modern, least antiquarian of all the early Romantics: adapting the sonata was the furthest he was prepared to go in accommodating himself to the recent past; otherwise he transformed contemporary dance idioms (such as the mazurka) or invented new genres (such as the ballade), in which the fantastic flowers of his melodies could find space to open and bloom. Wagner, in some ways the inheritor of Chopin's erotically-charged Romanticism, learned the art of fugue from Theodor Weinlig, a successor to J. S. Bach as Cantor of St Thomas's, Leipzig, and there is a fugue in the finale of the symphony he wrote when he was nineteen. His mastery of Bachian counterpoint in *Die Meistersinger* is flawless, above all in the wonderful fugato ensemble at the end of Act Two. But, as with Chopin, there was no place for a full-blown fugue in his mature music. Nor in Sibelius, who nonetheless showed sufficient mastery of counterpoint – and in particular the Palestrinean counterpoint of the openings of his Sixth and Seventh Symphonies – to demonstrate that he too could have written an interestingly individual fugue had he chosen to do so. Even Debussy, primarily a harmonist, might at least have begun to think about fugue if he had lived to experience the neoclassical revival of the 1920s and been able to pursue the more linear style he was developing in his last chamber sonatas.

~

The revival of the fugue after Bach had got properly under way with Haydn's finale fugues in the last two of his Op. 20 string quartets. Haydn may not have known Bach's fugues, but both Mozart and Beethoven revered Bach – as they did Handel – and made transcriptions of fugues from the '48'. Mozart transcribed three for string trio to which he added preludes of his own; Beethoven made a string quartet version of the C♯ minor fugue from Book 1, whose influence can be heard in his own great C♯ minor fugue in the Op. 131 Quartet. Mozart's own fugues sometimes seem to want to outdo Bach in sheer cleverness, as in the *Adagio and Fugue*, K. 546, where the tense fugue subject drives relentlessly through the music, as insistently memorable in inversion as it is the right way up. In the finale of the 'Jupiter' Symphony, Mozart dazzles the listener as he nonchalantly shows off every contrapuntal trick in the book. Here is the spirit of Apollo: pure delight in the form. With Beethoven, for whom the fugue became more and more important as he ventured into new areas of artistic aspiration at the end of his life, Apollo is joined by Dionysus in the duality that Nietzsche thought essential to the highest art. Dionysus prevails in the most extraordinary fugue of all, the 'Grosse Fuge' that Beethoven originally conceived as the finale of the B♭ major Quartet, Op. 130, but later detached to form a self-sufficient piece. As the opening Allegro charges along with manic exuberance, there is a feeling of exploring completely uncharted territory, like pioneers in the Australian outback. Huge vistas are glimpsed but are tantalisingly out of reach. The pace is relentless, the dynamics always *forte*. Then suddenly it stops, and a new fugue begins, slow and full of intense lyrical emotion. And then a third: a rough-edged, unbuttoned dance which sometimes loses all sense of key. So Beethoven has contrived to encompass all the elements of the symphony within the texture of the fugue. This music will always sound 'modern' because it is stretching the limits of the possible; it is still fiendishly difficult to play. No fugue since has ever been quite so adventurous on every level.

Many Romantic composers would have been wise to heed Schumann's warning: 'The emptiest head thinks it can hide its weakness behind a fugue; but a true fugue is the affair of a great master.' Liszt's fugues, for instance, tend to show up his deficiencies as a contrapuntist. His chromatic harmony sounds laboured, and he quickly runs out of steam. The whole philosophy of Romanticism, after all, was opposed to that of the Baroque: the individual, revolutionary voice, whose natural expression was heightened melody, in contrast with the voice of the community still grounded in political stability and religion, and symbolised by polyphony. The majority of later nineteenth-century fugues are choral, and are descended from Handel rather than Bach, a routine part of the ubiquitous oratorio which was the pious Victorian counterpart to Wagner's unleashing of erotic feeling in his operas. Most of them are dutifully dull, but the best composers, such as Brahms in the *German Requiem*, or Elgar in *The Dream of Gerontius*, overcame pedantry with intellectual passion. The choral fugue that opens Berlioz's *Grande Messe des Morts* is compellingly unorthodox, the subject making a dramatic downward swoop on the words 'Requiem aeternam' while the countersubject sets the same words to a tremulous descending chromatic scale. At one point each entry of the subject surges in a tone higher than its predecessor, producing great cumulative power. Berlioz too found a fresh and colourful use for fugato to portray the brawling Montagues and Capulets at the start of his *Roméo et Juliette*. Mahler, as a student at the Vienna Conservatoire, neglected his counterpoint studies and failed his examination, and this seems to have spurred him on later to become an ardent student of Bach and eventually the most accomplished contrapuntist of all the Romantics. The influence of Bach may be heard as early as the Second Symphony, and is all-pervasive in the finale of the Fifth. It reaches its climax in the central double fugue in the first movement of the Eighth Symphony, where Mahler also almost matches the striving intensity of Beethoven's *Missa Solemnis*.

The nineteenth-century vocal fugue finds its apogee in the finale of Verdi's *Falstaff*, the last operatic music he wrote. Verdi had already composed a remarkable and innovative fugue, 'a light-hearted Grosse Fuge', as Julian Budden has described it, in his E minor String Quartet, his only mature piece of chamber music. In introducing the fugue to the operatic ensemble, he was bringing to fruition what Mozart had hinted at in the final ensemble of *Don Giovanni*. At the end of *Falstaff* all the characters assemble on stage to pronounce their verdict on life: 'Tutto nel mondo è burla' ('All the world's a joke'). It is a compositional triumph: a last summoning up of all Verdi's powers in an effusion of contrapuntal jest.

In the twentieth century the instrumental fugue made an impressive return.[3] At the start of the century we find Bartók modelling the fugal first movement of his First String Quartet on Beethoven's Op. 131, like Schoenberg in his own First Quartet (though this contains no strict fugue) taking up the challenge of Beethoven's late quartets – the first two composers to do so since Schubert and Mendelssohn made their tentative response; even Brahms had been daunted. Bartók went on to incorporate a fugue into the Allegro of his Third Quartet in a very Beethovenian way, and to write a measured fugue of masterful order and precision as the opening movement of his *Music for Strings, Percussion and Celesta*. The neoclassical movement after the First World War brought the fugue back into fashion. Busoni, who had already found his own way to an independent kind of neoclassicism, had in 1910 completed Bach's unfinished fugue from *The Art of Fugue* in his *Fantasia contrappuntistica*, with masterly daring. Ives, another independent, working in isolation in New England, delighted in contrasting the wildest musical experiments with the orthodox harmony and counterpoint he had learned as a student at Yale. In his Fourth Symphony, he follows the polytonal second movement, probably the most revolutionary music he ever wrote, with a fugue based on the hymn 'From Greenland's Icy Mountains', whose orderly calm is only momentarily threatened by dissonance. Stravinsky, not a natural contrapuntist, absorbed himself in Bachian counterpoint in his neoclassical period and wrote an affecting, chromatic fugue in his *Symphony of Psalms*. Later in the 1930s he made an assiduous study of Beethoven's late fugues that bore fruit in the fugal finale of his Concerto for Two Pianos. Tippett studied Bachian fugue privately with R. O. Morris, an outstanding teacher of counterpoint. He took the composition of fugue very seriously and several fine examples in his string quartets show evidence of Beethovenian labours. His friend and rival Britten had studied sixteenth-century counterpoint at the Royal College with John Ireland: it was one of the few disciplines he had not learned already from Frank Bridge. In his young maturity, he threw off several brilliant fugues with apparent ease; in particular the concluding fugue of *The Young Person's Guide to the Orchestra* is an example of the kind of carefree cleverness for which, absurdly, he was criticised at the time. Hindemith's many fugues tend towards earnest academicism, in contrast to Shostakovich's fresh and expressive set of 24 *Preludes and Fugues* in all the keys, composed in 1950-51, a deliberate homage to Bach's '48' and an impeccable answer to the avant-garde of the time who were pronouncing that such things were no longer possible.

The nearest the fugue came to a modernist gesture was probably Ernst Toch's 1930 *Fuga aus der Geographie*. This is a four-part spoken fugue, whose rhythms follow the natural rhythms of the carefully-chosen words. The subject, given to the tenors and needing Savoy Opera dexterity to deliver, is:

Ratibor!
und der Fluss Mississippi
und die Stadt Honolulu
und der See Titicaca;
der Popocatopetl liegt nicht in Kanada
sondern in Mexiko, Mexiko, Mexiko.

… at which point the second voice comes in, and the standard fugal procedures are worked through. Toch's fugue has a distant cousin in the 'Sirens' chapter of *Ulysses*, where Joyce – who might have wished to be a composer rather than a novelist, had he been able – attempts to use some of the techniques of fugue in a striking display of sonorous prose. He sets out his thematic material in an introduction – 'Bronze by gold', etc. – and then develops it into rounded, musical sentences: 'Shrill, with deep laughter, after, gold after bronze, they urged each each to peal after peal, ringing in changes, bronzegold, goldbronze, shrilldeep, to laughter after laughter.' There is an illusion of counterpoint in the juxtaposition of overheard conversation, snatches of songs, and onomatopoeic sounds. At the same period, musical modernism could initially accommodate the fugue (in Berg's *Wozzeck* for instance). In 1936, Schoenberg wrote: 'In its highest form … nothing would claim a place in a fugue unless it were derived, at least indirectly, from the theme',[4] hinting at a connection with his twelve-note method of composition; and indeed, twelve-note fugues are quite feasible, though Schoenberg himself avoided them. It may be argued, however, that in denying the tonal basis on which the fugue had always relied, a great deal of its strength is lost.

Few composers today, however, are writing fugues, and it has to be asked if fugue can still make a valid contribution to contemporary musical language. My own answer would be yes, and I can point to several examples that, in my view, demonstrate its continuing vitality. Their composers will probably not become household names, but then I would hardly expect the art of fugue ever to be modish and popular when the art of serious contemporary music itself has become an unfashionable minority interest. First, the Scottish composer Alistair Hinton, who in the huge finale of his nearly three-hour String Quintet (1969-77), included a 20-minute fugue, or rather three continuous fugues, modelled on the 'Grosse Fuge' and rivalling it in its scope and emotional intensity, if not quite achieving its transcendental vision.[5] Hinton's first fugue, in similar dotted rhythms, has the fierce energy of Beethoven's opening fugue; his second fugue, in total contrast calm and sweet-toned and sounding like a piece from the Renaissance, begins and ends with a canon whose theme becomes a fugue subject in its central section; the third employs subjects and countersubjects from the first two fugues together with new themes of its own, and combines them all in the most learned (yet never pedantic) style, with the themes played backwards and in inversion, all the time gradually generating another volcanic eruption of Beethovenian energy. In the spirit of his friend Kaikhosru Sorabji, who wrote many gargantuan fugues in his still hardly known keyboard works, Hinton has continued to include large-scale fugues in his own pieces, including the *Variations and Fugue on a Theme of Grieg* and *Sequentia claviensis*, both for piano.

My second fugue composer is the Moravian, Pavel Novák, who has been working for the past seventeen years on another vast project, a set of 24 Preludes and Fugues for piano based on the Old and New Testaments (twelve for each part).[6] Novák has a radically unorthodox attitude to fugue: the first fugue, evoking the creation of heaven and earth, has only one voice, and no counterpoint; the sixth fugue is built on a one-note theme and employs only seven notes altogether. The music grows into greater complexity as the world grows with it. A fugue without counterpoint might seem a contradiction in terms, but Novák somehow contrives to give substance to his omissions. The background to his music is rich and firmly-rooted enough to enable him at times merely to sketch in the foreground.

Shostakovich's fugues had brought a new sense of spacious calm into the fugue: they are fugues for the unchanging landscape of Russia. In Howard Skempton's recent and remarkably beautiful string quartet, *Tendrils*, the texture is one of continuous canon and while the mood is one of sustained contemplation, Skempton's Shostakovich-like chromaticism keeps the music in a continuous state of mild tension, which the abrupt resolution into E♭ at the end does not altogether dispel. Skempton may now be ready to write a contemplative fugue; he certainly doesn't think it impossible.[7]

At this point I should declare an interest. I had used canonic devices in my own music for many years, but it was not until 1998 that I felt able to introduce a fugue, a contemplative one somewhat indebted to Beethoven, into my Eighth String Quartet. It seemed to work. The same year, at a concert in London, I heard my violinist friend Peter Sheppard Skærved play Bach's G minor solo Sonata, which contains an elaborate three-part fugue.[8] I wondered if it was possible to write a four-part fugue for solo violin, something that as far as I knew no one had attempted, for the obvious reason that four-part counterpoint on a violin is virtually impossible. I wrote a few bars and sent them to Peter, who to my surprise pronounced them playable. So I finished the piece, in a neo-Bachian E minor, and thought of it as a one-off technical exercise until Peter persuaded me to write more.[9] In 2001 I wrote another four-part fugue, in A minor but highly chromatic and almost atonal; then, over a period of nine months, carried on writing them occasionally until I had fifteen, cast in the more practical keys. Only five of them are four-part fugues, and even in these there is little continuous four-part writing, which would be almost intolerable for the listener, let alone the player. There are two two-part fugues and the rest are in three parts. I amused myself with the kinds of games that fugal writing seems to encourage: my first two-part fugue has a ten-note theme derived from the keys of all the fugues in my series in the order they appear (major and minor counted as one) and it modulates in turn through all these keys before returning home to C minor. One fugue was entirely pizzicato. Another was based on a blackbird's song. I was learning a new skill, like a painter learning how to etch. Because I hadn't been to a music college, I had never learned the art of fugue formally. Perhaps those who have to go through what at the time may seem merely an academic chore cannot associate it afterwards with living music. I'm grateful to have discovered the sheer pleasure of fugue by myself, without any prejudices.

Even if counterpoint is presently neglected, it will not die out: it is too rich a resource. In his exemplary little book *Counterpoint*, Edmund Rubbra, no mean practitioner himself of the art of fugue, wrote: 'The history of Western music is the history of the form-compelling power of counterpoint.' That is justification enough for its survival. Throughout Western music's history, composers who have possessed what Rubbra defined as 'an intuitive grasp of the essential spirit of fugue' have been able to renew this most intriguing and demanding of all contrapuntal forms, and there seems no valid reason why, if composers can learn to master it, the art of fugue should not continue to evolve in the future; in Rubbra's words, in 'an evolution that never destroys the basic nature of the form'.[10]

Notes

Source: Expanded version of 'Form-compelling', a review of *The Art of Fugue* by Joseph Kerman in: *London Review of Books*, 21 September 2006, pp. 27-9.

1   Joseph Kerman, *The Art of Fugue. Bach Fugues for Keyboard, 1715-1750*, University of California Press, 2005, p. xxvii.

2   *Ibid.*, pp. 139-40.

3   David Matthews writes (June 2013): 'Hearing Max Reger's superb Fantasy and Fugue on *Wachet auf* recently I realised I should have included him as perhaps the most prolific and arguably the finest composer of fugues since Bach, his closest musical ancestor. Reger's music is so unfashionable now that he is often – quite unfairly – passed over'.

4   Arnold Schoenberg, *Style and Idea. Selected Writings of Arnold Schoenberg*, ed. Leonard Stein, London, Faber and Faber, 1975, p. 297.

5   Alistair Hinton (b. 1950) studied at the Royal College of Music with Humphrey Searle and Stephen Savage. He has composed regularly throughout his life but destroyed much of his music from before 1985. A friend and advocate of composer Kaikhosru Sorabji (1892-1988), Hinton is now the curator of the Sorabji Archive. The String Quintet referred to in this essay was recorded in 1999 (Altarus AIR-CD-9066). Matthews has corresponded regularly with Hinton and wrote the following to the composer after hearing the String Quintet:

My first reaction was: you were only 19 when you wrote that first movement, and yet it's so assured. You'd already mastered the sort of complex lyrical counterpoint you get in Schoenberg's 1st Quartet. And his kind of incredibly sophisticated edge-of-tonality harmony too. But although the sound-world is of early Schoenberg, it doesn't sound at all like pastiche; that must be because it's such genuine expression of feeling, with real emotional warmth. I liked very much the sound of the ensemble, the depth you get from the prominent double bass. (Letter to Alistair Hinton, 30 January 2005)

6   Pavel Novák (b. 1957) is a Moravian composer, known as Pavel Zemek in the Czech Republic. His output includes five symphonies and several string quartets. The completed *24 Preludes & Fugues* have been recorded by pianist William Howard (Champs Hill Records: CHRCD016). Writing in the liner notes for that recording, Matthews commented: 'I have no doubt that these 24 Preludes and Fugues are one of the finest piano works of our time, a worthy companion to Ligeti's three books of Études, with which they have something in common, though the atheist Ligeti's strongly secular tone is in stark contrast to the intense spirituality of Novák's music.'

7   Howard Skempton (b. 1947) is a British composer and long-standing friend of Matthews. He studied privately with Cornelius Cardew, with whom he helped found the Scratch Orchestra. *Tendrils* won the Chamber Scale Composition category at the 2005 Royal Philharmonic Society Music Awards. Since the original publication of this article Skempton has indeed begun work on a sequence of preludes and fugues for William Howard.

8   Peter Sheppard Skærved is a British violinist and dedicatee of more than 200 works for violin by composers including George Rochberg, Judith Bingham, Michael Finnissy and Hans Werner Henze. He is a close collaborator with David Matthews and, as founder and leader of the Kreutzer Quartet, is engaged with the ongoing recording of Matthews's complete string quartet cycle and complete works for solo violin, both for Toccata Classics.

9   This is *Fuga* (1998), later incorporated into Fifteen Fugues for Solo Violin, Op. 88.

10   Edmund Rubbra, *Counterpoint*, London, Hutchinson, 1960.

Symphonic Traditions

5   Mahler's Tenth Symphony

In December 1960 my brother Colin and I heard the BBC broadcast of Deryck Cooke's then incomplete performing version of Mahler's Tenth Symphony. At that time we were both still at school; we were obsessed with Mahler's music, and had also begun ourselves to compose. Colin in particular was seized with the idea of making his own realisation of the Tenth, and to that end he obtained a copy of the Zsolnay facsimile through the local library and made a transcription of it. Although Colin eventually decided not to finish his own version, he did score the complete fourth movement and both of us worked on passages from the Finale. We saw the score of Deryck's version at the BBC and, perhaps rather surprisingly, they offered to lend it to us. In 1963 Colin wrote to Deryck, pointing out some errors of transcription that he had noticed in Deryck's score, and making some suggestions for changes in the orchestration. Deryck wrote back and eventually we both went to see him. He was rather taken aback to discover we were so young, but it was typical of him that this did not in the least affect his attitude to us. The three of us became friends and, over a period of about eight years from the late 1960s until the publication of the score in 1976, we collaborated on the extensive revision of the score that Deryck had already begun.

Deryck had been given a lot of help with the original orchestration by Berthold Goldschmidt, who conducted the 1960 broadcast performance and the first public performance in 1964. Although Deryck had been a composer himself as a young man, the majority of his compositions had been songs with piano, and he was inexperienced in writing for the orchestra. So he was very ready to accept advice on orchestration from others. The published score appeared with the three of us – Berthold, Colin and myself – listed as collaborators, although of course the vast majority of the work had been done by Deryck.

One of the first fruits of our collaboration was a decision to increase the size of the orchestra from the original triple woodwind and three trombones, which Deryck had used for the simple reason of economy, to one of quadruple wind, plus an extra clarinet, and quadruple brass. It could easily be deduced from the manuscript that this was the size of orchestra that Mahler had intended to use. The larger orchestra immediately enabled us to produce a more authentic sound. We could, for instance, exploit much more those powerful unisons of the upper wind that are so characteristic of Mahler. The inclusion of a fourth trombone gave us an interesting idea for the fourth movement, which probably not many people have noticed. In the first movement of *Das Lied von der Erde*, Mahler had originally used three trombones and a tuba, but in his orchestral draft score he crossed out the tuba part, and in fact the tuba now plays in only one place in the whole of *Das Lied von der Erde*, in the rowdy middle section of 'Von der Schönheit'. We decided to do something similar in the fourth movement of the Tenth, which is close in style to the first movement of *Das Lied von der Erde*. So we kept the tuba back until the coda, where it makes a dramatic entrance at bar 547 with a descending chromatic scale, ending on the low A, from which it begins its rising scale solo at the opening of the Finale. It is like a character making his appearance on the stage, a dramatic touch I think Mahler would have appreciated.

As is often pointed out, Mahler used a large orchestra in his symphonies not so much for volume of sound (though according to one of the orchestral players who played under him in New York he could never produce a sound loud enough to satisfy him) as for clarifying orchestral texture; and in rescoring the last two movements we always worked towards this principle of clarification. The elusive Mahlerian sound, which we could all hear when we looked at the bare notes of the short score, was extremely difficult to arrive at in practice, but I think that finally we did go a long way towards achieving it.

We used to meet three or four times a year to go over ten or so pages of the score very thoroughly. Colin and I would put forward our suggestions for revisions, Deryck would explain his, and eventually we would reach an agreement. Deryck's concern for details meant that he never tired of giving careful consideration to even the minutest suggestions for potential improvements. He was, I should like to emphasise, the right person in every way to undertake the task of making a performing version of the Symphony. He was a first-rate musician, who had at one time been a composer – and I do think that those who have composed themselves are best qualified to understand the thought processes behind the Symphony. But neither Deryck, nor Colin nor I had any wish to impose our own personalities onto the work. I am rather glad that neither Schoenberg nor Shostakovich responded to Alma Mahler's invitation to work on the score. Schoenberg in particular probably could not have resisted making the score as much his own as Mahler's, so that we might have been unable to hear the very personal tone of voice of Mahler's last work; and to be able to hear that voice is the main reason for making a performing version at all.

In order to illustrate the process of refinement of orchestration that the score went through in the fifteen-year period between Deryck's completion of his original version in 1961 and the publication of the score, I want to discuss two short sections of the Finale. The first is the opening of the recapitulation, the B♭ major section that follows the return of the dissonant chord from the first movement. Deryck's introductory talk to the 1960 broadcast gives some insight into the way he made decisions about scoring:

> When this chord leaves off, a high note is left hanging on marked 'trumpet', and the opening viola theme of the whole Symphony enters, marked 'horn'. The wheel has come full circle: the transformed restatement of the finale's introduction begins, pianissimo. This restatement ignores the lugubrious opening of the movement and takes up the hopeful violin theme, and here there's a passage which provides an example of how whole sections of the music score themselves. In the manuscript, it's essentially a five-part texture, with certain melodic and harmonic gaps in the lower parts. As it stands, played by the strings, this passage is entirely coherent in essentials, but slightly deficient in detail, and what's chiefly lacking is a low sustained octave on the dominant. In the realisation of the full texture, the cellos will set the octave going before the other parts enter. But this isn't string music. The melodic bass line lies too low for cellos, and the basses alone can't give it edge; and in any case the strings have to enter at bar 314. What instrumentation did Mahler have in mind? The feel of one particular bar –

> – brought to my mind the solemn sound of Wagner's music for horns and tubas in *The Ring*; and the sustained low octave is of the type commonly written for second and fourth horns. Furthermore, the bass tuba is the only instrument which can articulate the melodic bass line clearly, and the two upper parts form a characteristic dialogue for first and third horns. So the passage scored itself for four horns and tuba, with the first clarinet in the obbligato sixth part in the first few bars; and what had at first seemed a rather insignificant passage sprang to noble life in its true brass sonority. [this extract has been adapted for publication]

In the version used in the 1960 broadcast performance the first four bars of the B♭ major section are scored for wind and strings. Colin and I felt strongly that the entry of the violins should be delayed until the return to F♯ major at the end of the passage for horns and tuba, and Deryck agreed with us. At the same time we decided to double the pedal F in the second and fourth horns with cellos, and the tuba with basses, to smoothen the sound. A further refinement was that the clarinet part in bars 302-07 was transferred to the E♭ clarinet (this was Colin's idea). Mahler did not always use the E♭ clarinet in a shrill, satirical way: there is, for example, a wonderfully gentle E♭ clarinet passage at the end of the first movement of the Ninth Symphony, and that was the model for this passage.

The whole passage from the move into B♭ major after the horn and trumpet duet was a revision. The original sketch went straight into the closing F♯ major music, but in the key of B♭, and the Symphony originally ended in B♭. So the new music in B♭ is a second thought, and a very inspired second thought. It was in fact probably the last music that Mahler ever wrote. I have no proof except my intuitive feeling, but I think that this passage, more than some others in the work, is one that Mahler would have kept intact if he had completed the Symphony, and I also think – and I hope I'm not being presumptuous – that we have got somewhere very near what his own scoring would have been. Having said this I should like to draw attention to Kurt Sanderling's recorded performance, in which he not only doubles the first and third horns with violins in the second half of the horns and tuba passage, but he also doubles the horn theme from the opening of the Symphony with strings, and has the second half of the theme on strings alone. I do react rather strongly against what seems to me to be a wilful reinterpretation of Mahler's marked intentions here, and also against the later doubling which I feel spoils our carefully calculated effect.

The second passage I want to examine is the beginning of the Finale's central Allegro section. This passage is a development of some of the 'Purgatorio' motives that have appeared in the Finale's introduction. In the second half there are some exact quotations from the 'Purgatorio'. Like the central section of the 'Purgatorio' this passage is in D minor, but at the end it suddenly sweeps exultantly into D major. The musical character of this Allegro is similar to the Rondo-Burleske of the Ninth Symphony, which therefore provides a model.

None of us was convinced that this passage in the version of the 1960 broadcast performance really sounded like Mahler. The main flaw was that it lacked the necessary nervous tension. Consider what has happened in the Finale so far: there has been an introduction of the utmost darkness, punctuated by the funereal sound of the muffled drum. Out of this, the flute theme comes like a ray of light, and it develops towards a passionately affirmative climax. But this is beaten down by the muffled drum and the mood of the introduction returns. This is the starting point for the Allegro, which has to begin again from, at first, a state of pure negation, with the 'Purgatorio' motives chattering away malevolently. One is indeed slightly reminded of the 'Mephistopheles' movement from Liszt's *Faust Symphony*.

How could the sound of this passage be enhanced? The first obvious thing to do was to mute the strings, which had the immediate effect of making the music sound more spectral and sinister. It also partly solved the problem of what to do about Mahler's *sempre piano* marking, which he puts twice in this passage at bars 102 and 113, and a *wieder piano* a little later at bar 132 in places where one might have expected the music to be *forte*. By muting the strings, and stopping some of the horn figures – for example those at the very beginning of the passage – and lightening the texture generally (for instance some accompanying chords on strings were changed from *arco* to *pizzicato*), we were able to give the impression of a *sempre piano* even when some of the instruments were marked *ff*. As well as lightening the texture we also made it more varied. In his original scoring, Deryck had often kept the violins continuously on the upper line, as in bars 98-121. In the revision we divided the upper line between strings and woodwind, and the result is much more interesting and more characteristic. In bars 114 and 115 we added trills, and marked each of the trills *sforzando*. Dynamics, of course, were extremely important to Mahler and he was continually changing them, so we approached the question of the correct dynamics with particular care.

In conclusion I want to say something of my personal feelings about the ethics of making a performing version of the Tenth Symphony. As a composer, I ask myself what I would think if I had left a piece unfinished at my death in roughly the same state as the Tenth? I can see that I might have some misgivings about the quality of the music in its unfinished state; on the other hand, if others felt so strongly about what I had left that they wanted to hear it, I don't think I would have the right to stop them if, like Mahler, I had not destroyed my sketches nor asked for their destruction after my death (in the case of the Tenth there is, I admit, some residual doubt about the latter condition). Music is a mysterious gift that you receive; once you have received it and written it down, it then belongs to others, though ideally I should like to make some provisions about the realisation of my sketches.

I should not want anyone to make their own creative additions, but simply to fill in necessary gaps and to orchestrate: in other words what Deryck Cooke did with the Tenth. I should prefer that it was a composer who worked on my score, but one who was not only in sympathy with my musical language but who did not himself write in a musical language that was radically different. I should be worried about the distortions that might arise from someone working on my score who was not absolutely competent to do so. To return to the Tenth – and I haven't actually moved away from it – I must confess my serious misgivings about some other realisations, such as Clinton Carpenter's, which in my opinion seriously distorts the score. Carpenter's extensive contrapuntal additions are often ill-considered, and his orchestration is often overloaded. Quite simply, his realisation makes the music sound bad. Carpenter also set out to 'complete' the score (as if that were possible), in contrast to Deryck Cooke, whose more modest and reasonable aim was simply to present the score more or less as Mahler left it. This is an important difference that cannot be emphasised strongly enough.

I think that comparisons between the Tenth Symphony and other unfinished works like Mozart's Requiem, Bruckner's Ninth Symphony, Puccini's *Turandot*, Busoni's *Doktor Faust*, and so on, are not of any real value because all these works must be considered as independent cases with their own problems. The Tenth Symphony is a special case. Deryck Cooke pointed out that the Tenth is both more and less complete that most of the other pieces we have been discussing. It is more complete because you don't have to do any actual composition in order to perform it; but it is less complete because a great deal of it is an unrevised sketch. We were always aware, while we were working on the revision, of the paradox that what we were trying to make as perfect as we could was something that was intrinsically imperfect. It was only Mahler's draft score, which we knew he would have revised if he had lived, and perhaps quite drastically in places (in the second movement for example), just as he had revised the draft score of the Ninth Symphony. And that score, I should point out, represents a more complete stage in composition than any part of the draft of the Tenth, including the first movement. A further paradox was that the closer the score got to what we believed was a truly Mahlerian sound, the more likely it was that audiences would forget that what they were listening to was only the realisation of a draft and accept it actually as Mahler's Tenth Symphony, which it never could be, however much it sounded like Mahler.

I think there is always going to be a danger of misinterpretation by audiences, but I don't think that any of us has the right to protect audiences against possible aesthetic confusion. If the score was going to be played at all, we obviously wanted to make it sound as authentic as possible: there would be no point in deliberately making the orchestration un-Mahlerian so people would always remember that it wasn't Mahler's own. There is no absolutely satisfactory solution to these paradoxes. An unfinished piece of music is different from an unfinished painting or work of literature, where one is easily aware of what the artist has completed and what he has left incomplete. In the case of some unfinished paintings or pieces of sculpture – the Michelangelo *Rondanini Pietà* is a case in point – some people have found their very incompleteness curiously satisfying. Many people now prefer Constable's large-scale oil sketches to the finished paintings he made from them. The sketches contain more of the original inspiration; they are more alive. This cannot possibly be said of a work of music, where the performance of a sketch will always be tantalisingly imperfect. So the view of those who opposed performances of the Tenth Symphony for this reason is at least understandable; but what I cannot understand is why people are not converted when they hear the actual music, as happened with Alma Mahler.

For the crucial question is the one Deryck Cooke asked when he wrote: 'Is Mahler's final symphonic masterpiece, so essential to our understanding of his life's work, to be lost to us simply because, lacking his own perfect end-product, we refuse to accept it in the form of its whole main essence, made audible through some subsidiary assistance by another hand?'[1] Deryck told me that the first time he heard the flute theme in the Finale, he knew that what he had done was worth doing. The music of the Finale, in spite of all its imperfections, is great music; it has profoundly affected many of us who have heard it. The Tenth Symphony, once thought irrecoverable, has returned to life: it cannot be ignored.

Notes

Source: Originally published as 'Deryck Cooke's Performing Version of Mahler's Tenth Symphony: My own involvement, some notes on the evolution of the score, and some ethical problems', *Fragment or Completion? Proceedings of the Mahler X Symposium*, Utrecht 1986, ed. Paul Op de Coul, The Hague, Universitaire Pers Rotterdam, 1991, pp. 60-73.

David Matthews has written regularly about Mahler and his music, including CD liner notes for several recordings of the Tenth Symphony; he has also occasionally reviewed live performances of the Tenth (see 'Breakfasting with Mahler', *The Independent*, 21 November 1986). Following Deryck Cooke's premature death in October 1976, he co-edited a volume of his writings, published under the title *Vindications: Essays on Romantic Music* (Faber, 1982, reprinted 2008). He has remained active as an arranger of Mahler's music throughout his career, and between 1962 and 2002 collaborated with his brother Colin on arrangements of *Lieder und Gesänge* for voice and orchestra. He has also arranged *Fünf Lieder nach Rückert* for voice and 14 players between 1992 and 1995 and, again with Colin Matthews, Seven Songs by Alma Mahler for medium voice and orchestra to a commission from the Royal Concertgebouw Orchestra in 1996.

1   Deryck Cooke, *Vindications: Essays on Romantic Music*, London, Faber and Faber, 1982, p. 94.

6   In Search of Mahler's Childhood

I first visited what was then Czechoslovakia in October 1984, accompanying the Nash Ensemble who were including my Clarinet Quartet on a short tour of the country. The tour began in Brno, and as I had a free day there I decided to go to Jihlava – Iglau – by train and find the houses where Mahler was brought up. The train was old, dirty and slow and the fifty-mile journey took several hours. At Jihlava I discovered that I had only an hour and a half before my train back to Brno, and that the station was over a mile away from the town square, near which I knew the Mahler houses were located. I set off on foot and eventually found my way to the square (the largest town square in Europe) and located Malinovského – old Pirnitzergasse – a little street running off its southern end. The Mahlers lived at No. 4 from 1860 until 1872, and then moved next door to No. 6. On the front of No. 4 is a plaque with a bas-relief of Mahler's head in profile. I took photographs and hurried back to the station. On the journey back, equally slow, peasants got in at almost every station with full baskets of mushrooms they had collected from the forest.

In January 1986 I was in Brno again. I had been asked by Roger Scruton, a founder and trustee of the Jan Hus Educational Foundation, to give an unofficial seminar in Brno on Mahler and on my own music.[1] The Jan Hus Foundation at that time operated as an underground university in Brno, Prague and Bratislava. It had begun in 1980 with a request from the philosopher Julius Tomin at the Charles University in Prague to Oxford University for help with their philosophy course. This had been severely depleted after the Russian invasion in 1968, when most of the staff had been purged and forced to take menial jobs, such as street-sweeping or boiler-minding. The Foundation's work had rapidly spread to other disciplines, and eventually to music. In Brno, the seminars were organised by Petr Oslzlý, dramaturge, and unofficial leader of the Brno experimental theatre company Theatre a String, and Miroslav (Mikin) Pospíšil, an English lecturer at the university. These seminars took place in Petr's flat, and like all such potentially subversive meetings under the communist regime were illegal, though the secret police, whom I imagine must have been aware of what was going on, caused us no trouble (the only visitor ever to be arrested was the French philosopher Jacques Derrida, who was released after the personal intervention of President Mitterrand; perhaps the secret police got cold feet after that).

In Petr's seminar I introduced and played a recording of Mahler's Tenth Symphony in Deryck Cooke's performing version, on which my brother Colin and I had collaborated. The choice of Mahler was important to Petr: for him, Mahler was a true representative of that Central European culture which the state, with its narrow emphasis on nationalism and its distaste for 'cosmopolitanism' (a thinly disguised anti-Semitism), was suppressing by neglect. It was also moving for me to be talking about Mahler, my favourite composer while I was growing up, in the country of his birth. Many of the immediate emotions I had had when young, but which had since receded, came back to me as I spoke and listened to this marvellous, poignant music.

The following day, Petr and Mikin offered to take me to the village of Kaliště to see the house where Mahler had been born. Kaliště is an isolated village on the border of Bohemia and Moravia, about seventy miles north-west of Brno and five miles from the town of Humpolec. It looks much as it must have done in Mahler's time: a little red-roofed church and a cluster of houses about a village green with a pond, and opposite the church the pub (*zájezdní hostinec* – roadside inn) that Bernhard Mahler kept at the time Gustav was born. The original building was burnt down in 1937 after being struck by lightning, and a new one, similar in design, had been erected on its foundations. This unpretentious pub was looked after by a rosy-cheeked *babička* in her seventies, Mrs Kratochvílová. She showed us her visitors' book, photographs and sheaves of press cuttings, and kept up a constant, high-pitched monologue in which (as I learned later) her random thoughts about Mahler ("poor man, he died so young") were interspersed with complaints about her health and her own hard life. It was a bitterly cold day, with a thick layer of snow on the ground. We took photographs – there is another plaque on the outside wall of the pub, similar to the one in Jihlava – and drove to the Jewish cemetery in Humpolec to see if we could find the grave of Mahler's elder brother Isidor, who had died in infancy in Kaliště. But almost all the graves had inscriptions in Hebrew and we soon gave up.

That October I was in Brno again. The Foundation had asked me to arrange a series of seminars by British composers. The first one was by Nigel Osborne, and I was there too, primarily to attend the Brno International Music Festival. That year there was also, for the first time, a simultaneous festival of contemporary music. On my January visit I had already been impressed with some of the contemporary Czech music I had heard, particularly from the younger Brno composers, which still seemed infused with the lively spirit of Janáček, and I had conceived the idea of trying to get some of it played in Britain. I had some success in doing this over the next few years, but that is another story.

During my visit Mikin Pospíšil took me to Kaliště again and we also visited the new Mahler museum in Humpolec. This was the brainchild of a local headmaster, Jiří Rychetský, who had single-handedly set it up, with some generous state funding, on the theme of Mahler as a Czech. Rychetský, a tremendous enthusiast, knew all the Mahler associations of the local countryside and took us to Seelau (Želiv), a few miles to the west of Humpolec. On the way we passed an 800-year-old lime tree, under which Hussite sermons had been preached in the fifteenth century and which, Rychetský assured us, was the very tree under which the hero of the *Lieder eines fahrenden Gesellen* lies down to sink into Romantic oblivion at the end of the cycle. A nice story, and at least Mahler would have almost certainly known this famous tree. Mahler visited his friend Emil Freund and stayed with him at his parents' house in Seelau on holidays between 1878 and 1881. He also briefly fell in love with one of Emil Freund's cousins, an affair that had a tragic consequence, for in 1880 she committed suicide by throwing herself in the river that runs through the village. There is a splendid monastery behind the Želivka river designed by the Baroque architect Santini – the Czech Hawksmoor, as Nikolaus Pevsner called him.

My next visit to Czechoslovakia, in August 1987, was a holiday with Maggie Hemingway, who wrote her extraordinary novel *The Postmen's House* out of her experiences that month.[2] We stayed with Petr Oslzlý, his wife Eva and their two daughters in their summer house in another village also called Kaliště (the name means 'muddy pool'), south-west of Jihlava. Petr told us with relish of how some Japanese Mahlerians came to his village by mistake, asked where Mahler's house was and were innocently directed to a house near his which by coincidence happened to be owned by some people called Mahler. He believed that a photograph of the wrong house had subsequently appeared in a Japanese book on the composer.

The countryside around Petr's Kaliště is unspoiled and beautiful, a high hill country with woods, old-fashioned farms and small lakes. My first venture into the pine forest was revelatory: I heard the opening of Mahler's First Symphony. The wind whistling through the trees produced a sound uncannily like that six-octave A on string harmonics. The whole opening, with its bird calls and distant fanfares, derives from Mahler's childhood memories of being alone in the forests near Iglau. It took him a long time before he found the precise sound he had in his memory, for originally the strings played their A normally, without harmonics, a sound, as Mahler later told his friend Natalie Bauer-Lechner, that was 'far too substantial for the shimmering and glimmering of the air that I had in mind'.[3] For the work's second performance in 1893 he hit on the idea of harmonics.

I had another revelation when Petr played me a tape of a village band that specialised in performing old-fashioned band music. Here was the source of the trio of the First Symphony's Funeral March: clarinets and trumpets in thirds playing sentimental melodies, pizzicato bass, and a bass drum with cymbals attached. I had not realised before to what extent the music that Mahler heard as a child must have affected him. Mahler told Bauer-Lechner, in connection with the 'Fischpredigt' from the *Wunderhorn* songs, that 'the Bohemian music of my childhood home has found its way into many of my compositions'.[4] How much so is probably not yet fully understood.

We made another expedition to Mahler's Kaliště and met Jiří Rychetský who took us this time to Lipnice (Lipnitz), the home of Mahler's paternal grandmother and the probable birthplace of Mahler's father. Jaroslav Hašek, the author of *The Good Soldier Schweik* (Švejk), ended his short and dissolute life there and we saw his house. Lipnice is dominated by a ruined medieval castle, and I thought of the opening of the second part of *Das klagende Lied*, 'Vom hohen Felsen erglänzt das Schloss' ('The castle gleams from a high crag'). No wonder Mahler was attracted to *Des Knaben Wunderhorn*! His childhood landscape was a Romantic world of forests, songs, lakes and castles identical to the one in which the poems are set.

Exactly two years later I was once again in Mahler country with Petr, Mikin, and a cameraman, Aleš Záboj. Petr wanted to film Kaliště, the pub and Mrs Kratochvílová; I suggested that he should also try to film all the nearby places associated with Mahler's childhood. With copies of Donald Mitchell's *Gustav Mahler: The Early Years* and Henry-Louis de La Grange's biography in my bag and with my memories of Jiří Rychetský's guided tours, we went from place to place with our video camera: the linden tree, Emil Freund's house at Želiv and finally Jihlava.

Jihlava is a historic town mostly well preserved, though in the 1960s a communist party boss, disregarding preservation orders, managed to demolish a group of medieval houses in the main square and erect a hideous supermarket in their place. Most of the handsome Renaissance buildings lining the square, however, are intact. We knocked on the door of No. 6 Malinovského and introduced ourselves to the Navrátils, the present owners, who remembered a visit by Knud Martner some years back. They were a friendly couple and allowed us to film inside and out. In the back yard were the dilapidated remains of Bernhard Mahler's Schnapps distillery. They were about to be demolished, so our filming was timely. Rummaging in the piles of broken glass and other rubbish that was strewn around the brick buildings, Mikin found an intact spirit flask which he gave to me as a souvenir. From its appearance, it could have dated from Bernhard Mahler's time, and I was certainly willing to believe it.

We filmed Mahler's primary school, and the Gymnasium to which he was sent at the age of nine. We retraced his walk to school, across the square and down a side street. The building now houses the town archives, and the staff readily produced Mahler's school reports and essays for us and, with remarkable casualness, left us alone so we could film them. We went on to the theatre where Mahler heard his first operas, still in its original state but unfortunately about to be modernised and its nineteenth-century interior destroyed; then to the Dělnicky Dům ('Workers' House' – a social club), once the Hotel Czap where Mahler played in a concert on 12 September 1876 that included his violin sonata – since lost. The salon where the concert took place was still intact, but this too was going to be demolished, as the building was to make way for a new post office. Our last destination was the Jewish cemetery. We were not certain if Mahler's parents were buried there, though we strongly suspected they must be; but the cemetery was a forlorn place, with many graves destroyed by the Nazis and most of the others overgrown by bushes and trees. We could find no trace of Mahlers. It was a chilling reminder of the fate of the Jews in this largely German-speaking town.

During those August days none of us had any idea that in a few months' time there would be a revolution that would overturn the communist government. So much has changed since then. Mrs Kratochvílová has died and the pub in Kaliště is for sale; what will happen to it is uncertain.[5] Petr Oslzlý, after two years as an advisor to President Havel, is back in Brno as director of the new, splendidly equipped Theatre on a String. Mikin Pospíšil is head of the now official, Brno-based Jan Hus Foundation, which acts as an agent for further education in both the Czech Republic and Slovakia. Brno is once again a neighbouring city of Vienna; Prague is no longer, as Milan Kundera once wrote, 'gradually fading away into the mists of Eastern Europe, to which it never really belonged'. The idea of a unified Central European culture is being reborn: those who cherished it during the long years of cultural oppression will not, I hope, lightly give it up. Mahler's part in that culture is crucial, and within it he cannot any more be regarded as the thrice homeless figure he once called himself; rather, he is equally at home as a Bohemian and an Austrian, and is recognised as the greatest of Jewish composers.

Notes

Source: *On Mahler and Britten: Essays in Honour of Donald Mitchell on His Seventieth Birthday*, Woodbridge, Suffolk, The Boydell Press, 1995, pp. 89-93.

David Matthews was introduced to Donald Mitchell (b. 1925) by Deryck Cooke in 1965 and began to do editorial work for the newly-formed publishing house Faber Music that Mitchell had founded that year to publish the music of Benjamin Britten. Matthews's first job was to copy parts for Raymond Leppard's edition of Monteverdi's *L'incoronazione di Poppea*. Freelance work for Faber Music led to his working relationship with Benjamin Britten, and also to contacts with other publishers, for instance Boosey & Hawkes, through whom he met Nicholas Maw (1935-2009), for whom he made the vocal score of his opera *The Rising of the Moon*. He remembered:

... we [David and Colin] were both affected by Nicholas Maw. Colin was an official pupil of his, and I was an unofficial one. I think we were both influenced by his music – in my case, particularly by *Scenes and Arias*. And by the kind of harmony that he used – I learned a great deal about harmony from him; and obviously Colin did too. There was a time when we both sounded rather like him. Colin moved away into other areas, and I didn't go in the same directions. In particular, he moved away into minimalism, for a time, and I didn't go down that path.

(See: Mark Doran, 'Composer in Interview: David Matthews', *Tempo* No. 223, January 2003, p. 10)

Matthews would himself become a house composer at Faber Music from 1982:

> I talked to Donald about my music being published by Faber. They had taken a few pieces on for their hire library but had only actually published a carol. Donald said I had to prove myself by writing a big piece. Colin had written his Fourth Sonata and won a prize and he was taken up. I felt I had also to write a big piece, hence the Second Symphony. In 1978 I had gone to Dartington and met Simon Rattle who was then about 22 years old. His girlfriend was friends with my then-girlfriend. Rattle asked to see a piece of mine and I showed him my Second Symphony and he said he would perform it. It took four years, but he stayed true to his word. It was a real stroke of luck. As a result of that, I was taken up by Faber. Previously David Drew had seen quite a lot of me and Boosey & Hawkes had published two orchestral works, *September Music* and the *Serenade*, as well as *Duet Variations* for flute and piano. (Conversation with the editor, London, September 2011)

Matthews's Third Symphony, Op. 37 (1983-85) and the song-cycle, *Movement of Autumn*, Op. 98, for soprano and small orchestra (2003-05) are dedicated to Donald Mitchell.

1   Roger Scruton (b. 1944), English philosopher and aesthetician. He writes about David Matthews in 'The Emancipation of the Consonance' in Part Two of this volume.

2   Maggie Hemingway (1946-93) was Matthews's partner from 1983 until her death. Born in Orford, Suffolk, she grew up in New Zealand before studying French and English at Edinburgh University, graduating with an MA in 1967. She worked in publishing, including as Rights Manager for J. M. Dent before devoting herself to freelance writing. Her first novel, *The Bridge*, was published in 1986 and won the Winifred Holtby Memorial Prize; it was adapted into a film in 1992. She wrote three more novels, *Stop House Blues* (1988), *The Postmen's House* (1991) and *Eyes* (1993). She provided the text for three of Matthews's works: *Cantiga*, Op. 45, for soprano and orchestra (1988), the song-cycle *From Coastal Stations*, Op. 53 (1990-91) for medium voice and piano, and *Pride* (1993) for soprano, alto, tenor voices and string quartet. The slow movement of Matthews's Piano Trio No. 2, Op. 61 (1993-4) and *A Little Threnody* for cor anglais, Op. 63 (1993) are dedicated to her memory. Her poem 'Autumn' is published in Part Two of this volume.

3   Natalie Bauer-Lechner, *Recollections of Gustav Mahler*, trans. Dika Newlin, London, Faber Music Ltd, 1980, p. 160.

4   *Ibid.*, p. 33.

5   It is now a pension with a small concert hall where Mahler's music is occasionally played.

7   Sibelius and Living Traditions

When I was ten years old, I went to my first symphony concert: the Hallé Orchestra under Barbirolli in Walthamstow Assembly Hall. The overture was Rossini's *The Thieving Magpie* and I can vividly remember the shock of the opening side drum solo. Then I suppose there was a concerto, though I don't recall which one. But the symphony, after the interval, was Sibelius's Second, and I remember how powerful it sounded, and how strikingly different it was from anything I'd heard up till then. I was having piano lessons at the time but hadn't yet begun to compose. When I did so, a few years later, it was another symphony, Beethoven's Ninth, which provided the initial stimulus to write, with all the absurd confidence of youth, an hour-long symphony of my own, a world embracing everything I could cram into it. While I was making this first attempt, Mahler became, and remained for many years, the chief of my musical gods. But Sibelius was always there alongside him, and at some point he began to usurp Mahler's place. Mahler, with his emotional extremism, is an ideal composer for adolescence, but Sibelius, like Haydn and Mozart, is perhaps only properly understood by adults. Nowadays there is no symphonist since Beethoven whom I hold in higher regard than Sibelius.

Mahler's famous disagreement with Sibelius about the nature of the symphony might have been less apparently diametrical had he known anything of what his Finnish contemporary was doing with the medium, which he did not. Sibelius was right to emphasise formal severity and a logical 'interconnection between all the motives'. Yet Mahler's own symphonies display hardly less thorough motivic interconnectedness than Sibelius's. It is, however, Sibelius's particular solution to the problem of Romanticism (which in various ways still haunts us all) that seems to me especially important. The more Romantic one's approach to composition – and I make no bones about acknowledging my own highly Romantic temperament – the more important it is to discover ways of objectifying one's emotions. Sibelius's progress from the opulent Romantic nationalism of the First Symphony to the taut Classical grandeur of the Seventh has been an exemplar for me, for I am also much concerned with traditional forms and their renewal. His transformations of Classical sonata structure are extraordinarily inventive. This is especially so in the Fifth Symphony, with its combination of first movement and scherzo, the latter enormously extending the idea of a new departure inherent in Beethoven's codas into a continuously accelerating second development and recapitulation; and in the Seventh, with its compounding of the elements of all four symphonic movements into a seamless whole. Sibelius was not just prolonging the life of tonality at a time when it seemed to some that the most logical step forward was to abandon it; he and other like-minded composers such as Nielsen were showing conclusively that its potential was by no means exhausted, but could be comprehensively renewed. In migrating northwards, the symphony found new energy and vitality.

Although I was perfectly aware of what most of my contemporaries were doing, I did not wish to join them; I could not abandon my instinctive inclination to compose tonally. My conviction was strengthened whenever I listened to Sibelius and noted how he used tonal disruption and dissonance as composers had always done: as part of a larger scheme whose boundaries were tonal. There are many passages where tonal disruption and subsequent resolution are employed with immensely powerful effect. In the Fifth Symphony, for instance, in the transition from the first movement proper to the scherzo development, the music seems suddenly to lose its way, as the strings (at figure J) take up a little chromatic descending and ascending scale motif and wander aimlessly about with it. A *lugubre* solo bassoon increases the sense of anxiety as it climbs higher to E♭ (its thin voice in this register, now marked *patetico*, is a brilliant choice of tone colour), at which point the strings stabilise themselves on the tonic chord. But no sooner have they done so, and a timpani roll underlined the E♭, than the brass enters *pp crescendo* with the dominant seventh of D: one of the most hair-raising moments in all music. The strings confirm this new tonal conflict with their forceful entry on D, E♭, D, A, A♭; the music strains forward, slowly and painfully, but in anticipation of something momentous, until its exultant leap into B major and the recovery of firm ground. (Although this key sounds like a complete new discovery, the shift from E♭ to B has already been anticipated at the beginning of the movement, five bars after figure A.) Similarly, in the coda of the finale, the quiet attainment (*largamente assai*, eight bars before figure P) of E♭ major after a long passage in G♭ major and the tonic minor is immediately undermined by accumulating dissonance (note how the trumpets spell out the little descending and ascending chromatic scale from the first movement). This reaches another electrifying climax three bars before figure R, with repeated Cs against a B/F tritone. When E♭ major is triumphantly reaffirmed, it has the additional authority gained from this trial of strength. Now the music's forward momentum is so overwhelming that it takes all six hammer blows interspersed with hugely dramatic silences to bring it to a halt (conductors should have the courage to give them their full duration).

We live in a time of loose definitions, the symphony among them. I would not go as far as Robert Simpson, who, when editing the *Pelican Guide to the Symphony*, excluded a number of composers, including Stravinsky, who had called their works symphonies on the grounds that these works were un-symphonic. But I certainly think that Sibelius represents the ideal of a true symphonist, and has set a standard against which one can measure oneself. Elsewhere, in discussing the fundamental difference between *Tapiola* (which Sibelius called a tone poem) and the Seventh Symphony, Simpson quotes

Sibelius: 'the directly symphonic is the compelling vein that goes through the whole. This in contrast to the depicting.'[1] The fact that *Tapiola* is the depiction of, or more precisely a meditation on, a state of nature as embodied in the Finnish forests, has often been given to explain why it remains rooted in B minor and a single theme; and although there are shifts of mood and pace, the music is essentially static: the forest may change with the seasons and the weather, yet in essence it is always the same. But one would also expect monotonality from the form that Sibelius had chosen: a classical set of variations. The way in which each variation grows organically out of its predecessor is a final tribute to Sibelius's mastery of the art of transition. The Seventh Symphony, on the other hand, though almost as fixated on its home tonality of C, is always moving symphonically: evolving, changing direction, sometimes with slow deliberation, sometimes with athletic swiftness; and its ending is felt as an achievement, the culmination of some great journey.

There is a similar feeling of a journey in several pieces that are not symphonies, such as the 'symphonic fantasy' *Pohjola's Daughter*. In making a distinction in my own work between symphonies and symphonic poems (I have now written four of each), I have again had Sibelius's own criteria in mind. The first three of my symphonies were all attempts at combining the movements of the traditional symphony into one; my Third Symphony is the most concise and, I think, the most successful attempt so far, and the closest to the Sibelius Seventh model of an organic whole, though when I compare my own transitions from one tempo to another with his I see I still have much to learn. There is also a clear influence (as I now see) from the slow movement of the Fourth Symphony in my Third's discovery of its principal theme at the very end of the piece. My four symphonic poems all to some extent draw their inspiration from landscape – an obvious common link with Sibelius. Having just completed the fourth of them, I realise that they form a kind of quasi-symphonic cycle like Sibelius's *Four Legends*. The first of the *Legends*, 'Lemminkäinen and the Maidens of the Island', is, incidentally, one of Sibelius's most underrated scores: it has superbly sustained symphonic momentum and its long central string melody is one of the most inspired melodies in his early work. The opening chord in the horns, one feels, could only be Sibelius; yet it is exactly the same chord as that which opens Beethoven's E♭ major Piano Sonata, Op. 31, No. 3. Sibelius was obviously haunted by it: it also stands in the background of the horn-dominated E♭ major opening of the Fifth Symphony.

Sibelius was a master of endings. I have mentioned the Fifth Symphony's, and there are many other superb ones: the sudden ebbing away of vital power in *Pohjola's Daughter*, leaving the strings to brood on its absence; or the grave procession of chords that follows the wholly unexpected moment of vision in *The Bard*, ending with an unequivocal *tierce de Picardie*; or the weirdly dissonant coda of that neglected masterpiece *Luonnotar* with its unearthly resolution into F♯ major. There is a sense of inevitability about all these endings, none more so than in the eight inscrutable A minor chords on the strings that close the Fourth Symphony, once again after a long and grimly-fought tonal conflict. The B major chord, also for strings and also *mezzo forte* (who else has ended pieces *mf*?) that closes *Tapiola* is another *tierce de Picardie*, but one far removed from, say, the tender farewell to tonality implied by the ending of Schoenberg's Second Quartet. Sibelius's chord, with its very special sound that comes from the placing of the D♯ in the middle with bare fifths above and below, has an unchallengeable inner strength, as if it has always been waiting there to be reached. After such an ending, what more could Sibelius possibly have had to say?

All that I have been discussing is for me the real stuff of music, the kinds of thing the complex musical language that has gradually evolved over the centuries is best equipped to do. To cast aside this rich and versatile tonal language with its productive tensions between diatonicism and chromaticism in favour of a totally chromatic one has always seemed to me a curious choice – likewise, to adopt a simplistic tonality that takes no account of what has happened since the seventeenth century. Not that I necessarily reject the music of those who have made either choice: I admire many composers with radically different approaches to my own. I can see the advantage of restriction, of using a palette with only a few colours. But because of what I want to say in my music, and the kinds of piece I want to write, there is no choice for me but to work within the broad language of tonality. And so it is to Sibelius, who used such a language with such power, that I feel closest.

Notes

Source: *The Musical Times*, April 1993, pp. 189-91.

1   Robert Simpson, *Sibelius and Nielsen*, BBC Publications, 1965, pp. 33-4.

8   'Dark Pastoral'

All unfinished works are problematic, though each has its own particular problem. In Mozart's Requiem, for instance, the Sanctus and Benedictus composed by Süssmayr are markedly inferior to the remainder of the work, but they have been generally accepted and most performances still include them. Schubert's Eighth Symphony was apparently left unfinished: that Schubert intended a two-movement form like Beethoven's last piano sonata is not impossible, though unlikely as he wrote the greater part of a scherzo in short score. Most people, however, agree that the two composed movements are peculiarly satisfying by themselves, and attempts to finish the Symphony by completing the scherzo and using the *Rosamunde* B minor entr'acte as a finale, are in my opinion unconvincing. Bruckner's Ninth Symphony is almost always performed in its incomplete, three-movement state; many believe this to be entirely satisfactory, yet Bruckner would certainly not have considered it so. He spent the last two years of his life composing the finale, in failing health, and almost completed it; a large part is in finished score and only the coda is absent. Three recent completions, all with their own version of the coda, have shown that, despite its imperfections, the finale should be played with the other movements; only then can we hear Bruckner's mighty scheme come to fruition.[1] The case of Bruckner's Ninth is not unlike that of Mahler's Tenth, which was also once only played as a torso. Unlike Bruckner, Mahler's symphony has no gaps, though much of it is in a less finished state than the nine-tenths of the finale that Bruckner composed. Initial objections to Deryck Cooke's performing version, expressed by Klemperer, Walter and other conductors of the older generation, have now mostly been overcome and the Symphony is taking its place in the repertoire; it is not the Tenth as Mahler would have perfected it, yet much of its music is among the best he ever wrote, and it must be heard. Finally, Elgar's Third Symphony, less complete than any of the other works I mentioned, has been nobly resurrected by Anthony Payne, who pieced together the disparate sketches and filled in the gaps with extraordinary stylistic insight: 'It seemed as if I was being impelled by forces outside myself,' he writes.

What Payne achieved for Elgar was an inspiration for me in a piece I based on the slow movement of Vaughan Williams's unfinished Cello Concerto. I had no idea that this work existed until in 2002 Steven Isserlis, who had been told about it by Anthony Payne, asked me to look at the manuscript in the British Library.[2] Vaughan Williams intended the Concerto for Pablo Casals, who had premiered the *Fantasia on Sussex Folk Tunes* for cello and orchestra in 1930. Neither Vaughan Williams nor Casals was entirely satisfied with this work and the composer eventually withdrew it. It seems that he found the medium of cello and orchestra unusually difficult. According to Michael Kennedy, he wrote most of the existing material between 1942 and 1943 and 'was "looking at it" again from 1953 onwards'.[3] He originally planned it in four movements, but sketches for a scherzo were abandoned, reducing the work to three movements: a fairly large-scale opening 'Rhapsody' marked *Andante con moto*; then a Lento; and finally an *Allegro moderato*. The first movement was completed in draft score, with some instrumental indications. For the Lento there is a six-page short score headed 'fair copy' along with an earlier sketched version and some other sketch pages. For the finale there are a large number of sketches that do not add up to a complete draft. All the sketch pages are hard to decipher: Vaughan Williams's handwriting is probably the untidiest of any great composer and there are many places where it is impossible to say with certainty what note he intended.

When I examined the manuscript, the first thing I saw was a note from Ursula Vaughan Williams saying that because it was incomplete the work should not be performed. I did not know whether this was on her authority or her husband's. I could not conceive of attempting to complete the work because of the chaotic state of the finale. The fair copy of the Lento, however, was both legible and certainly performable, but the score breaks off at the end of the page. Here Ursula Vaughan Williams has written 'Nothing after here in fair copy' – though it is curious that there isn't any more, as the music ends in the middle of a phrase, and there is no indication for what was to happen next in any of the sketch pages. Could it be that some pages have been lost? What exists of the fair copy consists of a longish section of 45 bars in an unvarying modal G minor, which develops the initial melodic phrases in the orchestra and solo cello (Ex. 1). Towards the end of this section, a new triplet accompanying figure appears, and this leads the music first to F minor, and then to an agitated passage for the solo cello in C minor, and finally to an orchestral passage in E minor. After three bars of this the music breaks off.

Example 1: David Matthews, Dark Pastoral, *Op. 112, initial melodic phrases.*

Example 2: David Matthews, Dark Pastoral, *Op. 112,*
new melodic idea derived from Example 1.

I copied out the short score, and Steven made a recording with Stephen Hough. This he sent to the RVW Trustees, with a request for me to make a performing version with orchestra for him to play. The Trustees initially turned the idea down; but in 2008, after Ursula's death, they generously agreed to my making a completion of the slow movement as a separate piece, provided that I used none of Vaughan Williams's sketches. I was free to make my own decisions about the remainder of the movement. Vaughan Williams had left very few instrumental indications: apart from those for clarinet and violas at the start, there were no others except three for flute and one more for clarinet. A smallish orchestra seemed adequate, with double woodwind (including cor anglais), two horns and strings – in other words, the orchestra of *The Lark Ascending*, apart from the addition of a cor anglais and the absence of a triangle.

After orchestrating what Vaughan Williams had already composed, and adding some extra contrapuntal lines in a few places, I faced the problem of how to continue. I wanted a substantial contrasting section to follow the E minor passage, which I also began in E minor, based on a folk-like melody in compound time. Though this sounds quite new, I derived it from the first idea in Ex. 1, as Ex. 2 shows (to make things clearer I have transposed the melody from E minor to G minor).

I soon brought back Vaughan Williams's triplet accompaniment idea, now in E major. After an orchestral climax on Ex. 2, I reintroduced Ex. 1, in a faster tempo; this also reaches an orchestral climax which subsides into a restatement of Ex. 1, as at the beginning of the work. I followed this with a coda in which the solo cello rises higher and higher against a background of increasingly divided strings alternating chords of G minor and E minor, and ending in the home tonality of G minor. This passage may sound very like Vaughan Williams: I wasn't consciously trying to imitate his style, but neither did I make a deliberate decision to go against it. This is the opposite of what, for instance, Schnittke does in his piece based on the scherzo fragment from Mahler's early Piano Quartet: his music has nothing in common with Mahler's and he makes a virtue of the dramatic contrast. The middle section of my piece is probably more harmonically daring than Vaughan Williams would have made it – I wanted to introduce some chromatic harmony after the unvarying modality of the first part – but it remains essentially within the same kind of musical language.

So this piece is different from the other completions that I mentioned at the start. In the first place, it isn't an entire completion, but a single movement derived from what would have been a much larger work. In completing Mozart's Requiem, Süssmayr not only tried to write in Mozart's style, but was also hoping to pass the whole work off as by Mozart. With Bruckner's Ninth Symphony and Elgar's Third, the intention was to write the missing parts as Bruckner or Elgar might have composed them. My aims were somewhat different: I became obsessed with Vaughan Williams's material and continued as if it were entirely my own piece. The result, I hope, is a kind of collaboration, in which a fine piece of vintage Vaughan Williams is resurrected and placed in a compatible context.

The piece lasts about eleven minutes, and is approximately one third Vaughan Williams and two thirds me. I have called it *Dark Pastoral*, as the orchestral colours are often muted and the overall tone rather elegiac. After the piece was written, it became a true elegy: in May 2010 Steven Isserlis's wife Pauline died after a long struggle with cancer. I have dedicated *Dark Pastoral* to her memory.

Notes

Source: 'My New Music: David Matthews', *Musical Opinion*, Vol. 133, No. 1478, September-October 2010, pp. 16-17.

Dark Pastoral, Op. 112 was first performed on 5 September 2010 at the Royal Albert Hall as part of the BBC Proms. The soloist was Steven Isserlis and the BBC Concert Orchestra was conducted by Paul Daniel.

Dark Pastoral was not the first time David Matthews had been involved with the music of Vaughan Williams. In 2003, he had been one of five composers each providing an orchestral variation on the composer's hymn tune 'Down Ampney' for the Three Choirs Festival. This short scherzo was later incorporated into his Sixth Symphony, Op. 100, which takes the hymn tune as its basis: premiered at the BBC Proms on 1 August 2007 by the BBC National Orchestra of Wales conducted by Jac van Steen, it was met with acclaim by audience and critics alike. The subsequent recording, by the same performers, was issued by Dutton Epoch and went on to win the award for a Premiere Recording at the 2011 *BBC Music Magazine* Awards.

Matthews has been involved with editorial work for Oxford University Press on several new editions of Vaughan Williams's scores, including the Tuba Concerto, Third Symphony and *Sinfonia Antartica*.

1   David Matthews writes (June 2013): 'Simon Rattle's latest recording of the complete symphony with the Berlin Philharmonic, which uses the most recent version of the Samale/Phillips/Cohrs/Mazzuca edition of the finale, is by far the most plausible account I have heard, and should convince anyone who has doubts about the validity of playing all four movements.'

2   Steven Isserlis (b. 1958), British cellist. He has regularly collaborated with David Matthews and premiered *Concerto in Azzurro*, Op. 87, in October 2002. On the occasion of the composer's seventieth birthday, Isserlis wrote:

David is a delight to work with, and a delight to be with. As a composer, he has steadfastly followed his own path, never trying to be different – and has therefore managed to find his own voice and be different! As a man, he seems to be devoid of any malice (not always the case with composers …). Although a deeply sensitive and serious musician, he is great company, with a smile that can light up a room. We have worked together several times – on his atmospheric completion of the slow movement of Vaughan Williams's unfinished cello concerto; on a charming *Tango flageoletto* for cello and piano, written for young cellists; and on a major work, his *Concerto in Azzurro*. This concerto is one of the most beautiful contemporary pieces for cello that I know: poetic, exciting and sincerely touching. I hope that it will enter the repertoire; and I hope and trust that David will continue to compose for the next 70 years – at least.

3   Michael Kennedy, *A Catalogue of the Works of Ralph Vaughan Williams*, Oxford, OUP, 1996, p. 241.

On Composers

9 *This What You Call Music?*
(book review)

Music is ultimately inexplicable, yet its creation is a mystery that most people forever want to probe. Composers today are always being asked to talk about their work and the creative process: many of them are rather good at it. Some of the most eloquent, indeed, are able to make their music appear more interesting than it turns out to be. On the other hand, I cannot imagine Mozart would have had much to say in a pre-concert talk. Just occasionally, one longs to return to a time when music was expected to provide its own explanation.

Andrew Ford, an Englishman now resident in Australia and a composer himself, has interviewed thirty composers for this book. Eleven of them are Australian, eight British, the remainder all internationally known figures such as Carter, Boulez and Stockhausen. Only ten of the interviews are presented in strict dialogue form, and these are mostly the best. Some of the others, originally written as newspaper articles, are more brief biography than interview. In Ford's conversation with the Australian Ross Edwards (to take the most extreme example), Edwards is allowed only three sentences of his own. The majority of the other Australian composers are treated similarly, which gives the no doubt unintended impression that their voices aren't worth hearing, unless filtered through Ford's commentaries; a pity, since they are the ones most unfamiliar to us in Britain. Ford, as a composer, asks insider's questions and generally gets confiding answers. His subjects could trust him not to ask dinner-party non-starters such as 'What kind of music do you write?' He is none the less very interested in what sort of music each composer writes and in the fact that each composer here writes in a different style. That two near contemporaries (and incidentally both pupils of Lennox Berkeley), John Tavener and Brian Ferneyhough, can end up at the opposite extremes of the stylistic spectrum is a telling comment on the freedom of the contemporary music scene, one in which every composer can find a means of expression to suit his or her temperament. Does this mean we are all postmodernists? I don't think so: if postmodernism implies a careless detachment from the styles one plays with, the serious artist builds a musical language out of what he loves best from the past and the present, a process of attachment from which he only begins to break free once he has found himself.

A tradition in the old sense, however, no longer exists. When asked if he feels part of one, Harrison Birtwistle replies that, for him, "tradition is what is created". What is created nowadays is so diverse one cannot classify it, but its validity has nothing to do with style. The days when Boulez could dismiss a large amount of twentieth-century music on grounds of incorrect style are over. Boulez himself is more benign these days, though he can still make such sweeping statements as "I compare postmodernism with neoclassicism between the two wars. What remains of neoclassicism? Absolutely nothing." (Weill's Second Symphony? Tippett's Concerto for Double String Orchestra? *Apollo*?!) But one would hardly expect composers' opinions to be objective: how else could they achieve individuality? Some of Tavener's ("there's nothing sacred in late Beethoven", for instance) sound pretty loopy to me; but they accord with his view that Western music took a wrong turning at the Renaissance, a view that has been the starting point for his own musical language. Peter Sculthorpe similarly has no time for Beethoven or Mozart, and finds *gagaku* "the greatest music of the race", which provides a key to understanding his own music. Steve Reich's realisation that serialism had little to offer a generation 'raised on Chuck Berry' was the beginning of his radically original path.

To return to my initial mild regret about composers needing to explain their work at all, I suppose that just as long as all contemporary music is widely supposed to be prohibitively difficult (though Górecki's Third Symphony, if it has done nothing else, may have helped destroy that myth), composers will have to go on trying to persuade their audiences that it isn't, necessarily. The real value of a book such as this may be to encourage its readers to seek out the sounds that these many different and fascinatingly individual voices have created, and perhaps even to enjoy them.

Source: Review of: Andrew Ford, *Composer to Composer: Conversations about Contemporary Music*, in: *Times Literary Supplement*, 27 May 1994, p. 17.

10   Benjamin Britten

(a) 'Death in Venice' and the Third String Quartet

The recitative introduction to the passacaglia finale of Britten's Third String Quartet (1975) contains five quotations from his last opera *Death in Venice* (1973). These are: the Venice Overture motif, played in the quartet by the cello (bar 3); the motif associated with Aschenbach's pursuit of Tadzio in Act 2, on the second violin (bar 7); the harp phrase from the 'Phaedrus aria', on the first violin, pizzicato (bar 9); the agitated motif that appears in the scene of Aschenbach's persecution by street vendors and beggars in Act 1, on the viola (bar 16); and finally Aschenbach's 'I love you' from the end of Act 1, played by all four instruments (bars 23-7).

Why are these quotations here? The finale's subtitle, 'La Serenissima', gives one explanation. Britten composed the movement in Venice on his last visit there, in November 1975, and he intended it as a tribute to the city he loved above all others. The passacaglia bass, on which the movement is built, he derived from the sound of Venetian bells.[1] Quotations from *Death in Venice* were also appropriate; and the first of the quotations, the Venice Overture motif, is based on the notes to which the chorus repeatedly sing 'Serenissima' in the preceding boat journey scene. But this is certainly not the whole explanation, nor the only link between opera and quartet. It is clear that Britten identified with Aschenbach, more closely, I suspect, than with any other of his operatic protagonists. One wonders if, when he was composing *Death in Venice*, Britten imagined that he would share Aschenbach's fate. What is probable is that he hastened his own death by postponing his heart operation until he had finished the score – the operation from which he made only a partial recovery. The Third Quartet, the *chef-d'oeuvre* of the works he wrote in the three years between *Death in Venice* and his own death in December 1976 is, I would suggest, Aschenbach's quartet; it continues, on a purely musical level, his quest for transcendence, whose symbol in the opera is Tadzio and, in the Quartet, Venice herself.

At the end of *Death in Venice* Aschenbach dies a broken and defeated man, believing that his pursuit of ideal beauty in the real world has led him, in the words of Socrates that he quotes, 'to the abyss'. But the music of these closing pages tells us otherwise. Immediately after the 'Phaedrus aria' – the passage in which Aschenbach unequivocally condemns himself – comes the fullest statement of the 'view' motif. In its context and in its character this passage is comparable to the D minor interlude in Berg's *Wozzeck*: in both passages the composer, as it were, steps on to the stage to plead for his hero. The warmth and indeed nobility of Britten's music here serve to purge Aschenbach of much of his accumulated guilt. The orchestral postlude after Aschenbach's death takes this redemptive process a stage further. Over a deep, tolling bass, the strings gently restate Aschenbach's 'Hymn to Apollo', which he had sung exultantly at the end of Act 1; the Hymn rises yearningly towards Tadzio's theme which is suspended above it on the glockenspiel, the two themes reaching a high unison A in the very last bar.

The exotic sonority of Tadzio's music had always emphasised his remoteness from Aschenbach, though its tonality, an unvarying pentatonic A major, is close to Aschenbach's own E major – E is its dominant. When Aschenbach sings the exultant 'Hymn to Apollo' after watching Tadzio's victory in the games, it is in Tadzio's key of A;[2] the music then moves to the dominant for Aschenbach's climactic "I love you" and the subsequent prelude to Act 2.[3] Though the association of E major with Aschenbach was made at the outset with "I, Aschenbach, famous as a master writer," this is the first time E major has been firmly established, and the fact that it appears here as the dominant to Tadzio's key contributes to its security. It is a short-loved security, however; suspicion of his motives soon begins to undermine Aschenbach's idealism. Tadzio's theme disappears and A major becomes the key associated with Aschenbach's relentless pursuit of Tadzio through the streets of Venice (starting at Fig. 211 in the operatic score); while the stability of E major collapses as Aschenbach gradually loses his self-control. In the climactic dream scene – the vision of a Dionysiac orgy – Aschenbach's E major is finally overwhelmed by the shattering reappearance of Tadzio's theme, in its original A major but now cruelly overladen with dissonance. As the vision fades and the still sleeping Aschenbach takes up the Tadzio theme and distorts it, the theme becomes, quite literally, perverted.

The feeble stuttering of the 'I, Aschenbach' motif at Fig. 307 indicates how thoroughly Aschenbach's key has been destroyed. But this passage, showing him at his lowest ebb, turns out to be the prelude to his partial redemption. The orchestral postlude at Fig. 325 rehabilitates A major and restores Tadzio's music to its original purity. The trilling bass pedal on the leading note, G♯, however, makes the tonality uneasy until the very last bar, when the pedal lifts off. One of the advantages of a tonal composer is the subtlety of expression he can achieve: the precariousness of the affirmation that Britten wants to make here is precisely expressed by this last-minute resolution.

The ambiguity still present in this ending is underlined by the fact that Aschenbach's E major has not been reaffirmed. For this we must turn to the Third Quartet, and here E major is achieved only after a long and complex process.[4] The first movement begins with a motif related, as Peter Evans has pointed out, to the music of Aschenbach's unhappy wandering through Venice (cf. Exx. 1a and b).[5]

Example 1a: Benjamin Britten, String Quartet No. 3, Op. 94, first movement, bars 1-3.

Example 1b: Benjamin Britten, Death in Venice, *Op. 88, Fig. 106.*

In addition, the figure marked *x* in Ex. 1a happens to be a retrograde of the opera's 'I love you' motif at the same pitch that it is presented in the introduction to the passacaglia. It is impossible to say whether this is conscious or unconscious. The two-flat key signature of this movement would seem to imply B♭, which is at the furthest tonal remove (an augmented fourth away) from the quartet's E major goal. But the tonality is not defined; this is the least tonal movement of the quartet and consequently the least stable.[6] The quartet is about the rediscovery of stability, and it begins at a point that corresponds to Aschenbach's psychological condition at his death.

Stability is first sought in the key of C major, and that key is serenely achieved in the slow, third movement. The fourth movement, which is called 'Burlesque', begins in A minor, the relative minor of C. So E major is once again approached through A, though this A, both minor and (after the trio) major, is worlds apart from Tadzio's pure pentatonic A. The music of the 'Burlesque' is hard, satirical, the trio deliberately banal – as in the 'Rondo-Burleske' from Mahler's Ninth Symphony, to which it surely refers. After this movement, the finale can hardly begin without a long, tentative introduction, which presents the five quotations mentioned above. The last of these, 'I love you', is stated, appropriately, in C, from which key the music moves smoothly into E major and stays there for the longest purely diatonic passage that Britten allowed himself in his late works. We cannot but feel that the redemption of Aschenbach that had begun in *Death in Venice* is completed here, with the radiant resurrection of his true key: this makes Britten's intention clear, as does the obvious derivation of the main melody from 'I love you' (Ex. 2a) and the reference, in the second phrase, to the Hymn to Apollo (Ex. 2b; see the notes marked *y* in both examples).

Example 2a: Benjamin Britten, *String Quartet No. 3, Op. 94, Fifth Movement, bars 26-32.*

Example 2b: Benjamin Britten, Death in Venice, *Op. 88, Fig. 178.*

The questioning ending that Britten chose instead of the expected E major triad opens up a fresh perspective (Ex. 3). In *Death in Venice*, the last bar brought sudden clarification; here too something is glimpsed, but more mysteriously. What lies beyond death is beyond the scope of most artists, but Britten, close to his own death, came as near as anyone to providing a clue.

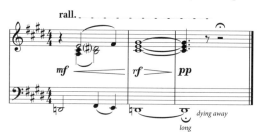

Example 3: Benjamin Britten, *String Quartet No. 3, Op. 94, fifth movement, bars 126-28.*

Notes

Source: 'Death in Venice and the Third String Quartet', Death in Venice, Cambridge Opera Handbooks, ed. Donald Mitchell, Cambridge, Cambridge University Press, 1987, pp. 154-61.

1   Specifically, the bells of Santa Maria della Salute, which are sounded once a year, on 21 November, to commemorate salvation from a plague (appropriately enough for a work indebted to Death in Venice).

2   David Matthews reviewed Glyndebourne Touring Opera's production of Death in Venice in 1989:

> The manipulation of the large cast on the small Glyndebourne stage is always adept. Even the Games of Apollo, the one universally criticised weak passage in the score, which can look embarrassingly like a prep-school sports day, are deftly choreographed here. If Tadzio's effortless victories in the games remain tiresome, that is part of the intractable problem of presenting a character who is defined only through his admirer's eyes. Infatuation will always seem absurd to the onlooker, and so it does here; but it is meant to. It was Britten's difficult task to provide music that would redress the balance, that would redeem his protagonist, after absurdity had led to degradation and death. This he did in the last pages of the score, which contain some of the finest music he ever wrote. ('A Master of Endings', Times Literary Supplement, 3 November 1989, p. 1213.)

3   The original intention, as is clear from Britten's sketch, is that Act 2 of the opera would follow on from Act 1 without a break.

4   David Matthews gives a fuller account of this process in his article 'The String Quartets and Some Other Chamber Works', in: The Britten Companion, ed. Christopher Palmer, London, Faber and Faber, 1984, pp. 383-92.

5   Peter Evans, The Music of Benjamin Britten, London, Dent, 1979, pp. 340-41.

6   Hans Keller provides an alternative reading of this movement, arguing that it is a subtle sonata scheme. See: Hans Keller, 'Britten's Last Masterpiece', Spectator, 2 June 1979, pp. 27-8; reprinted in: Hans Keller, Britten. Essays, Letters and Opera Guides, ed. Christopher Wintle and Alison Garnham, London, Plumbago, 2013, pp. 170-73.

(b) Benjamin Britten. A Biography by Humphrey Carpenter
(book review)

Britten would probably have been horrified by this book. He may have expressed the wish before he died for the truth to be told about him; yet the tiniest deviation from the truth as he saw it would have upset him enormously. The duty of the conscientious biographer, however, is to assemble all available facts and a diversity of opinions, in order to try to present as objective a portrait as possible. Humphrey Carpenter has done this with tremendous skill. For the most part he does not judge but lets the evidence of Britten's own words and those of his friends speak for themselves. The result is an immensely readable book which seems to me, as one who knew Britten during the last ten years of his life, to give a mostly true and fair account of the complex personality of one of our greatest composers.

The question remains, nonetheless, whether such an intimate biography – especially revealing of its subject's sexual life – should have been written at all. In Britten's case, I think the answer is yes. There are some composers – Bach or Stravinsky – knowledge of whose life adds little to the understanding of their music. But for Britten, as for Mahler, composing was, on one level at least, a kind of spiritual autobiography, a way of coming to terms with the deepest problems of life, which in Britten's case were sexual ones. There can be no doubt that sympathetic revelation of even the most private aspects of Britten's life sheds light on his music.

As a biographer of Auden, Carpenter is well qualified to show how the poet's influence on Britten persisted long after they had ceased to work together. The famous letter Auden wrote to Britten just before leaving the USA in 1942 urged him to confront his whole nature with its dark side – which Britten then proceeded to do in *Peter Grimes*. Carpenter, who has many fresh insights into Britten's music, shows clearly how the operas from *Grimes* onwards, with their doomed outsider heroes and innocent victims, relate to the dilemmas of his private life as a homosexual. Britten was not only liable for prosecution under the law for most of his adult life for his 'marriage' with Peter Pears, but struggled to sublimate his frequent infatuations with teenage boys into paternal affection (which clearly was also quite genuine). The guilt he felt about his sexuality profoundly affected his music; indeed, it is a source of its strength and individuality: only recall the extraordinary power of 'O rose, thou art sick'.

But the supreme moments in Britten's music are those where the guilt is transcended, either by achieving a state of peace, as in *Billy Budd* or *Death in Venice*, or by forgetting guilt altogether in the healing world of night and sleep. Had Britten been a carefree sensualist, he would not have written great music; neither would he have won our respect as a man, which I think from this biography, despite all his flaws, he does.

Source: Review of: Humphrey Carpenter, *Benjamin Britten. A Biography*, London, Faber and Faber, 1992, in: *BBC Music Magazine*, September 1992.

(c) Britten's Children by John Bridcut
(book review)

John Bridcut's BBC documentary *Britten's Children* was highly praised when it was shown in 2004. The film centred on Benjamin Britten's relationships with teenage boys, and dealt with this delicate subject with sensitivity, successfully avoiding any hint of prurience. Bridcut has now expanded the research he undertook for the film into a book, in which he is able to go into greater detail, resulting in one of the most enlightening studies of Britten that has appeared so far.

In his 1992 biography, Humphrey Carpenter first raised the subject of Britten's serial infatuation with boys. Carpenter interviewed a number of the boys in question, now grown up, all of whom testified that the relationships had been beneficial experiences, and that they had remained chaste, though most of the interviewees were aware that Britten had been in love with them. Britten's homosexuality accords very precisely with Freud's account of boys whose intense fixation on their mother leads to an identification with her, and thus to narcissistic love of 'a young man who resembles themselves and whom they may love as their mother loved them'. Large areas of Britten's personality seem to have been arrested at the age of thirteen, a time when, to quote the Hardy poem he was to set in *Winter Words*, 'all went well': he was head boy and *Victor Ludorum* at his prep school, pouring out reams of music, including his first orchestral works, and his adoration for his mother was at its height. In conversation with Imogen Holst in 1953, as Bridcut relates, Britten admitted that he thought of himself as perpetually thirteen. When he moved into adolescence and began to have crushes on younger schoolboys, they too were often at this age; the pattern recurred throughout his life.

The companion set of interviews in *Britten's Children* includes one that is especially revealing. Wulff Scherchen (now John Woolford) was one of the most significant figures in Britten's life, but until a few years ago he had been a shadowy figure. Britten met Wulff, the son of the conductor Hermann Scherchen, in Siena when he was twenty and Wulff thirteen. Four years later, in 1938, Britten learned that Wulff was living in Cambridge, and the pair quickly became the closest of friends. Britten's letters to Wulff in Volume Two of *Letters from a Life* were censored at Woolford's request, and Carpenter was thus constrained in his biography; but Woolford has now allowed Bridcut unrestricted publication of the correspondence, and of the poems he wrote to Britten. It is clear that both of them were deeply in love – the tone of their letters conveys an intimacy paralleled only by those between Britten and Pears a few years later – and that for both this was an experience without precedent.

The immediate musical result of this relationship was the song cycle *Les Illuminations*, the work with which Britten reached full artistic maturity. While he could now express in his music the whole range of his feelings, in his life he was unable fully to come to terms with adult emotions. Quite possibly the main reason for his departure to America with Peter Pears was his inability to cope with the Wulff affair. The Britten-Pears relationship, which began properly during their first few months in Canada and was to last to the end of Britten's life, was a safer haven, one reason being that the older Pears assumed the role of surrogate mother. Meanwhile, Britten was left free to fall in love with a succession of thirteen-year-old muse figures, many of whom also became for a while surrogate sons – for his paternal instinct was a side of him that continued to develop.

Britten's love of children led him often to use boys' voices: they are one of the most distinctively original sounds in his music. As Bridcut points out, they appear, astonishingly, in almost thirty of his major works, including twelve for the stage. He did not much care for girls' voices. Bridcut has much of interest to say about these pieces, notably *Noye's Fludde*. The presence of boys in Britten's operas, from *Peter Grimes* to *The Turn of the Screw* and from *A Midsummer Night's Dream* to *Death in Venice*, shows how much he was led to dramatise his obsession; and *Death in Venice* at least, in which Aschenbach's infatuation with the boy Tadzio leads eventually to his death, shows that Britten felt some guilt about it. He was innately puritanical, and in the 1930s had long resisted Auden's attempts to bohemianise him. It was courageous of him to be openly autobiographical in *Death in Venice*, and even though Aschenbach's idealised love is shown as becoming perverted, as the guardian spirit of Apollo is overcome by the savage sensuality of Dionysus, the music at the very end of the opera, evoking Tadzio's initial innocence, partially redeems him. In his almost last work, the Third String Quartet, Britten based the finale on the phrase to which, in the opera, Aschenbach sings his first, exalted "I love you", and develops it into a passage of transcendent radiance. In the end guilt is overcome by the ideal beauty that Britten worshipped all his life.

Paedophilia has become a modern obsession. It may not always imply a sexual relation, but the special nature of Britten's obsession with young male beauty and intelligence is nevertheless easily misunderstood. Many paedophiles were abused as children, and their dangerous desires are motivated by hatred. Britten's were motivated by love, which may have been to a large extent narcissistic – and, as John Bridcut's book reveals, often ended with an abrupt withdrawal of attention when the boy grew up – but which was fundamentally benign. *Britten's Children* is written with sympathy both for Britten and for the children; it is an important book, which anyone seeking to understand the personality and the music of the greatest English composer of the twentieth century should read.

Notes

Source: 'Lucky Thirteen', review of: John Bridcut, *Britten's Children*, London, Faber and Faber, 2006, in: *Times Literary Supplement*, 10 November 2006.

David Matthews began to work as Benjamin Britten's assistant in the spring of 1966 when Martin Penny, who was preparing the rehearsal score for *The Burning Fiery Furnace*, fell ill and someone was needed quickly to take over. Donald Mitchell, who was employing Matthews at the time as a copyist for Faber Music, asked him to undertake the job. After the first performance of *The Burning Fiery Furnace*, Matthews met Britten for the first time:

> Afterwards I was introduced to Britten who spoke very kindly to me. He said "Did you enjoy hearing your notes?" The atmosphere at the end seemed to be one of wholly uncritical adulation – Donald Mitchell in raptures, hordes of flatterers gathered round the poor composer. (*Journal*, 9 June 1966)

Matthews continued to work for Britten for the next four years as an occasional assistant to Britten's regular assistant, Rosamund Strode. Among his tasks, Matthews prepared the rehearsal score of *The Prodigal Son*, the vocal and full score of *Owen Wingrave*, and in 1976 made a vocal score and reduction for two pianos of Britten's first opera *Paul Bunyan*. Matthews also assisted with performing editions for Britten, including Mozart's *Idomeneo*. In his biography, *Britten*, he described his mixed feelings about working for the composer:

> I used to go to Aldeburgh to stay for extended periods, and was assigned an office in the former stable buildings beside the Red House which are now part of the Britten-Pears Library. Most days Britten would call in to say hello; sometimes I would join him for tea, and on one occasion I had supper with him and we talked at length about the contemporary music scene. I think he felt a little isolated from it but still concerned to keep in touch with what was going on. After supper he played me some gramophone records: Kirsten Flagstad singing Sibelius – I remember his enthusiasm for her voice – and the Indian flautist Pannalal Ghosh, whose playing greatly interested him at that time and influenced some of the melodic writing in *The Prodigal Son*.
>
> I was shy and somewhat in awe of Britten – not surprisingly, as he was the first adult composer I had met – and now feel that I could perhaps have made more use of the opportunities I was given. I could have shown him my music, for instance, but didn't. I was somewhat wary of the Aldeburgh scene, and a little afraid of becoming too closely drawn into it. I was also aware, as everybody was, of Britten's hyper-sensitivity and that one had to be careful not to upset him by venturing any rash opinions. He, I must say, was never anything other

than kind, considerate and helpful. (David Matthews, *Britten*, London, Haus Publishing, 2003, pp. vii – viii).

By 1975, when the Third String Quartet was composed, David Matthews's role at Aldeburgh had been taken over by his brother, Colin. Both brothers, however, played through the new quartet:

> Colin & I went to Aldeburgh to play Ben's newly composed 3rd Quartet to him in piano duet. He has not changed too much in appearance; his voice is just a little less firm, but otherwise, when seated, he looks extremely well. But he mostly has to be helped to walk, and he can only work a few hours each day. We made rather a botched job of the piece playing it through by ourselves before lunch – at least I did; I was rather self-conscious at making so many mistakes & tended to get worse instead of improve. But after lunch ... & a little more practice we did produce a reasonable through-performance for him & it was a moving occasion as the quartet is certainly a masterpiece & proves his creative powers are quite undiminished. The long passacaglia finale is especially fine, a serene piece in E major. After we had finished there was a silence and then Ben said, in a small voice: "Do you think it's any good?" We assured him that it was. (*Journal*, 17 December 1975)

Interviewed by Mark Doran when he was working on the biography, Matthews commented:

> ... there was a lot of influence that came from the Third String Quartet. I was 32 by then, but it represented so many things that I really 'believed in' about Britten: it was the piece that I wanted him to write. I was always wanting him to write more quartets, more instrumental pieces, and was disappointed, in a sense, that he was writing the pieces he was writing. And also the Third Quartet seemed to be doing just the things I was trying to do too. So I suppose that's why it was an influence. (Mark Doran, 'Composer in Interview: David Matthews', *Tempo* No. 223, January 2003, pp. 2-14.)

11   *Berthold Goldschmidt*

One of Berthold Goldschmidt's best-known anecdotes concerns the premiere of his First String Quartet. This took place in Berlin in 1926 at a concert Franz Schreker had arranged for those of his pupils, including Goldschmidt, who had completed their studies with him. Arnold Schoenberg had been invited, and, as Goldschmidt relates:

> My First Quartet came at the end of the programme and – I won't say was a success, but it got a lot of applause from the audience of students. Afterwards Schoenberg appeared backstage, came up to me and held out his hand: "Congratulations! Your piece was a great success – I am glad for you." His face twitched as he spoke, and I guess I looked a bit frightened and could not speak properly as I thanked him. There was a slight pause, and he shook my hand again: "It was a great pleasure – ", and off he went. Of course, what he wanted was for me to say, "Herr Professor, could I possibly continue my studies with you?" Which I failed to say: I was too scared. I knew all his pupils, and they were totally under his magnetic influence and in fact wrote as he wanted, whereas with Schreker there was a very liberal atmosphere.[1]

This crucial rejection of Schoenberg has, I think, a wider, symbolic significance. I should say that any criticism I make of Schoenberg here does not detract from the great admiration and respect in which I hold him and I should point out that Schoenberg did not, in fact, impose his ideas rigidly on his pupils, and certainly did not compel them to write twelve-note music. This was true in Berlin at that time and later on in Los Angeles. Leon Kirchner, who was one of Schoenberg's pupils there, has assured me that Schoenberg allowed his pupils to write in any style they wished.[2] Malcolm MacDonald has pointed out that even his famous remark in the summer of 1922 to Josef Rufer about the twelve-note method ("I have discovered something that will guarantee the supremacy of German music for the next hundred years"), though it sounds supremely arrogant, may well have been intended ironically. Schoenberg regarded his twelve-note method as a family matter, to be passed on to chosen initiates. That he thought of Goldschmidt as a possible disciple, and was therefore the more disappointed by Goldschmidt's declining to become one, seems to be confirmed by another Goldschmidt reminiscence. His friend Harold Byrns, some twenty years after this incident, was with Schoenberg when the latter saw Goldschmidt's name on a programme together with his own, and exclaimed: "Goldschmidt? Goldschmidt – that was another who betrayed me."

Schoenberg may not have seen his method as a universal one – after all, the most famous of all his sayings is that there is plenty of music still be written in

C major– but he did claim that 'every expression and characterisation can be produced with the style of free dissonance'.[3] It was only after the Second World War that Boulez, Stockhausen and the other young composers who attended the Darmstadt Summer School would proclaim that their own, even stricter serialism was now the only possible way forward for music. With Webern rather than Schoenberg as their hero, and echoing the pronouncements of Theodor Adorno, they believed that tonality was completely outmoded and consequently that composers such as Strauss, Sibelius, Hindemith, Prokofiev, Shostakovich, Copland, Britten and the neoclassical Stravinsky were more or less worthless. It was an attitude that contributed, in the 1960s, to a musical climate where Berthold Goldschmidt became so dispirited that he gave up composing altogether for almost twenty-five years.

We see things differently now. The path of serialism from Schoenberg to Webern to Boulez appears only one of many through the garden of twentieth-century music and, I would suggest, a somewhat narrow and cloistered one. If Berthold Goldschmidt had become a Schoenberg disciple and composed twelve-note music, I think it is doubtful that he could have written anything as direct and moving in its expressive power as the slow movement, called 'Folia', of the Second String Quartet.[4] This was the first piece he composed after his forced emigration from Germany to England in 1935. In his own words, it was 'an elegy for what had already happened in Germany' – which even at this early date had included the death of two of his cousins in concentration camps and of his sister Ruth under the neglectful 'care' of a Nazi nurse.[5] The three-note motif, which is repeated over and over again, seventy-one times in all, is taken from the Renaissance dance *La folia*, which had been used as a basis for variations by many composers, including Frescobaldi, Corelli, Bach and Liszt. It was typical of Goldschmidt that he should have turned to the past in order to express his most urgent feelings about the present – he pointed out that 'folia' means 'madness' – and also that he should have used a form based on repetition of a ground. The chaconne and passacaglia were his favourite forms, and behind his chaconnes there hovers, not just the acknowledged influence of the Bach C minor Passacaglia for organ, one of the seminal works of his youth, but also of another slow dance in triple time with a repeating ground: Busoni's 'Sarabande and Cortège' from *Doktor Faust*, the first orchestral piece of Busoni that he had heard. This was on a memorable day during the winter of 1920-21 when, as a schoolboy, he attended a rehearsal and concert in his home town of Hamburg at which Busoni also played Mozart's E♭ major Piano Concerto K. 482. Goldschmidt was introduced to Busoni, who advised him: "When composing, make this your rule: all counterpoint must be *melodious*."

Counterpoint like that to be heard in the 'Sarabande and Cortège' produced an orchestral sound and texture that had the profoundest effect on the young Goldschmidt. Indeed, he was to follow Busoni's advice about melodious counterpoint for the rest of his life, as, for instance, in his Passacaglia from 1925, which won the Mendelssohn Prize that year (when, incidentally, Schoenberg was a member of the jury). It was performed by Erich Kleiber in Berlin the following year and, after Goldschmidt sent the score to Universal Edition, was then lost for seventy years. He had already found his personal style, with its striking anticipations of the later Shostakovich, who at that time had only just finished his First Symphony. More importantly, there is a general adherence to the principles of what Busoni called 'Young Classicality', among whose ideals were 'the recapture of melody as mistress of all voices', 'the casting off of "sensuousness" and renunciation of subjectivity', 'the reconquest of serenity' and '*absolute* music'. This 'Young Classicality' was significantly different from Stravinsky's or Hindemith's neoclassicism, or from Schoenberg's attempt to tame his expressionist language by caging it within classical formats like the string quartet. Schoenberg, it seems to me, gets into difficulties because his language resists being tamed in this way: compare the awkwardness of manner of much of the Third Quartet of 1927 to the overt expressionism in the orchestral *Accompaniment to a Film Scene* a few years later, or to the String Trio of 1946, where again content gets the upper hand.

In avoiding Schoenberg's influence, Goldschmidt surely made the right choice, having already chosen a confident, classical, tonal language that seemed perfectly natural for him. He did hesitate: some of his colleagues chided him for his apparent conservatism; his next work after the String Quartet was a Piano Sonata that was the most radical piece he ever wrote, in which tonality often has only a precarious hold. Should he adopt the twelve-note method after all, he wondered? But he drew back, and in future if he was ever to use a twelve-note row, as in the first of the *Mediterranean Songs*, he used it in the same way as Britten did, in order to show how it might be turned towards tonal ends. In 1925, he had also taken part in the first performances of Berg's *Wozzeck*, playing the celesta in the orchestra. He admired the work, which appealed to him more than any of Schoenberg's music: and, of course, it does not entirely renounce the musical vernacular, but incorporates a wide-ranging expressionism that can accommodate triads as well as tonal clusters. Yet Goldschmidt must have realised that Berg, like Schoenberg, was a very different kind of composer from himself, and he had no inclination to follow a Romantic, subjective path when he had already discovered an objective, Classical one.

In the late 1920s, Goldschmidt's career blossomed: his First Quartet and Piano Sonata were published by Universal Edition and he was soon writing his first opera, *Der gewaltige Hahnrei* ('The Magnificent Cuckold') which was successfully produced in Mannheim in 1932. This period was a tumultuously rich one for music in Germany, and one of its outstanding features, of course, was the series of collaborative works by Kurt Weill and Bertolt Brecht. The stunning use of the popular vernacular by Weill, as well as by contemporaries such as Eisler and Hindemith, also had its effect on Goldschmidt: the two settings for chorus, percussion and piano he eventually called *Letzte Kapital* ('Final Chapters'), which he made in 1931 but which were not performed until 1984, used the popular vernacular in a sterner and more frenetic way than Weill to underline the tension that was building up towards the catastrophe of 1933. Weill, three years older than Goldschmidt, had been a pupil of Busoni, and 'Young Classicality' had a profound effect on him also, although this side of him has generally been passed over because of the fame of his theatre works. Yet Weill's Second Symphony is a perfect example of Busoni's aesthetic principles put into practice, as its neo-Beethovenian opening Allegro shows. It is a cruel irony that the Symphony was begun in the very month, January 1933, that Hitler came to power, so that its performance in Germany was impossible. Weill left Germany for Paris in March 1933, never to return, thus severing his links with the German culture to which this symphony so proudly and defiantly belongs. The Second Symphony has no successor, and Weill was to write no more purely instrumental pieces – a tragedy, I think. There is a parallel here with Goldschmidt, whose Second Quartet was the piece he wrote immediately after he left Germany two and half years after Weill. The first movement of the Quartet is another neo-Beethovenian Allegro, and its spirit of furious joy reflects Goldschmidt's immediate feelings of relief at having escaped from the Nazis, not a moment too soon.

"My wife and I were exceedingly happy to be in England. I could sit down and try to work again," Goldschmidt told Michael Struck in 1989. The trouble with England was that Goldschmidt was completely unknown and it was very hard for him to get his music played. The Second Quartet was not publicly performed for seventeen years after its completion, and though this belated premiere got good reviews, another fifteen years followed before its next performance. Yet I believe this is one of the few truly great string quartets of our time.

Despite these and other difficulties, including no longer having a publisher, Goldschmidt composed a substantial amount of music over the next twenty years: a ballet, *Chronica*; a Sinfonietta; three large-scale concertos; and, most ambitiously, his second opera, *Beatrice Cenci*. This produced perhaps the biggest disappointment of all, for after the opera had been one of the winners of the Arts Council's competition in 1949 for the Festival of Britain, the promised performance never materialised. How desperately frustrating this must have been for him can only be guessed, especially when the music was as good as anything he wrote. Undoubtedly the failure of *Beatrice Cenci* to reach the stage was a contributing factor to the long silence that followed the completion of the *Mediterranean Songs* in 1958. The last of these songs is a setting of a poem by Shelley, on whose play *The Cenci* his opera had been based. The poem is *Stanzas Written in Dejection near Naples* and it ends with the lines:

> I could lie down like a tired child,
> And weep away the life of care
> Which I have borne and yet must bear,
> Till death like sleep might steal on me,
> And I might feel in the warm air
> My cheek grow cold, and hear the sea
> Breathe o'er my dying brain its last monotony.

Although he surely must have chosen this poem for autobiographical reasons, Goldschmidt sets it with characteristic objectivity and avoids any hint of self-pity. In the German version he made for the score, he translates 'its last monotony' as 'ihr letztes Wort: Ade': 'Breathe o'er my dying brain its last word, farewell' – and this song was indeed that, for many years. If Goldschmidt had died at the respectable age of 79, he would have died in virtual obscurity. Fortunately he didn't, and instead there came an extraordinary Indian summer.

The Third and Fourth String Quartets that Goldschmidt wrote in 1989 and 1992 are, I think, the finest products of those later years, and make one regret that he did not write more quartets during his life. There is a fifty-three-year gap between the Second Quartet and the Third, but no sign of loss of confidence in the medium. In the 1960s Goldschmidt may have thought, and may have been made to think, that he was now hopelessly out of date. In 1989, in a more open artistic climate, he had no hesitation about beginning the Third Quartet on an E♭ major triad, with a warm gesture of comradeship towards Beethoven, most obviously to the Quartet in E♭ major, Op. 127, but in a deeper way to the 'Eroica' Symphony and the place that work holds in German culture. This opening passage may also bring to mind Strauss's *Metamorphosen*, which has its own association with the 'Eroica'; there is a parallel between these two composers in their eighties, looking back with sorrow on the tragedy of their country's recent history, but doing so with great warmth and humanity. Strauss and Goldschmidt shared a common tradition, the German Classical tradition. There is no nostalgia in Goldschmidt's late music, only a strong sense of continuity with the past and its importance to him: his own past, and that of German music. The same is true of the Fourth Quartet, which he wrote when he was 89. Both the Third and Fourth Quartets are composed as single movements, which distil the Classical forms he knew so well. The Fourth Quartet is especially concise, ranging in its thirteen-and-a-half minutes through every shade of mood from the skittish to the tragic. It closes with a passage of sustained eloquence, the counterpoint singing to the end, which culminates, appropriately enough, on a chord of C major, so proving the truth of Schoenberg's maxim.

Many composers are neglected, though few of them unjustifiably. Berthold Goldschmidt's neglect for much of his life was undeserved. It is right that he is now taking his place among the significant composers of the twentieth century, and gratifying that he should have lived long enough to see this beginning to happen. But what future for composers who, like Goldschmidt, choose to work within the mainstream, 'the middle way' as I call it? The middle way in music avoids the asceticism of the avant-garde on the one hand and the instant gratification of popular music on the other. The mainstream, which includes all those composers I named earlier who were condemned by the Darmstadt school, has in fact provided most of the best music of this century. It has adhered to tonality in some form or another, because those composers who contributed to it recognised the continuing validity of the musical vernacular. Schoenberg's rejection of it, and of tonality, was not the demonstration of a universal truth about the exhaustion of tonal language, but rather a solution to his own pursuit of Wagnerian chromaticism to its limits.

I admit that the mainstream is now at a crisis. Those serious composers who practice tonality today most successfully in terms of communication, the minimalists – both the holy and the unholy sort – have provided a clean new sound world, but no renewal of melody and no great intellectual depth. Few works at all are entering the repertoire. If there are solutions to the contemporary problem, they are in the hands of composers, and I can only conclude by advising them, with Goldschmidt as an admirable exemplar, to learn their craft thoroughly, to attend to the present forlorn state of melody as well as to the neglected art of counterpoint, to sense their debt to their predecessors and draw sustaining nourishment from the past, to endeavour to say what they have to say in music in as direct and clear a way as possible, and to stay loyal to their inmost beliefs, however unfashionable they may seem.

Notes

Source: Revised version of 'The Middle Way', *The Salisbury Review*, Spring 1999. Another version of this essay appeared as 'Berthold Goldschmidt' in the *BBC Music Magazine*, March 2003. David Matthews met Berthold Goldschmidt (1903-96) through their work on the performing version of Mahler's Tenth Symphony with Deryck Cooke. He recollects that:

Colin and I would go for tea with Goldschmidt from time to time. He was full of anecdotes about Schreker, Busoni and Schoenberg. He had an immaculate memory right until the end of his life. He wanted to play us his music and he had tapes of pieces like the Second Quartet and the three concertos. Neither of us knew at that time how much he had written. For fifteen years or so he had not really done much. The Germans gave him a state pension and he lived in one room, really. It was very modest. It always looked to me as if he had just arrived and hadn't unpacked. A grand piano and old furniture, an un-modernised kitchen. His wife died quite tragically and Colin and I didn't meet him regularly in his flat until after she had died. We did both meet her though. I am not sure quite why he gave up conducting, it just all sort of stopped. You would have expected him to conduct Mahler Ten a lot, but he didn't. Bernard Keefe did a lot to support Berthold and got a performance of his first opera put on at Trinity College. I managed to persuade David Drew to come and that turned out well as he was then offered a publishing contract with Boosey & Hawkes. The change in his fortunes from the 1980s onwards was extraordinary. Around the time of his 80th birthday it all started happening: David Drew had said "the revival must start in Germany" and Rattle played the *Chaconne* there and there was a five minute standing ovation. Berthold played us the recording including all the applause. It was very touching, as if he was being welcomed back to Germany. When he first went back he said he felt everything had changed. He had left in 1936 and not been back. He said he had great faith in young Germans; he wasn't bitter. (Conversation with the editor, London, October 2011)

Went to see Berthold in the afternoon (Colin & Jean came too). Jean [the composer Jean Hasse, David Matthews's then wife] was amazed by his energy, & his memory. He is very fortunate – I hope there never is a falling off. He is conducting again now – recently, the Violin Concerto at the RFH. This piece has had 11 performances in the past year – after 2 in the previous 40 years. It still all seems like a dream to him. He told us about his meeting with Hindemith in the 1930s – after a piece of his had been booed & whistled at, he saw Hindemith in the artists' room, about to play a viola concerto. H said "don't worry; for me now they only cough." In 1933 B went to H's flat to ask him what he should do. H advised him to stay, saying that the Nazis were so stupid they couldn't survive, the army would soon step in & arrest Hitler. (*Journal*, 16 January 1995)

1   Michael Struck, 'Evidence from a Fragmented Musical History: Notes on Berthold Goldschmidt's Chamber Music', *Tempo*, No. 174, September 1990, p. 3.

2   Matthews has written at greater length on Leon Kirchner in a book review. See: *Tempo*, No. 258, October 2011, pp. 60-1.

3   Arnold Schoenberg, *Style and Idea: Selected Writings of Arnold Schoenberg*, ed. Leonard Stein, London, Faber and Faber, 1975, p. 245.

4   Reviewing the first recording of Goldschmidt's Second and Third Quartet in 1991, Matthews wrote that: '... the high-voltage playing of the Mandelring Quartet brings out the spirit of furious joy in the first movement as I have never heard before ... they are equally responsive to the 'Folia' elegy – which seems to me quite simply the most profound commentary on the fate of his people under the Nazis that a Jewish composer has yet made.' (*Tempo*, No. 178, September 1991, pp. 46-7)

5   Struck, 1990, p. 4.

6   *Ibid.*, p. 3.

12   *Charles Ives*
(book reviews)

Debussy and Ives were the first major composers to form their musical language more from personal choice than inherited tradition. Debussy used chords that were not to be found in any textbook simply because he liked their sound. Ives went further: for him, *any* chords were permissible, nor did they have to relate to any kind of tonality. At the age of twelve or so, encouraged by his father, Ives would imitate a bass drum on the piano by playing clusters of low-pitched notes. Later, he would put such chords, and many others never heard before in music, into his compositions. Why not? It seemed perfectly natural to him, if not to any previous composer.

There seems no other way to explain how it came about that Charles Ives, the bandmaster's son from Danbury, Connecticut, brought up on his father's enthusiasm for experimentation, on hymns and psalms and on a few pieces from the standard nineteenth-century repertoire, should have single-handedly invented just about the whole language of contemporary music, from bitonality to polyrhythm, from quarter-tones to serialism. Ives was driven neither by historical necessity, like Schoenberg, nor by a wish to astonish, like Stravinsky. He was a visionary, like Whitman, his closest predecessor, and his vision was a wholly truthful one that encompassed all aspects of human life, from the trivial to the sublime. So every kind of musical sound had to be drawn into it and, as in real life, many events made to occur simultaneously, with the result that the texture of his music is often complex to the point of chaos. Curiously, although the sound of his music was, and remains, 'modern' to most people's ears, Ives was anti-modern in all his attitude; he hated the increasing mechanisation of American life, never owned a radio, didn't go to the cinema and disliked the camera and the automobile. Like Stanley Spencer and Cookham, Ives's vision was centred on childhood memories of a place, of Danbury before its small-town intimacy was irrevocably destroyed by 'progress'.

Jan Swafford's engaging biography provides the fullest and most sympathetic account that we have of Ives's remarkable life, together with much perceptive commentary on the music. As a composer himself, Swafford well understands Ives's tribulations, from the stuffy pedantry of his Yale teacher Horatio Parker (though Ives learned a lot more from him than he cared to admit) to the almost total incomprehension of his fellow musicians when faced with his music. The reaction of a German violinist called Milcke, who played through the First Violin Sonata with him in 1914, was typical, Milcke exclaiming "This is awful! It is not music, it makes no sense … I cannot get these horrible sounds out of my ears."

Not surprisingly, Ives grew increasingly wary, and ended up not daring to attend the rare performances of his pieces – so missing the ovations when John Kirkpatrick premiered the *Concord* Sonata in 1939 and Leonard Bernstein the

Second Symphony in 1951. By this time, Ives was not short of admirers, but his composing days were long over. Like previous biographers, Swafford relates Ives's creative decline directly to his illnesses: he had his first heart attack in 1906 at the age of thirty-two, and his second in 1918; between those years he wrote almost all his most important pieces. But Swafford also reveals that during the same time he had been gradually developing diabetes, inherited from his father who died from a stroke at the age of forty-nine, and that this was very likely the cause of his heart attacks and all his subsequent health problems. Given this inheritance and his manic life during his peak years, when as well as composing prodigiously he became a millionaire businessman, it is a wonder that Ives survived into his eightieth year.

That Ives did so must owe much to his wife, the delightfully named Harmony Twichell, who was a trained nurse and his inseparable companion. Like Schumann's, Ives's marriage was a tremendous stimulus to his creative powers. During its first six years, he wrote *Three Places in New England*, the *Holidays* Symphony, the *Concord* Sonata and much of the Fourth Symphony – in other words, almost all his greatest works. Whether Harmony really understood Ives's music must be doubted, but he could rely totally on her support. Swafford is the first Ives biographer to have access to the letters she wrote during their three-year courtship and their early married life; they are very touching, and reveal her exceptional serenity. Given Ives's increasing irascibility, that serenity must surely have been severely tested in later life.

Ives comes so vividly alive in Swafford's book that it is dispiriting to turn to Philip Lambert's *The Music of Charles Ives* and find ourselves in the laboratory world of higher musicology, where Ives's works are dissected like so many dead frogs. The title – a standard one as part of a series on twentieth-century composers – is misleading, as the works chosen for detailed analysis are not Ives's most important and tend to be his most wildly experimental – in several cases pieces that he only sketched, like *Chromâtimelôdtune* and the *Universe Symphony*. As Swafford remarks, Ives didn't always finish such pieces because he didn't think they were worth it. Lambert's analyses are almost impossible for anyone but a trained musicologist to understand, written in jargon derived from Allen Forte and Milton Babbitt. They are painstaking, and occasionally enlightening, but are so preoccupied with detail that anything of real importance gets submerged. If everything is seen to be significant, then, it could be argued, nothing really is. I can't believe Ives would have had any time for this book. Music is life, he told Harmony. If you put music under the microscope, the life disappears.

Source: 'To the Point of Chaos', review of: *Charles Ives. A Life with Music* by Jan Swafford, and *The Music of Charles Ives*, by Philip Lambert, in: *Times Literary Supplement*, 28 November 1997, p. 12.

13   *Igor Stravinsky*
(book review)

Since Stravinsky lived the richest life of any twentieth-century composer, he is a gift to a biographer; but the sheer amount of documentation that exists, along with the way that Stravinsky throughout his life attempted to revise his autobiography according to his current perceptions, poses complex problems of interpretation and judgement. Stephen Walsh, who has already written the best available introduction to Stravinsky's music, has now risen admirably to the challenge of the life in the first of two projected volumes. While acknowledging his debt to Robert Craft's invaluable biographical writings and also to Richard Taruskin's revelatory *Stravinsky and the Russian Traditions*, Walsh, who is fluent in Russian and has had access to Russian archives to an extent that no previous writer on Stravinsky has done, is the first to attempt to establish the full, true facts about Stravinsky both as a Russian and as an exile. His command of these facts is always impressive: this is one of the most intelligent musical biographies I have read.

Let me first get a reservation out of the way. There is a certain aloofness about Walsh's style, so that we never feel especially close to the composer, or his family and friends, even though we learn a great deal about them. This detachment is particularly noticeable when Walsh deals with sensitive areas of Stravinsky's life. After reading the account of his partial abandonment of his wife and family after he began his relationship with Vera Sudeykina, I reread Craft's essay 'Sufferings and Humiliations of Catherine Stravinsky' in his book *Stravinsky: Glimpses of a Life*, and immediately felt much more involved in Katya Stravinsky's pain and her sadly unrewarded devotion. There is also a slight coyness, which may well be a deliberate reaction against the sexual prurience of most modern biographies, but it perhaps goes a little too far. When we are introduced to Diaghilev, for instance, we are not told that he is homosexual, so that when Nijinsky – whom we have not at this point been informed was his lover – leaves him to get married, the innocent reader might wonder why Diaghilev is so excessively distraught. Admittedly, almost all readers of this book will know the facts already, but a few may not – the book is intended for the general reader – so it does seem unnecessarily prim to withhold them.

Walsh's aloofness matches the tone of Stravinsky's music. In many ways Stravinsky is hard to get to know, so that we seize eagerly on the occasional detailed observation, like the French attaché Paul Morand's in 1916: 'very much the dandy, mustard trousers, black jacket, blue shirt and collar, yellow boots, clean shaven, slicked-down blond hair, bad teeth, myopia, thick lips' (discussing photographs of Stravinsky with a friend recently, I remarked on how he always kept his mouth severely closed, never smiling; she said it was probably because he had bad teeth, a point Morand confirms). If Walsh is short on intimate detail, he does make many astute comments, as when, observing near the start of the book how much of Stravinsky's life was spent on trains, he adds: 'Nobody has yet seriously examined the effects on those incessant anapaests of iron wheels over track connectors and points on the consciousness of the greatest rhythmic thinker since Beethoven.'

On the larger canvas, Walsh is constantly illuminating. He draws vivid portraits of Stravinsky's oppressive family; his Chekhovian youth, when he gradually discovered his gifts as a composer during endless summer days on country estates; his thorough training under Rimsky-Korsakov, who made Stravinsky score sections of the opera that he, Rimsky, was currently orchestrating, before comparing the two versions; the fortuitous entrance of Diaghilev into his life and his amazingly astute grasp of the opportunities he provided; and of the young composer with a growing family, constantly on the move but somehow always managing to work obsessively. Later, Walsh makes it very clear why, in the chaos that followed the Revolution and the end of the First World War, with exiled relatives descending on him for support in addition to his family, Stravinsky became understandably preoccupied with earning money, especially as he was not prepared to sacrifice his aristocratic lifestyle; and why he readily escaped from this cloistered domesticity into the heady atmosphere of 1920s Paris, surrounded himself with new chic friends, and deliberately changed all his attitudes to Russia, folklore and anything that derived from his Rimskian past. The hostility of his old associates towards his music encouraged this, as did his mother's continuing admonitions to respect his betters: i.e. Scriabin – whom Stravinsky once hero-worshipped but whom later, like so many figures from his past, he could not tolerate.

Walsh is, as he admits, basically on Stravinsky's side, and the composer's many faults are always made explicable from the internal and external facts of his life. So that even when, at the end of this volume, in 1933 we find Stravinsky making a pilgrimage to Rome to see Mussolini, 'the *one man who counts* nowadays in the whole world', and not being prepared to stand up for the recently banished Bruno Walter and Otto Klemperer (who had championed his music in the 1920s), Walsh, while not excusing him, at least has an unprejudiced understanding of his motives. It will be fascinating to see what he makes of the second half of Stravinsky's life: we await Volume Two with impatience.

Source: 'Debts and Credits', review of: *Stravinsky: A Creative Spring* by Stephen Walsh, in: *The Musical Times*, Vol. 141, No. 1871 (Summer 2000), pp. 72-3.

14   Michael Tippett

(a) 1979 (book extract)

It might seem premature to sum up Michael Tippett's achievements while he is still so much alive and active among us. Nevertheless, since his earliest published works are now over forty years old – and he himself feels very detached from them – we can put these at least into some kind of historical perspective, and can go on to bring his music as a whole into provisional focus.

Tippett's musical language in his early works is markedly conservative, even in the then context of English music. Of the major Continental innovators, Hindemith alone is a felt presence in Tippett's early music; and it is significant that by the 1930s Hindemith was in the process of renouncing what he had come to believe were the sins of a misspent avant-garde youth and adopting a traditionalist stance, which he attempted to justify by massive theorising. To judge from the music alone, we could well imagine (though we should in fact be wrong) that Tippett was then unaware of Stravinsky (whose influence on other members of his generation such as William Walton or Constant Lambert had already been considerable), and also of Bartók or Schoenberg. What is certainly apparent, and true, is that there is a strong continuity with the previous generation of English composers, Vaughan Williams in particular. This is emphasised by Tippett's belief in the continuing validity of folk music as a musical vernacular, at a time when such a belief was rapidly going out of fashion.

Tippett's conservative beginnings are, however, misleading; for he was to become a very different kind of composer from Edmund Rubbra or Gerald Finzi, to name but two thoroughgoing conservatives among his contemporaries. Yet certainly his overriding aim in the late 1930s was conservative *par excellence*: it was no less than the re-creation of Classical tonality. Such an aim tells us much about Tippett's confidence in his own powers, a confidence which was largely to be justified by the achievement of the next decade. In an article he wrote in 1938, Tippett traces the degeneration of the tonal system since Beethoven's time, remarking that: 'Since the nineteenth century composers have ceased to produce the sort of themes that demanded Beethoven's clarity of tonal structure ... the tonal system related to sonata form is a highly polarized system. Modern people are not polarized, they are split.'[1] Clearly Tippett saw his personal quest for psychological wholeness, which he was undertaking through Jungian self-analysis, as related to a necessary rediscovery of Classical, i.e. Beethoven's, tonal values. The re-creation of a Classical language was achieved with remarkable success in the works of the 1940s, culminating in *The Midsummer Marriage*, perhaps the most tonally stable of all large-scale works written this century. Its resplendent A major close (with a Wagnerian sustained final triad) is a precise musical parallel to the psychological stability that Mark and Jenifer have attained. In all the music of this period, the final cadence on to the tonic triad has the unforced strength of a true Classical work. Tippett's Classicism sounds absolutely natural: outwardly directed emotions are expressed in music that is both gracefully lyrical and vigorously athletic. In contrast, the neoclassicism of Stravinsky, despite its brilliance, seems studied and inhibited; it never quite lets go. Tippett's music of the 1940s comes very close at times, not only to the Classically poised world of Beethoven, but also, in a wider context, to that of Goethe, who, in a similar spirit, revitalised the classical elegiac couplet:

> Froh empfind ich mich nun auf klassischem Boden begeistert;
> Vor- und Mitwelt spricht lauter und reizender mir.
>
> *(How happy and inspired I feel now on classical soil;*
> *Both the past and the present speak to me with more eloquence and charm.)*

By the mid 1950s, Tippett realised that he could do no more with traditional tonality without repeating himself; he also felt a need to expand his musical vocabulary. It was at this point that he turned (there is some irony here) to the neoclassical Stravinsky of the 1930s and 1940s, just at the period when Stravinsky himself was turning towards serialism in an attempt to reinvigorate his own language. In Tippett's Second Symphony of 1956-57, the first major piece to show Stravinskian influence, the writing is generally more sectional, the tonality more static, the harmony more astringent. But the music still has a more continuous, integrated flow – it is more symphonic – than one ever finds in Stravinsky. This is not to say that Tippett is a better composer than Stravinsky; only that Tippett has done things with Stravinskian language that Stravinsky himself was incapable of doing, just as, say, Bruckner used Wagnerian language in a quite different way from Wagner.

Tippett has continued to generate genuine symphonic movement in subsequent works up to and including his most recent, the Fourth Symphony; he has managed to do so despite his gradual abandonment of the tonal language which he had so impressively mastered. Whether his present synthetic language, with its Americanised, blues-based vernacular and widely allusive range, and its use of tonal gestures within a generally non-tonal background (one can usefully employ Rudolph Réti's term 'pantonality' to describe it), is a wholly adequate substitute for the Classical tonality of his earlier works is an intriguing question; but one that it is yet too early to answer with any certainty.

The grammar of Tippett's language is an obvious key to his individuality, but his tone of voice is no less distinctive. The exalted, ecstatic tone of Tippett's most idiosyncratic music is what singles him out from almost all his contemporaries. The only figure with whom he can properly be compared is Olivier Messiaen, though they are very different, both as composers, and as representatives of two totally distinct cultures. Messiaen's Roman Catholicism, awesomely transcendent and at the same time deeply sensuous, pervades and characterises all his music. In so far as Tippett is religious, his is the humanistic religion of the divine latent in man (as proclaimed by Nietzsche and preached by Shaw), enriched by an empathy with the pantheism of the early Romantics and with the unorthodox mysticism of such figures as Blake. Tippett had to struggle long and hard to win his vision; Messiaen's seems almost to have been born with him. In his music, Tippett most often achieves a state of ecstasy through a dense counterpoint of melismatic melody; in Messiaen, the melody is characteristically propelled into ecstasy by the luxuriant progressions of the underlying harmony, as for example in the 'Louange à l'immortalité de Jésus' from the *Quatuor pour la Fin du Temps* of 1940-41. It is the difference of approach between the contrapuntist (Tippett) and the harmonist (Messiaen). Despite their fundamental differences, there are moments when their voices are strikingly similar: to cite another example from the *Quatuor pour la Fin du Temps*, the 'Danse de la fureur, pour les sept trompettes', an unharmonised, unison melody in fast tempo and complex additive rhythms, invites a most interesting, direct comparison with the same features in Tippett generally. Tippett and Messiaen are the only authentic visionaries amongst living composers, and each has produced some of the most life-enhancing music of our time.

Tippett's own solutions to two of the chief problems of twentieth-century music – the problem of language and the problem of movement – are, I believe, of great importance. In the first place, despite assertions to the contrary, the musical language Schoenberg formulated, and from which most currently fashionable styles are descended, is limited in expressive range. It is an ideal vehicle for the depiction of extreme emotional states: hence the total success of the monodrama *Erwartung*. It is hopelessly unsuited to comic opera: hence the total artistic failure of *Von Heute auf Morgen*. Of those composers who have used a Schoenbergian language, the most successful have been those who have expressionist things to say: Peter Maxwell Davies, for example. In short, serialism (under which blanket term one can broadly classify all styles ultimately derived from Schoenberg) cannot easily evoke states of joy, gaiety, exuberance. If composers still want to express such emotions in their music, they might profitably consider how Tippett's language in its development from orthodox tonality to pantonality has always been a potent vehicle for the widest range of expression. In the second place, Tippett has continued to compose music that is not only in a fast tempo but whose harmonic progressions generate a real sense of dynamic movement. Within serialism it is hard to prevent genuine movement being clogged by a too densely chromatic harmony, and most composers faithful to this language can only create what amounts to a procession of static blocks, whether the tempo they specify is fast or slow.

As soon as we try to define Tippett's place in the history of twentieth-century music, we realise that he does not fit. He is a maverick (he has approvingly described Blake as such), an eccentric in the proper sense of the word. Our age is supposedly one in which artistic originality is sought after more keenly than ever before; yet much of the music of the present day is marked by a grey uniformity of expression (sometimes concealed by a surface gloss), as well as by a depressing lack of vitality. The international language of serialism has tended to foster these traits, and to provide an easy retreat from the rigours of developing a true artistic personality. Against this background, Tippett's exuberant individualism stands out in startling contrast. His music may sometimes disconcert, for Tippett has the true original's power to disturb. But it is certainly never conventional, and never superficial.

Tippett unashamedly assumes a prophetic role. Like his mentor Beethoven, he finds it an inseparable part of his calling to voice the aspirations of ordinary people; for, Tippett would claim, the artist has a deeper insight into the collective unconscious than most of us, and thus a surer understanding of our psychological needs. Tippett has taken upon himself the immense task of discovering new images of reconciliation and hope for a spiritually barren age; he wants, in his own words, 'to renew our sense of the comely and the beautiful. To create a dream.' That this is no unattainable aim is abundantly proved, I believe, by his music.

Notes

Source: David Matthews, *Michael Tippett. An Introductory Study*, London, Faber and Faber, 1980, pp. 101-05.

1   'Music and Life', in: Michael Tippett, *Music of the Angels*, London, Eulenburg Books, 1980, p. 32.

(b) 1999 (book review)

Michael Tippett's life (1905-98) spanned our troubled century, and he did as much as any artist to 'blithe' it, as Auden hoped artists would. At its best, Tippett's music surpasses that of almost all his contemporaries in its imaginative power and quality of inspiration. There are effusions of lyrical beauty that catch the heart, passages of intense and invigorating energy, infectious outbursts of sheer exuberance. He was a life-enhancing presence, and the sense of loss felt at his death last year is still acute.

Tippett's music has always taken time to be accepted. It was only when he reached his sixties that he was generally recognised in this country as a major composer rather than a brilliant but eccentric amateur. Much of his earlier work – up to and including *King Priam* – has now achieved classic status. It is still too soon to say for certain whether the later works are up to the standard of the earlier ones, although a number of Tippett's admirers have had doubts about the quality of some of this later music. These doubts were in the main not expressed publicly until Derrick Puffett's article 'Tippett and the Retreat from Mythology' appeared in the *Musical Times* in January 1995 – the month of Tippett's ninetieth birthday. Puffett was devastatingly outspoken in his criticism: the 1991 Yeats setting, *Byzantium*, was 'the most utter failure ever achieved by a thoroughly respect-worthy musician'. The nub of his argument was that most of Tippett's later music fails to realise its intention to provide a collective imaginative experience – an aim specifically stated by Tippett in connection with *The Midsummer Marriage* – and instead is only too inclined 'to go off into a fantasy world of eccentricity'. Tippett, Puffett harshly concluded, joined a number of composers who had lived beyond their time.

Tippett Studies, the latest addition to Cambridge University Press's handsomely produced surveys of composers, avoids controversy in being mostly analytical rather than critical. The book originated from papers presented at Newcastle University's International Tippett Conference in 1995. As might be expected, sadly, the majority of the analyses are written in the unattractive language – 'pitch-classes' and so on – that contemporary musicology has encumbered itself with; nor are they especially illuminating, apart from Arnold Whittall's hard look at some of the unifying motifs of *King Priam*. Any composer can now be analysed in this way, but the instinctive nature of Tippett's composing methods makes him a less than ideal subject. The music resists the laboratory. There are a few essays on broader topics: David Clarke's on the Concerto for Double String Orchestra is a fascinating account of Tippett's links with the folk-song tradition and is informative about the incomplete monograph on folk-song that Tippett's friend Francesca Allinson wrote, which Tippett for some time intended to complete after her death, though he never did so. Clarke notes that the folk element in the Concerto is in no way nostalgic, as it is in the music of some of Tippett's English predecessors, but presents 'the image of an invigorated future rather than a mythologised past'. Indeed, the piece is extraordinary in its ability to sound fresh while remaining so indebted to the past.

Two of the essays do touch on criticism. Wilfrid Mellers, whose thoughtful and characteristically engaging memoir of the composer reminds us, late in the book, what really fine writing about music can be, expresses some credible misgivings about *The Knot Garden* and *The Ice Break*, but puts up a strong case for the last opera, *New Year*. In his discussion of the Fifth String

Quartet in the final chapter, Peter Wright attempts to refute Puffett's claim, asserting that there was no demonstrable decline in this or any of Tippett's later works. The Fifth Quartet, Tippett's penultimate piece, is indeed one of the best of the later works; yet I don't think Wright's account, interesting as it is in showing the links with Beethoven and particularly Op. 132, succeeds in proving that it is as good a piece as the Second or Third Quartet, both of which seem to me to have superior thematic material and tighter intellectual control of that material. However, it has a serenity that makes it a precious addition to his *oeuvre*.

While we should be wary of accusations against Tippett of eccentricity, bearing in mind that similar things were once said about the earlier music and, in particular, the work that most critics would now acknowledge as his masterpiece, *The Midsummer Marriage*, it would not be surprising if there had in fact been an overall decline in quality. To put it another way, why should a composer necessarily be expected to go on improving all his life, and especially if he lives to a great age? There have been few examples of this happening in the past: the outstanding one is Verdi. Bruckner almost qualifies, but his mind severely deteriorated in his final years and he was unable to finish the Ninth Symphony. Janáček, rejuvenated by falling in love, produced his best work in his sixties and seventies. There are others who maintained consistency into old age, but until this century relatively few composers lived beyond seventy, and the phenomenon of the active composer in his eighties is a new one.

Comparisons between Tippett and Stravinsky are inevitable, especially since Tippett revered Stravinsky above all his immediate predecessors, and was deeply influenced by him. Puffett asked why Tippett could not, like Stravinsky, have been 'content with making beautiful objects'. Stravinsky's last works, especially *Requiem Canticles*, are moving in their acknowledgement of the limitations of old age. The intellectual fire is still there, but most of the physical energy is gone; it is condensed into a single gesture, a single chord. Stravinsky remained a perfectionist; every sound is perfectly imagined. In middle age, Tippett inherited that perfection of the sound-object from Stravinsky, as the Second Symphony in particular shows. But later he began to adopt a freer, more sketchy attitude towards the notes and the sounds he chose. Some great painters in old age, for instance Titian and Monet, have been able to loosen their technique and achieve a liberating freedom without abandoning any sense of control, but it is difficult to do this in music without simply sounding careless. Listening to the Triple Concerto recently – which does, in its slow movement, contain one of the most inspired melodic passages in all the later works – I thought how imprecise much of it sounded in comparison with, say, the slow movement of the Second Symphony, with which the Concerto's first movement has a lot in common. And the awkwardness of the solo parts continues to sound awkward, however brilliantly they are played.

In the last thirty years of his composing life, the scale and range of Tippett's work remained as ambitious as in the previous thirty years – perhaps more so. *The Vision of Saint Augustine* is a valiant attempt at expressing the unsayable, comparable with – and possibly influenced by – Schoenberg's *Moses und Aron*. I cannot understand why Tippett added a third part to this oratorio, which seems to add nothing to the first two parts: the exalted ending to Part Two would have been a wholly appropriate place to stop. Here, as elsewhere, the didactician in Tippett seems to have got the better of the artist. The same kind of thing happens in *The Mask of Time*, which, as Wilfrid Mellers notes, is 'in total effect more tract than a living organism'. Its attempt to encompass just about everything in a single work proves too ambitious for the structure, which collapses under its own unwieldiness. There are marvellous moments, but as a whole the work is a noble failure.

It is fair to ask if Tippett's failures are not preferable to another's more modest successes. I do not wish to condemn his pretensions out of hand. When he wrote, in an article before *The Mask of Time* was completed, 'I have tried to confront and consider fundamental matters bearing upon man, his relationship with time, his place in the world as we know it and in the universe at large', I may have been somewhat apprehensive, but my expectations were keenly raised. My disappointment at hearing the finished work was tempered by admiration for the attempt, and the final compensation of the radiant ending. It might have been more sensible for Tippett to have followed Stravinsky's example and produce a succession of perfect, smaller works. That he was capable of doing this seems proved by the example of *The Blue Guitar*, a modest, wholly successful companion to Britten's *Nocturnal*. But Tippett was Tippett, and it is useless to regret a path not taken.

It is hard to think of any other major composer whose output is so uneven as Tippett's, though there are comparable writers – Shelley, for instance. This fact surely has to be faced before any proper estimation of Tippett's oeuvre can be made. We can be grateful that there is still much to praise unreservedly, and if he achieved his best work in middle age – *The Midsummer Marriage*, the Piano Concerto, the Corelli Fantasia, the Second Symphony – then that only brings him into company with most of the major British composers of this century – Elgar, Delius, Vaughan Williams, Walton, probably Britten – who did the same.

Notes

Source: 'His Relationship with Time', review of: David Clarke, *Tippett Studies*, in: *Times Literary Supplement*, 21 May 1999. As a young composer, David Matthews had hoped to study composition with Tippett, but as Tippett did not take pupils, he studied instead with Anthony Milner at Tippett's recommendation. Matthews first met Tippett in 1974:

Went to Nockett's Hill for lunch with Tippett. He is astonishingly youthful still, small boned, with beautifully expressive, slender hands. He talked for 2½ hours with hardly a stop, about an enormously interesting composer called Tippett & his equally interesting music – no I'm not being facetious: it's just that his self-knowledge has brought him such a remarkable degree of objectivity when he talks, fascinatingly, about himself. And he has good reason to find himself interesting, unlike most self-centred men. (*Journal*, 4 September 1974)

However, some of Matthews's doubts about the later Tippett pieces expressed in both of the articles printed above are to be found in a journal entry he made the following day:

Listened to my tape of *The Knot Garden* for the first time, I think, since the 1st performance-time in winter 1970-1. I badly wanted to find it better than it seemed when I left it: well I can say that Act III seems much more substantial (musically) than I thought & none of it is as weak as the 1st Dov-Mel scene in Act 1. Denise's aria, the Act II finale & Thea's aria in Act III are all very fine things. The jazz finale of Act 1 now seems a mess, & little else … As a whole I still can't say it's a success. I was trying to leave dramatic & verbal questions on one side & concentrate on the music & I don't think overall it's great music. I hope I'm wrong, I hope it's simply the shrinking back from the novel & unfamiliar that makes me yearn for *The Midsummer Marriage*. (*Journal*, 5 September 1974)

Looking back in June 2013, David Matthews wrote:

If in 1999 I was unwilling to pass judgement on Tippett's later works, I think I can now say with certainty that they are inferior to the earlier ones. Tippett's best music was composed between 1935 (the First String Quartet) and 1961 (*King Priam*); all his subsequent works are flawed in various ways, some of them very seriously. I say this with reluctance, but I am also certain that in his best work (above all *The Midsummer Marriage* [first performed in 1955]) Tippett is a great composer, and that if his star is ever to shine brightly again – for in the years since his death it has been almost eclipsed by Britten's – it is vital to sort out the wheat from the chaff.

15   *Pieces in Our Time*
(book review)

When people think of musical sketches, they often think first of Beethoven and his struggles to realise perfection out of a confusion of ideas, some of them so banal that one can hardly associate them with the finished masterpiece. 'The genesis of a work of music is an enigmatic and, from the lay person's point of view, even a magical process,' as Tomi Mäkelä writes in his chapter on Stravinsky's sketches in this *Handbook to Twentieth-Century Musical Sketches*. A few composers – Shostakovich, for example – never used sketches at all, but wrote straight into full score; others, notably Brahms, destroyed almost all their working material. Most, however, have left to posterity their first attempts at notating their 'vision', as Hindemith called it.

When people ask me, "How do you compose?" they often mean, "how do you begin to write a piece?". "Usually with a very brief melodic idea," I say, "just one or two notes." If asked for more details, I explain how a piece will usually start when I am doing something else: out for a walk, or in a train. Sometimes a first idea has had to be written down on a London Underground ticket, or on the back of an envelope. I was amused to discover from this book that Kurtág has composed a whole piano piece on Post-it Notes.

In the past two days I have composed the draft of a short piece, a setting for unaccompanied chorus of lines by Auden.[1] Its thirty-eight bars are written in pencil on both sides of a single sheet of paper. Using pencil means that much of the compositional process will be hidden, since you rub out as you revise, and I rub out a lot. There was only one tiny preliminary sketch, of the first bar, which I noted down in the middle of the night. I had been thinking about the piece, and reading the text, before going to sleep; waking, I reached for a sheet of manuscript paper and a pencil, and wrote down something which I had either been dreaming or thought of immediately I woke up.[2] Looking at these few notes in the morning, they seemed a good beginning, so I used them, after transposing them down so they would better fit the voices. As this was a fairly straightforward piece, I was able to write directly into four-stave score – it seems better to write *something* down even if while writing you know that you will have to make changes. At this moment it seems finished, though tomorrow I shall probably find that it needs more revisions. At a certain point you give up trying to make a piece better: as Valéry famously said of poetry, it is never finished, only abandoned.

This *Handbook* is, in the first place, a practical guide for scholars and students who work with sketches. Various skills and techniques are touched on in a series of chapters, uneven in quality, dealing with individual composers from the twentieth-century European and American avant-garde, from Bartók and Berg to Cage and Carter. Regina Busch's chapter on transcribing Webern's sketches, for instance, is seriously marred by the small-scale reproduction of three pages of sketches written in light pencil, which are virtually illegible. The final chapter, and the longest, is a puzzling inclusion. Larry Austin's detailed description of how he made a new realisation of Cage's octophonic tape piece *Williams Mix*, while an engaging account of Austin's devoted work, has nothing really to do with sketches. Cage's score, the 'dressmaking pattern' that Austin used to make his own realisation, is a finished product, not a sketch, however 'sketchy' the means used to create it (chance operations derived from the *I Ching*, in fact).

A handwritten score is often in itself a vital key to the composer's working method. The draft manuscript of Janáček's Second String Quartet, which I have seen in Brno, is written on many small sheets of landscape-format paper, on each of which Janáček ruled about three-bars' worth of staves in the centre of the page. On these he wrote, at white-hot speed and with characteristic near-illegibility, a single, explosive idea; usually he then added another three bars or so on the right-hand side on additional staves drawn freehand, revealing that his way of composing was in short moments of inspiration – moments of intense feeling – which were then linked together. This accords with the way the music sounds: the piece 'works' as a large-scale composition because the tension is never relaxed as it proceeds from moment to moment.

In a somewhat similar way, Elgar sketched in separate 'paragraphs' which he later brought together to form a seamless whole. It was Anthony Payne's uncanny skill in assembling the sketched paragraphs for the Third Symphony that enabled him to produce such a convincingly integrated work. In their introductory chapter on the nature of sketches in general, Giselher Schubert and Friedemann Sallis appear to cast a somewhat cold eye on this and other attempts to complete an unfinished work from sketches and drafts. They are right to be cautious, even with a work such as Mahler's Tenth Symphony, which is unlike most unfinished works in that there is at least an unbroken line from start to finish. Yet the resurrection of the Tenth has added immensely to our understanding of Mahler's work as a whole. In the case of Bruckner's Ninth Symphony, it is a poignant experience to hear its 'completion' and to realise that it doesn't really work, because at this stage in his life Bruckner's compositional powers were failing.[3] So we must largely be content with the three movements he finished, though it is certainly worth hearing how, with many piercing glimpses of a future never quite grasped, he finally lost his way.

Stravinsky's sketches, as Mäkelä shows, are always precisely notated for the instruments that will for the most part eventually play them. This is unusual: even a composer as concerned with the nuances of instrumental colour as Mahler was content to write his first detached sketches and his first complete drafts with virtually no instrumental indications. They were, at this stage, pure music, like Bach's unspecified score of *The Art of Fugue*. This is not to say that Mahler didn't have an orchestral sound in mind as he was composing, but rather that these details did not concern him until he had got the notes right. The drafts of the last two movements of the Tenth Symphony are tantalising in that, looking at them, one can imagine Mahler's orchestral sound, but in practice this is very hard to achieve. Several of the 'completions' of the Tenth fall flat in this respect: they fail to evoke a convincing Mahlerian sound-world. It is a problem that did not arise to nearly the same extent, for instance, in the case of Mozart's Requiem.

Perhaps the most interesting chapter in the *Handbook* is László Somfai's on Bartók's sketches for the First Violin Sonata. The sketches are clearly written in ink, but not dated; they fill the pages, but at first glance it is hard to see their continuity or establish a correct sequence. By a scrupulous examination of Bartók's pen strokes, Somfai is able to suggest a convincing order, which sheds much light on how the material and the shape of the work began to evolve from these first ideas. It is exciting to see the compositional process at work so vividly, something one would not be able to deduce from the finished score. So while, as Schubert and Sallis point out, a musical sketch cannot have the same kind of autonomous aesthetic value as a visual artist's sketch – which will often possess more 'life' than the finished work based on it – there are occasions when, as here, the composer's mind and personality will be revealed to us in a unique way.

It is rather touching to see that Bartók and Berg at about the same time – the end of the First World War – were using the same type of sketchbook, bought from Josef Eberle in Vienna. Berg's sketchbooks for *Wozzeck*, carried around on mountain hikes and train rides and stained and damaged by their constant use, are now preserved in the most clinical surroundings. There is a curious irony in the contrast between the treatment of these sketches as sacred relics, to be guarded and protected with the utmost care, and the world around us, where music is treated so carelessly. Degraded by its constant and insistent presence, music leaks indiscriminately into every area of our lives, while advertisers ransack the great music of the past as part of their campaign to sell us their goods. Surely a balance needs to be found and rectified, so that living music may be felt to have an equal value and be treated with as much respect as our preservations from the past?

Notes

Source: 'Pieces in Our Time', review of: *A Handbook of Twentieth-century Musical Sketches*, ed. Patricia Hall and Friedemann Sallis, in: *Times Literary Supplement*, 12 August 2005, p. 26.

1   This piece became part of *Two Choruses*, Op. 101 (2005).

2   This is not the only example of such nocturnal inspiration in David Matthews's creative life. The opening idea of the Violin Concerto No. 1, Op. 31 (1982-83), emerged in a similar way.

3   Matthews also promotes this view in Chapter 14 on Michael Tippett ((b) 1999), but has changed his mind in recent years: see Chapter 8 on his own completion of Vaughan Williams, *Dark Pastoral* (2010).

Part Two

Tributes

David Matthews, 8 April 1993 (Milein Cosman)

A Birthday Tribute

Colin Matthews

"What's it like to have a brother who is also a composer?" The same question is often asked of both of us. To have more than one musician in a family is a commonplace; but to have more than one composer is something of a rarity. Yet since the two of us have known nothing different for by far the greater part of our lives it has always been something that we've taken for granted.

What is uncommon, though, is that there is no strong history of music in the family. Apart from a second cousin who became a cathedral organist and choir director, there is no member of our family, going back for at least four generations, who had more than a superficial musical ability. Our parents saw to it that we had early piano lessons, but this was only in the same spirit of aspiration that led them to be the first of their respective families to move from the heart of East London to somewhat more genteel suburbs. For us they hoped to provide – and succeeded in providing – a far better education than they had had, which brought with it the opportunity to make our own decisions about what we wanted to do with our lives. I suspect that they might have been just as happy, if not happier, had we become moderately successful bank managers: but they never raised any objections to our unlikely and unexpectedly identical choice of career. And we benefited greatly, of course, from growing up at a time when the state was both wise and generous in its education policies, and when libraries were places of enlightenment.

David has always seemed to me to be the more natural musician. He was a good enough pianist in his early teens to play chamber music publicly, and as soon as he started to compose, to have had the ability to write down what he wanted to write. However unsophisticated the results might appear now, he wrote with immediate facility and fluency. This ability seemingly came from nowhere, because there was no real preparation or grounding – he simply turned himself into a composer. Equally surprising was the immediate elegance of his musical handwriting: most musicians take some while to achieve an adequate musical hand, some never do; but to David it came naturally. My own early musical handwriting is embarrassing; David's seems to me to have hardly changed over the years.

Most composers start on a small scale, perhaps largely through an awareness of their limitations, or because their teachers insist on it. David, enthralled by Beethoven's Ninth Symphony, and having discovered Mahler in the centenary year of 1960, decided, wholly untaught and without any guidance, that he should be writing symphonies; and, of course, he has never looked back. I can still visualise the opening page of the first symphony that he committed to full score after several earlier attempts: a majestic A♭ triadic statement over a deep pedal D, along with pages that had to be sellotaped together to give him the sixty or so staves he needed for multi-divided strings playing trilled clusters. Where the latter came from I have no idea: we certainly knew nothing about Ligeti at that time.

My own early efforts were much more modest and far less assured. But I was able to contribute one of the building blocks for David's future when, in 1963, I got in touch with Deryck Cooke, instituting a long-lasting collaboration with him on Mahler's Tenth Symphony in which David soon joined. David in turn made contact with Donald Mitchell, and this, once he had left university in 1965, led to editorial work for the then embryonic Faber Music, and thus a connection with Benjamin Britten. An apprenticeship that had started from nowhere had, within a few years, led to connections with two of the century's greatest composers, giving us both the solid background that we had hitherto lacked. I think both of us realised how fortunate we were, but perhaps not what exceptional and implausible opportunities we had been given. Needing to complete the picture by finding a composer to study with, David turned to Anthony Milner, whose strong personality and rigorous approach added the final touches. The rest, I'm tempted to say, is history – which others can tell as well as I can.

In fact, better than I can, or at least from perhaps a more impartial standpoint. Because the question of what it's like to have a composer for a brother doesn't really have a simple answer. I am not only full of admiration for what he's achieved so far – and if he doesn't succeed in beating Haydn for quartets I expect he will more than match Shostakovich; as for symphonies, who knows? – but am also reassured by the scale and scope of this achievement. The insecurity that sometimes arises from our lack of a musical background is dispelled when I look at what he has accomplished – if he can do it, so can I! And so if one of us at any time is doing better professionally than the other I don't believe this has ever resulted in anything like jealousy – only pride in what the other has succeeded in doing. In dedicating my Fourth Quartet to David, 'il miglior fabbro', a brother not only superior in craft in this particular medium but far outstripping me numerically, I am expressing my admiration for a composer for whom I would have unconditional respect were he to have no connection to me at all.

David Matthews in Australia – a Memoir

Peter Sculthorpe

When I was in London in 1966, I signed a publishing contract with Faber Music. I was very excited about this. The company had just been established through a trust left for the purpose by T. S. Eliot, and I was the second composer to join it after Benjamin Britten. The first piece of mine to be published was my String Quartet No. 6. It was hand-copied by Margot Toplis, one of David's early girlfriends.

I spent a good deal of time with Margot. While our conversations were mostly about matters concerning musical notation, it was from her that I first heard about David. She was in love with his music and his smile. Donald Mitchell was the founding managing director of the company. He believed that David had an exceptional future as a composer, as did his brother Colin. David was then twenty-three and Colin twenty. I was surprised to learn that they were both composers and certainly I looked forward to meeting them one day in the future.

My String Quartet No. 6 includes some wordless settings of poems by D. H. Lawrence. Margot thought that David, with his enthusiasm for poetry, would like this particular compositional device. At the time of the composition of the work I was very much influenced by D. H. Lawrence, especially his novel *Kangaroo*. The early part of it is concerned with an Englishman coming to Australia and his initial dislike of it. He found its vastness quite unapproachable. He 'longed for Europe with hungry longing'. But over a period of some months, he comes to love 'the country he had railed at so loudly'. It's a kind of antipodean *Pilgrim's Progress*.

When David first visited Australia, he was certainly in awe of its vastness, but he didn't find it unapproachable. He embraced the country from the very beginning. His was no *Pilgrim's Progress*. D. H. Lawrence's protagonist remained a little uneasy about what he regarded as the secretiveness of the bush. It readily yielded its secrets to David. He came back many times.

$\sim$

I finally met David when I returned to England in 1971. In addition to his position at Faber Music, Donald Mitchell was Professor of Music at the newly-established University of Sussex. He'd invited me to be Visiting Professor. David was then living in Sussex, at Burwash, and Donald decided that he should be my assistant. Having already edited music for Faber, he had the skills needed for preparing my works for publication.

In the early part of my stay in Sussex, I lived at Glynde, near Glyndebourne, in a thatched Elizabethan cottage. It had a rambling garden, full of old-fashioned roses, and a rivulet trickled into nearby marshes. The morning after I moved in, I drove across to Burwash for lunch. Often, if one looks forward too much to meeting somebody, there's a little disappointment when the meeting finally takes place. This was certainly not so with David. Indeed, I felt as though I'd always known him. He and his then-partner, Vivien Southon, welcomed me with home-made bread, English cheddar and the best French red wine they could afford.

I very much liked David's unbridled enthusiasm for music, painting and literature, and for life itself. I liked his generosity whenever he spoke of people he knew. I also liked the fact that he and Vivien had initiated a private printing press. They'd published some poems by T. E. Hulme, whose work I'd known for many years. They even designed the marbling on the covers. I still treasure the slim volume that they gave me.

After lunch, David and I discussed what needed to be done for Faber. He seemed to be drawn to the Australian orientation of my work and it was clear that he liked my music as much as I did his. Later, we went for a walk. We walked past Bateman's, the house in which Rudyard Kipling once lived. We then went to parts of 'The Weald and the Marsh and the Down Countrie'. It's the setting of *Puck of Pook's Hill*. We talked about music, especially Mahler's *Das Lied von der Erde*, the Ninth Symphony and the unfinished Tenth. We also talked about Australia. David's curiosity had been aroused by John Betjeman's view of it, then being presented in a BBC television series. By coincidence, my orchestral piece *Sun Music I* was used in it.

That day with David and Vivien was the first of many happy and productive days in Sussex. The days were made even more pleasurable when Anne Boyd and David's brother Colin were appointed to the music staff at the university. Both were just beginning to make their way as composers. Anne, one of my very dearest friends, had been a student of mine at the University of Sydney. I was heavy of heart when I had to return to Australia early in 1973. All the same, it was good to be back home and back to my teaching duties at the University of Sydney. Anne returned within eighteen months or so and David made his first visit within a year.

~

It was so good to see David again. He was able to afford the visit because Faber paid him a small retainer to work as my assistant. In those days none of us had much money. While he was clearly invigorated by the country and the people, he was initially a little disconcerted by some of our habits. He stayed with me in Sydney and on the day after his arrival he was quite surprised when I gave him crumpets for breakfast.

I hadn't realised that he was a serious bird-watcher. He bought a copy of the Australian publication *What Bird is That?* Almost every morning, he'd take the book to nearby Centennial Park and he soon knew far more about our birds than I did. This reminds me of the time that Olivier Messiaen was here. He'd been given a copy of the book by at least thirty people. I suggested that he open another Australian bookshop in Paris. As far as I know, Messiaen didn't use Australian birdsong in his music but David later did so in his orchestral *Aubade*.

David often ventured far beyond Sydney. With *Kangaroo* as his only guide, he even located the house in which D. H. Lawrence lived when he was here. The house is on the coast, at Thirroul, some miles south of Sydney. It's called Wyewurk, a misnomer considering that the first draft of *Kangaroo* was written there in six weeks. On another occasion, with my good friend Jane de Couvreur, David made the long train journey to the outback town of Broken Hill. He was astonished to come across an authenticated Rembrandt drawing while there. It was in the collection of the bush painter Pro Hart.

David made some life-long friends here, notably Ross Edwards and his wife Helen, Jane de Couvreur, Adrienne Levenson and Michael Hannan. Michael is a connoisseur of fine wine and food and David was delighted to be introduced to the best Australian vintages. These enlivened plans for our collaboration on a score for a short feature film. Called *Essington*, and with a script by Thomas Keneally, it was made by the ABC. It tells of the attempt to establish a settlement at Port Essington, on Australia's northern coast, in 1838. It was abandoned in 1849. The settlers were unable to adapt to the climate and the peculiar conditions of the land. The soldiers, for instance, at all times wore uniforms more suited to an English winter than an endless Capricornian summer. Finally, a ship was sent to rescue those who'd survived. It was a disastrous episode in the story of English colonisation.

In the colonial era, the piano was regarded as a symbol of taste and refinement, a symbol of the civilised world. We decided that our music would be for piano, using both the keyboard and the strings. By the time we'd convinced the producer of our intentions, we had only a week or so in which to complete the score. David wrote the keyboard music. It consists of a series of variations suggesting the music of early Victorian times. Underlying the variations, however, is a deeply-felt yearning for life in the Mother Country. During the course of the film, David's music is eroded by alien sounds played on the piano strings. Michael was responsible for these. At the end of the film, after the settlers have left, his arrangement of an Aboriginal chant, 'Djilile', sounds as though it's played on a gigantic Aeolian harp. It then becomes clear that the theme of David's keyboard variations is based upon the chant.

My tasks were mostly concerned with overseeing the project and maintaining the belief of the director, Julian Pringle, in what we were doing. Actually, we were so excited by what we were doing that we finished the score well before we had to record it. Our carefully-planned sequence of music was fundamental to the structure of the film. The producer, however, insisted that parts of it be rearranged. Even though I felt that it still worked, Julian resigned, and David and Michael wanted me to withdraw the score. Fortunately, Julian was reinstated.

David went to Melbourne after the music was recorded. He managed to identify the architects of some of its late Victorian ecclesiastical buildings. We share a passion for architecture, but I much prefer Georgian to late Victorian. In Australia, because of the climate, wide verandas were often added to Georgian houses. It may be our only contribution to world architecture. Modest verandas were added to my own house in Sydney.

While he was here, David always found time to compose. Unlike me, he doesn't always need to refer to the piano and he'd sit happily writing music on my back veranda. He wrote the last movement of his String Quartet No. 2 there. After a London performance of the work, the music critic for *The Daily Telegraph* wrote that its 'savage … rhythmic resource makes rock music seem tame'.

⌇

David continued to write music when he returned in late 1979. He thought that Australia seemed a good place for beginning pieces and he started *The Company of Lovers* here. The work is for unaccompanied SATB chorus with texts by two of our best-known poets, David Campbell and Judith Wright. It was written for the Sydney-based Leonine Consort and its conductor, Charles Coleman, to whom it's dedicated. They wasted no time in making a recording of it.

Shortly after his arrival, we collaborated upon a work for multiple guitars and string quartet called *Cantares*. While some of the music is quite engaging it's not a very good piece. I still like the title, which was David's idea, and at least David was able to come to know John Williams, who played in it. After *Cantares*, we collaborated on music for another film, *Magnaninnie*. Set in Tasmania, the island of my birth, it provided us with a good reason to go there.

In colonial times, the settled parts of Tasmania were an attempt to replicate the architecture and landscapes of England. David was surprised to see neo-Palladian churches, streets lined with Georgian houses, oaks and elms, and fields surrounded by hawthorn hedges. In the capital, Hobart, he met the director of the film, John Honey. He was reassured about the film when he discovered that John loved music and even played the cello. John drew us a map, showing the various locations for the film. We then drove from the mists of the highlands to the green midlands and the sunlit beaches on the eastern coast.

We finished our travels in Launceston, my home town. Arriving later than expected, a surprise party for us, given by my brother and his wife, was already in progress. My mother thought that David looked like Rupert Brooke and she mentioned how much she liked his and Vivien's small book of poetry by T. E. Hulme. She didn't know that Hulme was also killed in the First World War.

Manganinnie, like *Essington*, is a story about two different worlds. It concerns the Aboriginal genocide of 1830. Separated from her tribe, Manganinnie meets Joanna, a ten-year-old white girl lost in the bush. In search of her people, she takes Joanna on a journey across the island and they establish a loving friendship. Following the massacre of her tribe, Manganinnie is wounded. The two then find their way back to Joanna's world and Manganinnie dies there.

The music for Joanna, her parents and the so-called civilised world was written by David. Again, it's a series of piano variations. Tenderly lyrical, the variations are somewhat Schubertian. We'd decided that somebody had given Joanna's mother some newly-published pieces by Schubert. I wrote Manganinnie's music. It's for solo cello and, in order to mirror the landscape, I also wrote music for string quartet. We both devised some *musique concrète*, suggesting Aboriginal spirit voices. Towards the end of the film, Manganinnie's and Joanna's music come together in an affirmation of their feelings for each other. Unlike *Cantares*, we took much pride in the score. It later won a number of awards.

With the first performance of his Third String Quartet impending, David wasn't able to be here for the recording of the music. Before leaving, he arranged several works of mine, including a version of the chamber orchestra piece, *Small Town*, for string quartet. The work was inspired by D. H. Lawrence's description in *Kangaroo* of Thirroul, which David had visited when he was first here.

~

Early in his career, David decided that he wanted to be a symphonist and, in particular, to be a part of the tradition that he'd inherited from Elgar, Vaughan Williams and Bax. I cherish the day that he showed me around the

Elgar house outside Malvern. With characteristic enthusiasm, he led me to a carefully organised collection of Elgar's pens and other writing materials. I was surprised to discover that Elgar had considerable skills as a graphic artist and a carpenter. David shares the former with him, if not the latter.

By the time he returned to Australia in 1979, David had already completed his Second Symphony. Then, on a short holiday in 1983, he began his Third Symphony. It had been commissioned by the Hallé Orchestra for performance in 1985, European Music Year. While it's much shorter than the Second Symphony, it's also a single-movement work. It was begun, not on my back veranda, but at Pearl Beach, north of Sydney. David was staying there with Helen and Ross Edwards. I've always felt that he inspired Ross to embark upon his own journey as a composer of symphonies. Alfred Hill wrote thirteen and Carl Vine has written seven, but few other Australian composers have set out on this journey.

After Pearl Beach, David continued work on his symphony at my place. Because he was eager to see more of Australia, I drove him around parts of New South Wales. One small part of the state, the Riverina, is the size of England. He was always puzzled by the fact that whenever he'd go walking in the bush, I'd stay in the car. When he mentioned this to Helen, she thought that Ross would probably have done the same. Both Ross and I had long satisfied our curiosity about the bush. David, however, must have felt as Darwin did when he was here. In the Blue Mountains, he even followed in Darwin's footsteps.

The Sydney Opera House was opened in 1973, the year before David's first visit. It's one of too few twentieth-century buildings that doesn't seem to be imposed upon its site. Embraced by the blue waters of the harbour, it's as though the site was waiting for it to appear. Admittedly, the appearance was long-delayed, owing to government wrangling and the unforgivable sacking of the architect, Jørn Utzon.

I think it was during David's visit in 1985 that he and I went to the opera house to see Benjamin Britten's *A Midsummer Night's Dream*. He wondered what Ben would have thought of the production. Oberon and Titania, and all the fairy people, inhabited the mortal world and the mortals, including the mechanicals, inhabited theirs. David thought that this kind of reversal was exactly right in the Antipodes.

In 1985, there was no time for sight-seeing. We were both too busy with a score for the film *Burke and Wills*. At least it contained footage of seemingly-endless parts of the continent that David had seen only from the air. In 1860, travelling from south to north, the explorers Burke and Wills were the first to cross it. Tragically, they perished on their return journey. The expedition is very much a part of the Australian psyche. There's even an image of Burke sitting on a camel on our twenty-dollar note.

The dramatic sweep of the story, with flashbacks to Melbourne and elsewhere, demanded much larger forces than our other films. The score is for full orchestra, theatre orchestra, brass band, string quintet and quartet, unaccompanied mixed chorus, solo soprano, mouth-organ and didjeridu, the quintessential Australian instrument. As always, collaboration was exhilarating. On one occasion, David dared me to write a music cue in the time that it took him to cook pasta for dinner.

Once again, our approach to collaboration was very straightforward. On the whole, David wrote the music for Wills, a well-born Englishman, and I wrote the music for the wild Irishman Burke. Wills, a man of science, sought the Holy Grail. Burke, on the other hand, sought fame and the love of his sweetheart, Julia Matthews, an opera singer. David even reconstructed the orchestration of the ballad 'Scenes that are brightest' from William Vincent Wallace's opera *Maritana*. He wanted it to sound exactly as it did when Burke heard his sweetheart sing it in Melbourne's Princess Theatre. We probably spent too much time on historical accuracy. Without last-minute help from Ross, we might well have been late in delivering the score.

The director, Graeme Clifford, tended to be easily influenced by others. There's a scene in the film where, sitting under the night sky, Wills tells Burke about his search for the Holy Grail. For this, David wrote music in the style of Haydn, a composer much admired by Wills. It's for string quartet and has the nobility of Haydn's best slow movements. Suddenly, when it was being transferred to film, one of the sound engineers exclaimed, "Geez! It sounds as though they're having it off together!" "Oh well," declared Graeme, "we can't have that!" The Holy Grail music was removed from the film.

David began an arrangement of some of our *Burke and Wills* music while he was here. It was written especially for the Magpie Musicians, a chamber ensemble directed by Vincent Plush. He called the work *The Burke and Wills Waltzes* and finished it in London, having returned for the first performance of his Third Symphony.

Some months later, in Melbourne, *Burke and Wills* was given its premiere. Prince Charles and Princess Diana were there, and afterwards there was a grand reception. In honour of the occasion, I arranged David's croquet waltz for big band. Princess Diana seemed to like the music for the film. Jokingly, I told her I'd heard that she only liked Rachmaninov.

After 1985, David no longer came back to help with my work and collaborate upon film scores. While I missed his help, I was overjoyed that he'd achieved whole-hearted recognition as a composer, just as Donald Mitchell had predicted. All the works ahead of him were significant commissions.

Fortunately, that year didn't bring an end to his sitting on my back veranda happily writing his own music.

David's initial visits were devoted to music and to his love of Australia. His subsequent visits were concerned with sharing this love with those dear to him, Maggie Hemingway, Jean Hasse, and Jenifer Wakelyn. In many ways, these visits were even more special to me.

~

I often stayed with David when he lived in his apartment overlooking Clapham Common. It was overflowing with books and music, and a large collection of works of art, including a Sidney Nolan lithograph. There, I was able to take an objective view of Australia and my direction as a composer. I'd like to think that David's visits to Australia helped him to affirm his own particular direction.

Just as I look to Asia, David looks to Europe, especially to Mahler, and this contributes very considerably to his compositional identity. Above all, however, he embraces his English inheritance. It seems to me that this is at the heart of his work. All the same, as Stephen Walsh has written, '... though he may breathe the air of green pastures and forest paths, there is nothing of the baggy corduroys about his music!'

During our walks across Kipling's 'Down Countrie', so many years ago, David often talked about Tippett. Because he'd always felt close to Tippett's music, Donald Mitchell asked him to write a book on it. This appeared in 1980. David once stated that his music, like Tippett's, 'has lots to do with physical energy.' More than anything else, energy and enthusiasm are ever-present in his work. For that matter, his personality brims over with them.

Unlike Delius, and Elgar in his Second Symphony, and many of his compatriots before him, David has little inclination to yearn for the past. Growing up after the devastation caused by the Second World War, he's more concerned with renewal. In *Burnham Wick*, written for the Britten Sinfonia, he gives us the song of Vaughan Williams's ascending skylark in terms of the present. His Sixth Symphony makes eloquent use of the Vaughan Williams hymn-tune 'Down Ampney'. It reaches an apotheosis in the final pages of the score. For me, this work brings the English symphonic tradition to its culmination and to a new beginning.

Dark Pastoral is lovingly based upon a surviving fragment of Vaughan Williams's Cello Concerto. After its first performance at the 2010 Proms, I told David that the mantle of English music had been passed on to him. Being David, he was somewhat embarrassed by this. To all of us who know his music, it's clear that he's been blessed in this way.

The Emancipation of the Consonance

Roger Scruton

During the twentieth century, English composers emerged as a distinctive breed, inspired by profound feelings for their homeland and its landscape, and also by a certain cultivated and philosophical distance from the modern world. Like their Continental contemporaries, they experimented with polytonality, heterophony, atonal harmony, and forms and rhythms borrowed from other places and other times. But – until recently at least – modern English composers have held back from the repudiation of melody and harmonic sequence. Serialism has had little appeal for them, and for the most part serious English music in our time has shown an acute awareness of the distinction between the art of music and the skills of the sound engineer. In particular, English composers continue to aspire towards melody – or at any rate melodiousness – and towards music that moves forward on a path that the listener can follow and to which he can respond with sympathy.

The attempt to unite modernist harmony with robust melodic thinking is exemplified in the symphonies of Vaughan Williams, the Concerto for Double String Orchestra and Corelli Fantasia of Tippett, the early operas of Britten, the lyrical concertos of Walton, not to mention those all-but-forgotten works by Arnold Bax, Havergal Brian, George Lloyd and Edmund Rubbra, which were aimed at a kind of audience that has now largely disappeared from our concert halls. But the desire to combine modernism and melody continued into my time as one part of the Englishness of English music. And in Robert Simpson and Malcolm Arnold we have seen a determined attempt to retain the Romantic symphony as a paradigm of musical form.

English composers of the post-war generation have been strongly influenced by the kind of melodic thinking that we find in Britten's later work (the *War Requiem*, for example, *Curlew River* and the Third String Quartet) and in the remarkable Triple Concerto and *Rose Lake* of the aged Tippett. But they have also developed a tonal language of their own. In the concertos for orchestra of Robin Holloway, in the operas of Oliver Knussen and Judith Weir, in the concertos and symphonies of the Matthews brothers, and in many other works by composers of their generation we find what might be called an 'emancipation of the consonance', and a tunefulness of inspiration that have been a refreshing experience for the music lover. English music in our time offers a new proof that music has an intrinsic grammar, and that this grammar has nothing to do with permutational algorithms, but everything to do with the conquest of musical space by voice-leading and harmonic progression.

No one more clearly exemplifies this current of musical craftsmanship than David Matthews, who is not merely one of the most prolific composers of his generation, but also perhaps the one who has carried forward with the greatest conviction the traditions of modern English music. David's indebtedness to Britten and Tippett is evident, not only from his music, but also from his brilliant critical appraisals of both composers, whom he knew, admired and (in Britten's case) assisted during their later years. But – like those two great men, and like so many modern writers and artists in the English tradition – David is a man of universal culture, whose love of the English specificity goes hand in hand with a profound respect for German and Austrian music, for the literature of Greece and Rome, for the art of the Renaissance and for the artistic and philosophical sensibility of Central Europe – not only the Central Europe of Mahler, Bartók and Janáček, but that of Kafka and Zweig, of Havel and Kundera.

His boundless admiration for Mahler shows itself everywhere in his music, not least in the meditative accumulations of melody, such as that which opens the Second Symphony and lasts for a whole movement, or that of the last movement of the Sixth Symphony – an Adagio of Mahlerian proportions in which voice after voice is summoned out of the orchestra to weave its contribution into the elegiac atmosphere. This movement is in fact a set of variations on Vaughan Williams's hymn-tune 'Down Ampney' ('Come down, O Love divine') and works through many cries of pain to a serene coda, in which VW's lovely tune appears like a thread of light under dark clouds at the end of day. This, perhaps the most English of all the many English works that David has produced, is also a remarkable tribute to a composer who was for decades regarded with disdain by the musical establishment, precisely on account of the idea of England that inspired him.

As with other English composers, landscape has been of fundamental importance to David, and he has explained its influence on his musical thinking and experience in *Landscape into Sound*, based on his Peter Fuller Memorial Lecture of 1991. But the landscapes evoked in his works are of many different kinds and inspired by many different associations. That which sparked off the powerful *Chaconne* for orchestra is the battlefield of Towton, scene of the most horrendous conflict in the Wars of the Roses in which twenty-six thousand men died (not to mention the horses). In the preface to the score David quotes Geoffrey Hill's evocation of a field after battle, which

> utters its own sound
> Which is like nothing on earth, but is earth.

'A medieval battlefield such as Towton,' David writes, 'has long since mellowed into the peaceable English landscape, the kind of landscape celebrated by our greatest painters and, in music, by Elgar, Vaughan Williams and Tippett. If that pastoral tradition can no longer be sustained in its innocence, perhaps another might replace it, which reconciles our romanticised sense of a picturesque past with the brutal facts of history.' That last sentence captures a vital current in David's thinking, both as a modern Englishman and as a modern composer: the search for an undeceived reconciliation between the romantic and the real, and for an experience of landscape which will not be a form of self-centred illusion, but an objective response to the world as it is. One way to achieve this is to concentrate on what is immediate, without specific human meaning, a matter of atmosphere and far-flung suggestiveness. Thus the cello work entitled *Concerto in Azzurro* evokes a suffusing blue, a synthesis of sea and sky, inspired by a visit to the island of Lundy in the Bristol Channel, but also connected through the Arabic word 'azure' to places where colours are stronger and more enamelled than they ever are in England.

David may be right that our pastoral tradition 'can no longer be sustained in its innocence'. But he is capable of writing landscape music that has an innocence of its own, such as the short piece for chamber orchestra *From Sea to Sky*, which has some of the joyful expansiveness of Tippett in his Double Concerto, and which was inspired by David's own early morning walks on the beach in Deal. It should be said here that the reference to landscape is not used to invoke sentiments of a nationalistic kind. His country of birth is only one of the many places that are visited in David's scores, which are the lyrical responses of a wanderer, who is never fully at home but always resonating to new places under new skies. He is possibly the only composer to have including a tango as the scherzo movement of a symphony – and it sweeps along with Latin panache, until stumbling over rhythmically contrary woodwind chords scattered like broken glass on the dance floor. He has gathered Mahlerian cowbells and Steve Reich-ish marimbas into his scores, and ranged widely in the geography and history of Europe for his inspiration. His settings of Sappho (*A Congress of Passions*) draw heavily on Cretan folksong. And he has also been profoundly affected by the landscape of Australia, with its slowly unfolding contours evoked by his friend Peter Sculthorpe, whose music always has to me the character of someone slowly drawing aside a heavy curtain from a scene that consists of another heavy curtain. David's *Aubade* for orchestra, by contrast, draws the curtain from a living landscape, full of the strange birdsongs of Australia, which question the presence of this wanderer from the Northern hemisphere but bubble with life regardless.

∿

Perhaps the most striking feature of post-war intellectual life in our country has been its catholicity. The inter-war generation fell under the spell of T. S. Eliot, Pound and Wyndham Lewis, and the post-war generation was brought up by schoolmasters and university lecturers saturated in the Eliotian view of European culture. Dante and Baudelaire were our heroes, while we regarded Tennyson and Browning as Victorian relics whose works we did not have time in the urgency of our modern commitment to read. We were introduced to the censorious criticism of F. R. Leavis, under whose light we wriggled without ever quite escaping from the glare; we read Rilke in Leishman's editions, and the extracts from the existentialists collected by Walter Kaufmann. I did not know David until very much later in life; but the influences that were brought to bear on me were also brought to bear on him, and this created in us an immediate rapport when we finally met. The excited discovery of Stravinsky, Bartók and the Viennese school, the worry over tonality and whether it was still permitted, the astonished encounter with Rilke, Kafka, Mahler and the Central European soul, the longing for experiences outside the bounds of our Anglican upbringing, and at the same time the stunning message of *Four Quartets*, which told us that those experiences were not out of bounds at all, but could be blended with the spiritual heritage of England – all these we shared and all these had a lasting influence on both of us. Although it is possible to exaggerate the importance of *Four Quartets*, there is no denying that it changed things utterly for literary young people of my generation. It brought together the subterranean current of Anglican Christianity with the questioning search for a purified and modernist art that would seek redemption in the immediate moment, observed, internalised, and expressed without lies. As the title declares, Eliot had before his mind the great example of Beethoven, whose late quartets show religious questions answered through aesthetic discipline, and redemption achieved by the hard path of artistic truthfulness.

For people of my generation no musical medium has been more important and more personally challenging than that of the string quartet. All the crises of twentieth century art come to a head in the quartet, whose four voices mimic the four voices of the choir, and can be used to set out with exemplary clarity the sequential harmonies of the tonal tradition. The greatest of chamber works in the classical style have been quartets – not those of Haydn, Mozart and Beethoven only, but the comparable masterpieces of Schubert, and the not quite comparable achievements of Brahms. There is something about the clarity of tone, and responsiveness to the life and emotion of the performer, which gives stringed instruments a special authority when it comes to exploring abstract forms. In the string quartet tonality is put to the test, and all its devices placed under an auditory microscope. At the same time the instruments converse with each other on equal terms, exchanging the most intimate thoughts and feelings, like members of a family, who will come together after every quarrel. Not surprisingly, therefore, the early modernists used the string quartet both to explore new tonal regions and also to challenge the repertoire of the Romantic concert hall. The quartets of Debussy and Ravel take us into a new sound world, as do those of Zemlinsky and Schoenberg. But for us English schoolboys in the 1950s and early 1960s it was the quartets of Bartók that hit us most violently in the stomach, as though it were our own guts that were being pulled around by horsehair.

David was no exception. Not only has the string quartet featured in his creative output as a favourite medium; he has used the medium to explore his own art and the possibilities that are open to a composer today. The frame created by the four voices invites tonal treatment; yet the enormous range of intonations available to string players encourages experiment in the realm of colour, timbre and the upper sonorities, both natural and harmonic, of the strings. Moreover, the tradition that began with Mozart and Haydn has consecrated the string quartet as the crucible in which musical sequences, modulations and key relations are tried. In all his quartets, therefore, David has been engaged in an exercise of self-exploration, trying out new forms of tonal thinking, and aiming at the kind of formal continuity and internal cohesion that characterise the classics in the medium. His latest quartet, No. 12, is a conscious attempt at late Beethoven, spread over seven movements, each punctuated by adventures into adjacent territory. The quartet contains introductions, cadenzas, two minuets, a serenade and a tango, the whole set in motion by a magnificent prelude and fugue, and carried out with something like Beethoven's combination of meditative seriousness alternating with bursts of unaffected joy. Every now and then, as though overcome by wonder at its own world, the quartet ascends into Messiaen-like birdsong, the birds themselves named in the score as in *Le Catalogue des oiseaux*, and the four instruments striving to escape from their natural sonorities into the clarified air above music.

Over the years it has been one of my great pleasures to discuss music with David, and at a certain period he even gave me some lessons in composition – lessons which made a lasting impact on my way of listening to music, and which saved me from whatever errors I do not make in composing it. I did not need any convincing that tonal order is fundamental to music. But David helped me to appreciate that with a due respect for the bass line, and proper voice-leading in the middle parts, it is possible to colour music with every kind of dissonance and still maintain an intelligible structure. He told me to respect the old rules of harmony and counterpoint, and lessons with him were like lessons with Hans Sachs, constantly reverting to the masters and the need to respect the tradition even when departing from it.

And that, I think, has been the most important and inspiring feature of David's own music, and why he has been a model to so many of my generation.

As schoolboys we were told by enthusiastic gurus that the symphony was dead, that the string quartet ended with Bartók, that tonality was exhausted, and that tunefulness was middlebrow, philistine and in any case no longer 'available'. We were also told (whether or not in the venomous tone of Adorno) that popular music was a commercial imitation of music, a kind of candy floss on sale in dubious holiday resorts, the sound of which is repulsive to the educated ear. David stood rock-like amid this tide of prejudice. His musical sensibility had been shaped by the symphony and the string quartet, and he thought and felt within the bounds that they defined. Therefore he would compose symphonies and string quartets, and would work to hear them performed. He enjoyed the pop music that was sounding around us in our youth, and found in the Beatles an example of tunefulness and harmony from which there was everything to learn. In his symphonic works we do not hear much pop; but we are given an unusual wealth of melodic ideas, bound together by cogent harmonic progressions, and set in the grand structures that David had learnt from Bruckner and Mahler.

The real problem for the tonal composer in our time is how to respect the principles of tonal organisation without writing music that is either banal or short-winded. And the importance of David, for me and for many others, is that he has faced up to that problem, and set an example that can be followed. True, there is a late-Romantic, or more accurately post-Romantic sensibility expressed in his work, and this makes it very personal in its impact. But the treatment of musical elements – of harmony and melody especially – is rigorous and objective, so that each of his movements tends towards a conclusion that is already implied in the opening material. This feature marks David's music as a vindication of the tonal tradition, and also establishes a connection with Sibelius, the great composer singled out by Adorno as the despised voice of reaction in a time that needed revolutionary change.

The many rhythms that accumulate in David's orchestral works can all be fitted, as a rule, into a single metrical frame, from which they derive by division in the traditional way. The listener never loses hold of the measured bar-lines; and it is because of this that the simultaneous voices hang together, moved not only by their own melodic lines but also by the harmonic sequences that they collectively form. Hence David's music, however dissonant, never disintegrates into sound effects and 'simultaneities' but always gives the impression of confluent voices, flowing through successive harmonic regions, guided by the chords as clearly as a melody in jazz or a theme in a Classical symphony.

David is a master of the orchestra, one who has studied all the achievements of the modernists and their immediate predecessors, and who can make use of every instrument to produce exactly the sound that he wants. Nothing has escaped his ear, and in his orchestral writing he draws on a data bank extracted from the entire twentieth-century repertoire. Of course, certain effects have a particular appeal for him. He is especially drawn to the use of quiet chords on *divisi* strings, in which the pitches lock together like the knitted fingers of hands in prayer – an effect used consummately by Elgar in the slow movement of the Second Symphony, and constantly recurring in David's symphonies and symphonic poems. Figure 45 of *A Vision and a Journey* is an instance, with violins divided into twelve, violas into four, cellos into two, and double basses playing a sustained open fifth – foundation to an enchanted tower of thirds and seconds touching Heaven with its Gothic finials.

David loves the cantabile of unison strings too, especially when they burst through a swarm of flapping woodwind. His harmonies are for the most part adapted from the tonal repertoire, as are his scales. Indeed, there is usually an identifiable tonal centre, and sometimes, as in *A Vision and a Journey* and the Twelfth Quartet, a dominant key (in both cases D major/minor, though much of *A Vision* is in E major). However, rarely does the music bear a key signature, and even when it comes to rest on a firm tonic triad, there is usually a foreign note squeezed in somewhere, as at the end of *A Vision*, where a C, E and B knock the heart out of the D major triad, or at the end of the *Vespers*, where a triumphant B major chord, repeated again and again, is unable to rid itself of the C♯ that has somehow got trapped inside. This way of treating tonal harmony is reminiscent of jazz, and also of the 'thickening' recommended and practised by Janáček. As in Janáček, thickening, properly introduced, imparts tonal structure, while forbidding the cliché-ridden closures of common-practice harmony.

It would be fair to say, nevertheless, that David's music has become more tonal, not less, as he has matured, the Twelfth Quartet abounding in unashamedly tonal tunes, harmonised with triads, seventh chords and clear progressions in the bass, and the most lyrical of the melodies often sounding over accompanying figures, as they might in Mozart or Schubert. It would be hard to guess on hearing the two works alone that this Quartet was written by the same person who wrote the harsh and often grating First Symphony.

Tonality is not a matter of effects, nor even of grammar only. It is primarily a matter of form – a way of developing ideas over a long span of musical argument. Musical ideas, for David, have consequences, and the labour of composing is that of spelling those consequences out. His symphonic writing shows the influence of Bruckner, with long paragraphs held together by continuous lines in the bass. But, like the Baroque masters, he never loses sight of the connection with dance, introducing dance-forms whenever they seem appropriate, and always allowing rhythmical elements to stand out from the flow. This is an aspect to which I return, since it serves to distinguish David's music from much that is composed today.

During the 1980s I got to know David in two other connections: as a philosophical thinker, and as a public-spirited defender of the oppressed. I was teaching in the University of London – my last full time academic position, which ended in 1990. Although I appreciated the academic life, and the philosophical discussions among colleagues, I felt the need for another kind of intellectual companionship: one in which art, literature and music would have a central place, and which would be neither academic nor political in its focus. I invited a few friends, chosen for their interest in the arts and in the big questions of our contemporary way of life, to meet regularly at my flat for dinner and discussion. Thus was born a circle which has been a great support both to me and to others who have belonged to it. David was an obvious choice, as was Peter Fuller, the erstwhile Marxist critic, tragically killed in a car crash in 1990 (and commemorated in one of David's most poignant works, the lovely second movement of the Sixth String Quartet). Anthony O'Hear and Norman Barry were also invited, together with Juliet Mitchell, the psychoanalyst; later Ian McEwan the novelist joined us, and later still the philosopher Sebastian Gardner. Our discussions were wide ranging, and David's immense culture and learning helped to focus them in a creative way.

It became gradually clear to us, during the course of our meetings, that *Four Quartets* had left a kind of 'cognitive pathway' in our thinking. (It is from *Four Quartets* that David took the title for his harrowing symphonic poem, *In the Dark Time*.) All our discussions seemed to lead back to religious ideas: not the idea of God only, but more general, and more anthropologically conceived notions, such as ritual, sanctity, piety and the idea of the holy. Not all of us chose to stray onto this 'overgrown path' that lay partly hidden in our consciousness. Norman Barry had little time for religion, being a robust libertarian and an empirically-minded political scientist, and Ian McEwan was inclined to an evolutionary explanation of this, as of so much else in the human condition. But David and Peter were articulate defenders of the kind of 'intransitive religion', as Erich Heller once described it, that we find in the late poetry of Rilke, and in much of the English music of our time (notably in Vaughan Williams and Benjamin Britten). And it was just such an intransitive religion that David heard in the music of Janáček, whose 'overgrown path' has been such an important influence on both of us.

In the course of our meetings David often articulated a vision of modern life that made room for the sacred and for the idea of redemption, but divested of the metaphysical commitments of traditional religious belief. During the years of our discussions he composed two remarkable religious works: the above-mentioned *Vespers* for choir and orchestra, setting poems by Rilke among others, and articulating in a most moving way the religious feelings of a post-religious person; and *The Music of Dawn*, a symphonic poem inspired by the mystical painting of that title by Cecil Collins. Collins had been a favourite painter of Peter Fuller, who had spoken about him to our discussion group. In Peter's view Collins typified the neglected tradition of figurative symbolism in English painting, the tradition that reached through Bomberg, Sutherland, Ivon Hitchens and the London Group, to Miles Richmond and Cecil Collins. This tradition stands to the English soul in painting as composers like David Matthews to the English soul in music. David was drawn to Peter in part because they both rejected the cult of desecration and flippancy that had arisen through the art schools and which led in our time to the moral and aesthetic disaster of 'Young British Art'. Although neither David nor Peter could be described as believers, they were united in their respect for sacred things, and in their belief that it is the duty of art in our time to rescue the sense of the sacred from the ruins of formal religion. The sustained melodious enchantment of *The Music of Dawn* conveys some of the intense religious experience that we find in Collins – not an experience that can be contained within the doctrine of any faith, but a kind of wonder at creation, and at the consciousness which makes wonder possible.

David often addressed our little discussion group, and it is pertinent in this connection to recall one of his talks, which he subsequently refashioned as an article. It concerned the great painting of the flaying of Marsyas by Titian, now in the Archbishop's palace in Kroměříž. David raised the question how this painting, of a subject-matter so horrifying that in other contexts it hardly bears thinking about, achieves an atmosphere of such serenity. The flaying, he suggested, is portrayed as a kind of loving act, and the composition is imbued with calm, as though all conflict had been overcome and reconciled. The savagery of Marsyas is being disciplined and overcome, in a ritual sacrifice that is also a purification.

The painting should be seen, David suggested, as a Renaissance alternative to the Crucifixion. Christianity suggests that man is helpless until he puts his trust in God; but Titian is insisting that man can rescue himself by learning from his mistakes. Hence this image has more to say to us, now, than the Crucifixion, even though it is communicating on the same level as a Crucifixion scene, showing the truth of life in the moment of sacrifice. Christianity, David argued, cannot survive in the modern world, since the ideas of atonement and redemption through faith no longer have a place. But here we find the humanist equivalent, and that is why modern people are so powerfully drawn to this picture.

Titian, he said, shows us becoming rather than being – the process of change and the getting of wisdom, a subject that is ignored by contemporary art, which has forgotten that human beings come into the world in order to perfect themselves. In much modern art, and in modern music especially, there is a tendency to reject becoming and to return to a pre-Renaissance idea of being, as something fixed and unredeemable. But in all great post-Renaissance art it is becoming that is emphasised, and being is seen as something to be achieved through becoming. Stasis comes through *dunamis*, as in Beethoven's late quartets (and especially that in E♭). The C♯ minor Quartet, David added, is the only one that begins in stasis and moves to *dunamis*. And this same Quartet ranks with *The Flaying of Marsyas* as one of the supreme achievements of our civilisation. Take the two together and you will understand what is lacking in so much contemporary music, namely the dance, that which inhabited the aged fingers of Titian in the same way that it inhabits the voice-led movement of Beethoven's quartet.

Titian's painting inspired David to write one of his most original compositions, *The Flaying of Marsyas*, for oboe and string quartet, in which the contest between aulos and lyre, represented by oboe and violin, is gradually subdued and reconciled, and absorbed into the texture of the string quartet. For all the philosophical reflection that went in to this piece, it is by no means an academic or 'learned' composition. On the contrary, like all of David's music, it shows reflection reworked as emotion, and has a spontaneity that is entirely musical. It exemplifies what I think is the most important feature of David's artistic persona, that he is immediately and totally engaged in whatever is before him, whether it be a painting, a landscape, an idea or a drama.

David's modest manner and his way of bearing his immense learning lightly and discretely have ensured that he has remained a private and not a public intellectual, easily though he could fill the latter role. His ability – astonishing in the times in which we live – to support himself as a professional composer of serious music, has freed him from any need to brand himself as a celebrity, and his quiet presence at musical gatherings testifies to the serene pleasure that he takes in the success enjoyed by others. His undemonstrative manner is not a sign of timidity, however. At a certain point during the period of our first acquaintance I asked him whether he would be willing to travel to Czechoslovakia (as it then was) in order to talk to a group of musicians and composers in Brno, who had been cut off from contact with their Western colleagues and also, in certain cases, excluded from official recognition and performance on account of their dissident profile. David readily agreed, and was profoundly affected by the experience – in particular by his meeting with Petr Oslzlý, founder and director of the Theatre on a String, a company that existed on the edge of things, neither permitted nor forbidden, but acting as a door into the underground, which would be opened to those who knew the password. David's seminar to the musicians and others who had assembled to meet him was on the topic of Mahler's Tenth Symphony, which he had worked with Deryck Cooke on reconstructing from the sketches. The seminar lasted six hours, and was received with great emotion since, although Mahler was a Moravian composer, son of the innkeeper in the village of Kaliště, who began his conducting career in Olomouc, his symphonies were rarely performed in the land of his birth, and the Tenth had not yet received its premiere there.

David returned from Brno resolved to do what he could to help the musicians and composers whom he had met. He at once set about organising exchanges and visits 'on the edge', through which to secure the privilege of travel for composers who had been marginalised. He volunteered to take on the task of coordinating the musical side of our slowly growing underground university, and thereafter travelled frequently to visit his Czech colleagues, and to provide them with the resources needed to further their creative activities. It was thanks in part to David's support, both before and after 1989, that the Brno school of composers has achieved international recognition. In particular, David's support for Pavel Novák has been crucial, first in encouraging Novák to stick to his calling during the difficult years on the margins, and subsequently in securing commissions outside the country, which have led to international recognition not only for him but also for those of the older generation, such as Miloslav Ištvan and Alois Piňos, and indeed for the entire Brno school, in whose music some of the eager life-force of Janáček still breathes. David also organised visits to Brno of important British composers, including the indefatigable Nigel Osborne, Judith Weir, Anthony Powers, Michael Berkeley and several more. The story is told by Barbara Day in her history of the underground university in Czechoslovakia, *The Velvet Philosophers*, and it records an exemplary effort by one concerned artist to offer a lifeline to colleagues less fortunate than himself and, in doing so, to experience a new kind and new intensity of inspiration.

David's experience of communist Czechoslovakia was emotionally intense; but it was not, psychically speaking, a new departure. Perhaps his most remarkable feature, both as a person and as an artist, is that he does not have experiences: rather experiences have him. They take possession of him completely, and use him as a vehicle in their search for expression and form. I don't mean to suggest that there is something demonic about him: on the contrary. He has the capacity both to surrender to experience and also to discipline and humanise it. His music has many dissonant and angry passages; but they never triumph, and are always overcome by a kind of distancing forgiveness. Even in the *Chaconne*, which marked a transition in David's style, and which contains some of his most superimposed dissonances, the mesmerising ground bass imposes an order which subdues the music to its rhythm, so that this work, which begins with hallucinatory shrieks in the upper range of the double basses, introducing startled cries from across the orchestra, settles at the end on a serene rumination on the ground bass theme, with soft strings in their natural register, accompanied by harp and celesta. The effect is clearly reminiscent of the long-drawn out 'ewig' that ends *Das Lied von der Erde*.

And maybe this is an appropriate point on which to end this tribute too. Mahler's 'ewig' summarises the religious feelings of an artist for whom the source of meaning is earth and her beauty, and who finds redemption, not in hoping beyond this world, but in being reconciled to leaving it, and leaving it forever. In Mahler's vision, redemption comes through beauty; but the awareness of beauty is not merely an aesthetic thing, existing in fleeting moments of delight. It is a stance of the whole person and informs the whole of life. It has its moral and political expression; and it is best explained, to those who do not know it, as the ability to bless, and to be blessed by, the things of this world. That ability was Mahler's; and it is David's too.

A Festival Friendship

George Vass

David Matthews first visited the Presteigne Festival in 2000 when he was featured as that year's composer-in-residence. It was the beginning of an important association for both the Festival and my own musical life. I had come to know David Matthews's music before I met the man himself. Recordings of the Fourth Symphony and the dramatic cantata *Cantiga* had made a strong impression on me (as did the *Concerto in Azzurro* – a masterpiece – which thrilled me at the premiere, not long after we first met). Here was a composer who carried on the musical line of Britten and Tippett, but who developed his musical language very much on his own terms.

At Presteigne, featuring music by living composers has always been a vital strand in the identity of the Festival, and we try to maintain a healthy commissioning policy. David was an ideal composer-in-residence: his music was immediately taken to the hearts of the Festival audience. His pieces sit comfortably alongside Classical and Romantic works of the past and twentieth-century masterpieces, from which he often draws inspiration, as well as those of his contemporaries, of whom he is such an active supporter. However, David's pieces always have something new and fresh to say. David has been at Presteigne every year since 2000 and he now acts as one of the Festival's more active vice-presidents. His music is regularly featured and we have hosted the premieres of a sequence of new works. The first of these was *Winter Remembered* (2002), a concertino for viola and strings, written for Sarah-Jane Bradley, and jointly commissioned with the Deal Festival. The following year David contributed a small song, 'For a Wine Festival', to the *Garland for Presteigne* (a cycle of twelve songs by ten composers) to celebrate the twenty-first anniversary of the Festival in 2003; this song was then incorporated into his orchestral cycle, *Movement of Autumn*, commissioned for the 2005 Festival. In 2007 I commissioned *Adonis* for violin and piano, setting David the unusual challenge to base a work not only on a Welsh folksong, but also on something from Greek mythology, as requested by the violinist who premiered the piece, Sara Trickey. Amazingly, David found a Welsh folksong that refers to the story of Venus and Adonis. In 2010 it was David's skills as an arranger that came to the fore in his orchestration for string orchestra of Elgar's String Quartet. In his careful treatment of the well-chosen sections for solo instruments, we see the natural musicality David brings to the work without ever distorting Elgar's original thoughts.

In my work as a conductor, I find David's music especially fascinating to prepare. His ability as an imaginative orchestrator has never been in doubt, and though his music can be technically intricate – particularly his string writing, which often needs careful rehearsal – it is always crystal clear how the music needs to be shaped. Recording the First Violin Concerto, for example, I realised that often the key to unlocking the true power of his music is to find the emotional peaks and troughs of the work, in order to bring the music's formal journey into focus. Collaborating with David is a joy, as he has the rare knack of letting go of the music sufficiently for performers to find their own way into it, while continuing to be a source of support. If you believe, for example, that a tempo marking should be faster or slower than indicated in the score, David will support you as long as he is convinced you have understood the essence of the music. My recording of *The Sleeping Lord* came in at over four minutes longer than the score suggests, but it worked: we had found the right tempi for that particular performance in that specific recording venue. As with Tippett's music, I think David's metronome markings need to be treated as considered approximations – his scherzos are often marked a little too fast, sometimes making it technically difficult for instrumentalists to play all the notes. What matters is capturing the mood and character of the music; his pieces always come together beautifully, and when I conduct his music I always feel as if I am with a good friend and in a very safe place.

In the past decade, much of David's music has been commercially recorded, ensuring his work is now reaching a far wider audience than ever before. I am honoured to have played a continuing role in this part of his life; making the first recording of the revised version of the First Symphony with the Ulster Orchestra (for the BBC), and recording commercially several chamber orchestra pieces and concerti including, most recently, the Piano Concerto with the Finnish virtuoso Laura Mikkola.

In this, his seventieth birthday year, David will return to Presteigne where we will give the Welsh premiere of his Double Concerto for violin, viola and string orchestra, jointly commissioned with the Cheltenham Music Festival and the Amsterdam Sinfonietta. It is my sincerest hope that there will be many more collaborations in the future, as well as opportunities to rediscover works he has already given us. There is so much in his output to cherish and treasure.

A Birthday Tribute

Paul McCartney

David and I met quite a few years ago when I was working on a full-length orchestral piece of mine called *Standing Stone*. I was working on my computer and needed someone to translate my rather clumsy work into something that the orchestra would be able to make sense of. He was always very supportive of what I was writing, and we had many fun times and interesting conversations about the daily life of a composer. He assisted me as we took *Standing Stone* through to completion with the help of other musical associates such as Sir Richard Rodney Bennett, John Harle and Steve Lodder. We talked about his love of Deal and its Music Festival that he would organise annually.

David also contributed a choral piece for the project known as *A Garland for Linda*, where nine contemporary composers donated choral works in aid of Cancer Research. His piece *The Doorway of the Dawn* was really well received, and it was a further pleasure to work together on this recording.

It is with great pleasure that I congratulate him and his work over the years on this special birthday.

Autumn

Maggie Hemingway

Autumn

A snail shell hangs on the wall
Like a lantern
The sun spiralling through caverns of amber
And the snail gone.

From lily to lily to rose
Spins the spider
Gossamer lace clouded with diamonds
In shadowy corners.

Beyond in the drowsing orchard
Lie the pears
Deep in soft grass gleaming like ingots
A glittering mosaic.

Warmth fades and the light dies
Over the garden
And none of our longing, our prolonging of days
Can hold back winter.

The Dream's Awakening

James Francis Brown

For David Matthews, on the occasion of his 70th birthday

April Sonatina for Solo Violoncello

John McCabe 2011/12

Gold Thread for solo violin

Pavel Zemek Novák

Partita for solo viola

Judith Weir

Partita for solo viola

Judith Weir (2011)

to David, in admiration
Judith xx

Birthday Tribute

Dmitri Smirnov, Elena and Alissa Firsova

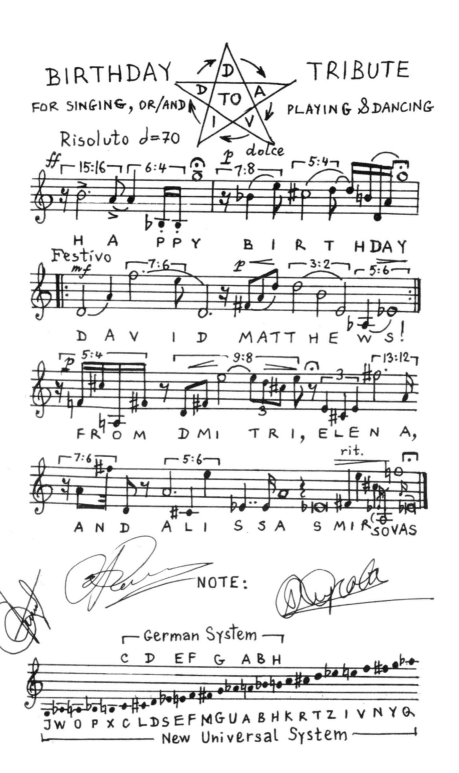

70-note Melody for David's 70th

Robin Holloway

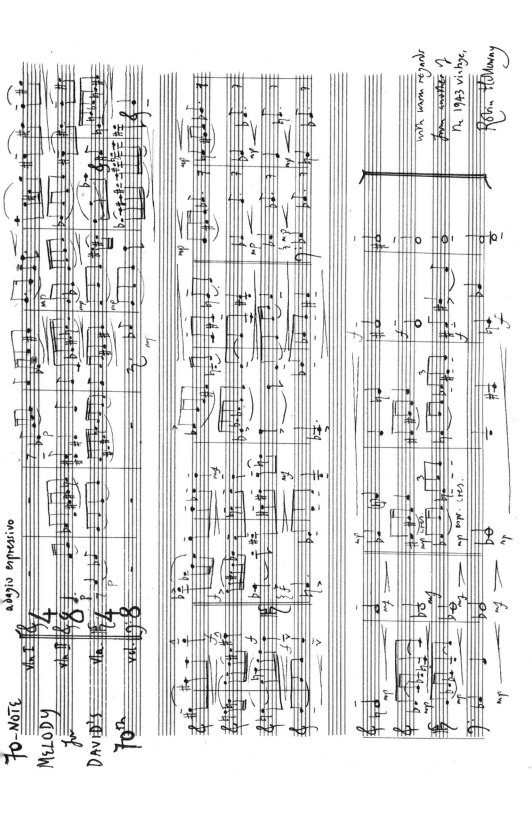

Sand Martins at Dunwich

Robin Leanse

For David Matthews

Now the east wind and the cliff
put on for us a Suffolk play,
cast a bright bird, and a cave,

and in roles close to their hearts,
a bird in the wind, a cave in the cliff,
coming together, loose yet tight.

But watch that cliff and this east wind
vying over the African bird:
it acts like a dream in the air

lines that pulse – a gust off the sea –
a dance to thrill an applauding wind …
How could wind not take it hard

when bird posts head – body – and legs –
into the sand …? But the cliff's spirits rise
when the bird is in the cave;

only then can it feel this shore
kind at last: the warmth of the bird,
the storm of feeding, the cradle of the cave –

seem to the cliff a better world,
the bird from abroad come safely home
cheating the nest-destroying wind

pacing outside. Weeks pass – food
flares in each chick – in the dark –
beak meeting beak like the spark of a song

till each flies from the riddle of homes;
the notes of folksong written in a cliff
a memory now – of a residence.

The sand martin; all the grace,
and young in the skies (for the next frontier)
not to mind its birth-place, ground

down more, each year, by that wind;
nor its clag caves letting in
the air – the homes destroying home;

heads in the sand they still perform
this cliff-hanger of a play –
still up-in-the-air today.

Part Three

Criticism

*Above: George Vass, David Matthews, Hugh Wood and
Thomas Hyde, December 2009 (Jenifer Wakelyn)
Below: Peter Sculthorpe with David Matthews, January 1983*

1   A View into the Landscape: David Matthews at 70

Malcolm MacDonald

By the age of seventy, David Matthews has established himself as one of the most distinctive voices in British music, with one of the most substantial oeuvres. He rates as a leading figure in the generation of British composers born in the 1940s, composers who had to define themselves, not only against the tonally and traditionally focussed achievements of their forerunners in the first half of the twentieth century, but also against the much more obviously radical generation born in the 1930s – such as Peter Maxwell Davies, Harrison Birtwistle, Alexander Goehr and Nicholas Maw – who in their different ways embraced and built upon the modernist aesthetic of Schoenberg and Stravinsky. As Matthews's Sixth Symphony attests, his solution to this aesthetic challenge has been to some extent to re-engage with the older British traditions, at least as represented by Vaughan Williams, Britten and Tippett; but also to draw strength from a thoroughgoing assimilation of the great European traditions of craft and expression extending from J. S. Bach to Mahler.

His achievement is all the more remarkable in that he emerged from 'outside' the conventional paths to British musical eminence. He has avoided teaching, but to support his composing career has done much editorial work and orchestration of film music, collaborating, for example, with Carl Davis and Peter Sculthorpe. Matthews is probably best known and most highly regarded as an orchestral and instrumental composer: his imposing series of (to date) seven symphonies – eight, if we count the 1996 *Sinfonia* for a severely classical orchestra (actually a larger body than that required for Symphony No. 4) – and twelve string quartets make that case rather unanswerably. Yet he has composed in most genres (except ballet and opera), and his achievements as a vocal composer, of both choral music and song, are just as significant.

Given that Matthews characterises himself as a composer who thinks primarily in terms of melody – the very idea would have sounded slightly archaic at the time he was setting out on his creative journey – it's arguable that the lyric impulse, the desire to sing, engenders much of the orchestral and chamber music. The epic Second Symphony, for example, grew out of the materials for an abandoned choral and orchestral work that would have been called *Ad Lucem*; the core and goal of the Sixth Symphony is a Vaughan

Williams hymn tune. Matthews has not yet introduced a singer into a symphony, but one can quite imagine him doing so: he has introduced a tenor into his Seventh String Quartet, *Skies now are skies*, setting D. H. Lawrence, e. e. cummings and *The Song of Songs*. Indeed the long, ecstatic final span (and the compositional starting-point) of the Third Symphony (1983-85), with its haunting oboe solo, is a wordless transcription of his Kathleen Raine setting 'Spell of Sleep' from the 1983 song-cycle *The Golden Kingdom*.

Matthews's music could at first be characterised – with drastic over-simplification – as a potent distillation and development of certain qualities that distinguish the Tippett, Britten and Maw generations of English composers: notably their ecstatic melodic writing and vibrantly expanded tonal harmony. Sometimes the debt is very directly expressed, as in the *Midsummer Marriage*-like opening of the Second Symphony, or the first movement of the Fifth Symphony, so reminiscent of the muscular neoclassicism of the first movement of Tippett's Symphony No. 2 (but also, beyond that, of the first movement of Stravinsky's *Symphony in Three Movements*). Although his concern for large-scale structure connects rather to the central European tradition, back through Mahler and ultimately to Beethoven, he has also, perhaps more consistently than any other British composer of his generation, engaged with perennial British themes: with landscape, with the pastoral as an ideal, with the change of the seasons and the changing spiritual aura that they engender in us – placing him in a line that stretches back through Maw and Tippett to Elgar, Delius, Bax and Frank Bridge.

It would be fatally easy, therefore, for a hostile critic to characterise him as merely a traditionalist (and therefore conservative) composer; but that critic would be very wide of the mark. Certainly Matthews is nothing if not a composer fiercely committed to the power and the enduring validity of traditional, and indeed national, conceptions of music. But his attachment and depth of commitment to tradition-heavy genres does not indicate any slavishness of approach to them. In fact, one of the most remarkable things about his symphonies, quartets and concertos is their variety of form, and how little Matthews depends on the classical three- or four-movement archetypes. Huge single-movement designs, unequally weighted diptychs or unusually proportioned triptychs are at least as common. Even when the classical pattern emerges, it is treated in unusual ways, and in recent years there has been a tendency to replace the function of the scherzo with a tango, a dance that fascinates Matthews for the versatility discovered in it by such masters as Astor Piazzolla. A strong interest in jazz and popular idioms manifests itself in other ways, as in the 'blues' movement of the Oboe Concerto. Above all, he is aware, as any intelligent composer in the early years of the twenty-first century must be, of a bewildering multiplicity of competing traditions, with their competing meanings; of the impossibility of a grand synthesis that would reconcile all the fruitful paths; and the importance nonetheless of a synthesis of that which means most to him personally.

An obvious case in point is Matthews's Sixth Symphony, a signal success at its premiere in a 2007 Royal Albert Hall Promenade Concert, which seemed in one sense in stark opposition to the temper of the times. There's something not merely traditionalist but practically archaic in the idea of a symphony (in C, no less) based upon Vaughan Williams's famous hymn tune 'Down Ampney' from the English Hymnal: one that develops from its motivic premises a large, three-movement design reflecting something of the idea of pilgrimage that infuses most of Vaughan Williams's symphonies. Yet that pilgrimage is articulated through formal structures and deep harmonic ambiguities that draw upon the examples of Bruckner and Mahler: Mahler, whose music has fascinated Matthews since his earliest years – Mahler, whom Vaughan Williams merely considered 'a very tolerable imitation of a composer'. A cowbell, redolent of Mahler composing his last works in the Dolomites, has already been heard in Matthews's first movement; and in the finale, a 'dawn chorus' of birdsong the composer had heard in Fremantle, Australia assuages the acutely dissonant climax. Nature and art here extend themselves geographically, from Gloucestershire (where the village of Down Ampney, Vaughan Williams's birthplace, unassumingly stands) through Europe to the ends of the earth.

So if style is the man, style in Matthews's case is wrought from those things he most loves, even when they seem to be contraries. As a result of that awareness of competing traditions, as also of his formidable breadth of culture in literature and the visual arts, there is almost always much more going on in one of his works than immediately meets the ear; each score demands (and rewards) repeated hearings to yield its fullness of meaning.

Consider for a moment a short yet highly significant work: *The Sleeping Lord*, a setting of a late poem by David Jones for soprano and the same instrumental septet that Ravel uses in his *Introduction et allegro* (flute, clarinet, harp, string quartet). The 'sleeping lord' of the poem, typical of Jones's lifelong, and in old age intensified, fascination with the Celtic/Romano-British nexus out of which British identity arose, is both Arthur – the 'once and future' king whom legend says will eventually arise from sleep to deliver his country – and also the landscape within which he sleeps, into which he has somehow been transubstantiated. The setting of the poem, though apparently the work's raison d'être, occupies little more than a fifth of it: ten pages out of the score's forty-eight, plus a few piercing melismas and repetitions in the closing bars. The rest is pure tone-painting, vibrantly evocative and intricately patterned: an introduction depicting the state of sleep and a main movement – too substantial to be termed an epilogue – full of the sense of awakening. There's also the seasonal metaphor in play, Winter's stasis giving way to Spring's sense of rebirth, a cycle Matthews has often explored, most extensively in the symphonic poem *In the Dark Time*. Finally, Matthews has stated that the elaborately decorative style of Jones's late drawings such as 'Tristan ac Essyllt' and 'Annunciation in a Welsh Hill-setting' was a direct influence on the texture of the instrumental music.

The Sleeping Lord is significant because the poem embodies a perfect metaphor for what seems to be happening here and very often elsewhere in Matthews's music: 'Does the land wait the sleeping lord / or is the wasted land / that very lord who sleeps?' The work is at one and the same time a song and chamber music; a setting of words and a tone-poem of landscape; illustrative and yet aspiring to that decorative intricacy of Jones's pictures in which form is created by an infinitude of detail and symbolism. Clearly we are not meant to choose between formal or expressive alternatives but to accept them both, accept them all, for what they can give us. And it's the same with his non-vocal works: are his symphonies, quartets and concertos primarily abstract designs or evocations of landscape and spiritual states? Are his symphonic poems primarily evocations of their avowed subject-matter, or symphonic designs? For the musical language and the expressive stance seems to be the same in each genre. Matthews seems to have arrived at a rare balance, almost an interpenetration or deliquescence, of the form/content, structure/expression conundrum that every composer must consider. (Even if that dichotomy is ultimately a false one: 'Form is expression', as Robert Simpson used to say.)

An equally complex case is presented by the *Chaconne* for orchestra (1986-87), a key work in Matthews's output. Here, a poem by Geoffrey Hill – one of Matthews's most admired poets – was the stimulus: a poem about the bloody battle of Towton during the Wars of the Roses showing how the medieval battlefield, with its dreadful freight of suffering and slaughter, has mellowed into the deceptive innocence of a peaceful English landscape. The strict form – not merely a set of variations on a ground bass, but also two such sets placed within a symphonic sequence of episodes including introduction, scherzo with trio and coda – generates a kind of 'anti-pastoral', the chaconne principle providing the motive power for meditation on the remorseless aspects of time and nature, and the ephemeral, but apparently everlasting, follies of mankind.

Response to landscape, therefore, can take many and sometimes unexpected forms. *Chaconne*, though it has the form its title proclaims, is also one of a cluster of orchestral works, such as *September Music*, *In the Dark Time*, *A Vision and a Journey* and *Winter Remembered*, that shows Matthews can handle large and small orchestras with a skill rivalled by few others of his generation. In these and other works, he seems to have revived the sometimes-derided genre of the symphonic poem, and they illustrate the inspiration he has drawn from both nature and the other arts, particularly painting and poetry. Indeed, in his 1991 Peter Fuller Lecture, published as *Landscape into Sound*, Matthews discusses how often his music has been prompted by visual stimuli. The *Concerto in Azzurro* for cello and orchestra, inspired by a holiday on Lundy Island and the 'vision of blueness' he experienced there, is but one example among many.

Landscape, then, and the seasons: the moods of *September Music* and the dramatic trajectory of *In the Dark Time*, spanning the cycle from late autumn, through winter, to the onset of spring, are patently linked to times of year. We see this also in some of his concertante works – notably the First Violin Concerto (1980-82), with its intriguing two-movement form and an inspiration partly autobiographical, partly derived from an atmospheric Dostoevsky story set in the bright summer nights (the 'White Nights') of St Petersburg, and the concertino *Winter Remembered* for viola and 16 strings (2002). The latter work can be enjoyed without any knowledge of its background, but nevertheless relates back to a potent nexus of poetry, song and string music. In 1982 Matthews wrote a solo violin piece, *Winter Journey*, based on two songs from Schubert's *Winterreise*: the first, 'Gute Nacht', and the seventeenth, 'Im Dorfe'. He later arranged it for solo viola, which partly prompted *Winter Remembered* – a composition that also, in its second theme, makes explicit reference to Schubert's 'Gute Nacht'. The title *Winter Remembered* refers to a poem by the twentieth-century American poet John Crowe Ransom, which, says Matthews,

> makes a nice allusion to *Winterreise*, as well as being not too far distant in its subject matter from the Wilhelm Müller poems that Schubert set [...] Although there is no overt description of stormy weather in the piece, there are some chill winds, and an overall feeling of melancholy that most of us associate with winter.

The result is an intensely personal, deeply-felt and deeply-expressed work which must rank among the finest contemporary compositions for viola.

There is also a clutch of pieces inspired by the times of day: *The Music of Dawn* (perhaps the finest and most 'symphonic' of all his symphonic poems), *Aubade*, *After Sunrise* and *Darkness Draws In*. The Tenth Quartet is another 'music of dawn' that, like *After Sunrise*, presents its own 'dawn chorus' of Australian birdsong, with the Munro magpie melody having pride of place. Matthews's interest in the songs of birds both Antipodean and European provides material for quite a few of his works, and is another and very direct example of his response to nature. He uses them not quite in Messiaen's quasi-ornithographical manner, but with greater or lesser literalness as the musical situation demands. Sometimes, indeed, the song is only imagined: when he composed *Marina* he had never heard a wood-thrush, so the basset-horn's quintuplets stand purely for a bird of the imagination.

At least as important as the symphonies are the string quartets. Robert Simpson apart, Matthews is probably the most important British quartet composer of recent decades. They are very varied works indeed, ranging from the sheer melodic generosity of the Fourth Quartet – a 'great C major' quartet if there ever was one – to the knotty intensity of the Fifth, the elegiac affirmation of the Sixth, the lyric fervour of the Seventh (with voice), and the dawn chorus of Australian birdsong that opens the Tenth. But it is the very recent Twelfth (2009-10) that is the revelation, and a kind of summa of aspects of the previous quartets. Its seven movements, incorporating short pre-written pieces – a Tango, a Serenade, two Minuets – are poised on the more massive foundations of an opening prelude and fugue, a deeply-felt-and-thought slow movement, and a jubilant finale, not to mention evocations of European and Australian birdsong at salient points. Like the late Beethoven quartets that are so clearly one of its inspirations, it seems to cram into the form almost more than it can take; yet the result is an imaginative enlargement of the genre that has a kind of Olympian relaxation, weighty yet practically angst-free, which makes this work, for me, one of Matthews's most important achievements.

So impressively do the quartets bulk in Matthews's output that it is easy to forget that he has contributed valuably to several of the other great chamber genres – with, for example, the Piano Quintet, the Clarinet Quartet and the piano trios and string trios. Interestingly, there is no duo sonata for a string or wind instrument with piano; but there is a powerful Piano Sonata (1989) and a small group of solo piano works such as the *Dionysus Dithyrambs* that attest – as do his song accompaniments – to an intimate and sympathetic acquaintance with all the keyboard's challenges. And Matthews's involvement with the piano has surely reached a new stage with the very recent Piano Concerto, Op. 111.

Matthews has written no opera, but he has composed a number of works that are in essence scenes which we could imagine fitted into some much larger dramatic design. None approaches the operatic state nearer than *Cantiga* (1987-88), the powerful (and highly theatrical) cantata on the true, pathetic and terrible story of Inês de Castro, secretly married for love to Pedro, crown prince of Portugal, who was murdered on the orders of Pedro's father King Afonso IV. When the prince succeeded as king in 1357 (the Portuguese know him as Dom Pedro the Just), he had the murderers executed and Inês's corpse exhumed, crowned and enthroned by his side as queen, forcing the entire court to pay her homage and kiss her hand. She was then splendidly interred in Alcobaça Cathedral, where to this day her tomb can be seen next to that of King Pedro. Matthews's cantata, to a vividly-imagined text by Maggie Hemingway, is a virtuosic vocal showpiece that graphically runs the gamut of moods engendered by this tragic love story.

A very different queen is evoked in *Terrible Beauty* (2007) for mezzo-soprano and seven players (flute, bass clarinet, harp and string quartet). This ravishing feat of vocal chamber music is largely a setting of Enobarbus's famous eulogy of Cleopatra in Shakespeare's *Antony and Cleopatra*, describing her progress down the River Cydnus to Tarsus in a gilded barge, attended by servants dressed as sea nymphs and watched by all the citizens of the town. This was the prelude to Mark Antony's first meeting with the Egyptian Queen, which set their tragedy in motion. As Matthews points out, Shakespeare's text is modelled on a passage in Plutarch's life of Antony; and Plutarch in turn is quoting from Homer's account, in Book 14 of the *Iliad*, of the goddess Hera's seduction of her husband Zeus. Matthews has therefore prefaced his setting of Shakespeare with some lines from the passage in Homer, in the original Greek. The title itself, *Terrible Beauty*, comes from W. B. Yeats's poem 'Easter, 1916', a record of a different kind of tragedy. Just as Enobarbus's speech is a virtuoso exercise in word-painting, so is Matthews's work a virtuoso piece of word-setting. This is immediately clear from the opening, where Homer's Greek is made both archaic and exotic by being set as a floridly-decorated vocal incantation with the sole accompaniment of harp (standing in no doubt for the Homeric lyre). Only once it is finished does the full ensemble enter, in music marked 'slow and languorous', to begin to resonate Shakespeare's great speech in plashing rhythms and colours. The whole piece is a dramatic *scena*, though as in *The Sleeping Lord* plenty of space is given over to purely instrumental music.

Other examples of such 'vocal chamber music' include the T. S. Eliot setting *Marina* for the unusual combination of baritone voice, basset horn, viola and piano, a commission from the 1988 Bath Festival. Eliot's text appears to be a dream-poem that refers to Marina, the daughter of Pericles in Shakespeare's and George Wilkins's play *Pericles, Prince of Tyre*. Lost at sea as a child, she is reunited with her father in the play's miraculous happy ending. Her name, too, evokes the sea; and the imagery of Eliot's poem seems to reflect his own memories of the New England coast where he had sailed and watched the birds, and the rhythm of the sea, a symbol of ancient time. Matthews has commented that the 'sea-green and blue-grey colours of the poem suggested the sounds of the viola and clarinet', but that he used the basset horn – the alto clarinet, the viola of the clarinet family – for 'added mellowness'. As well as the sea-sounds evoked by the ensemble in the short instrumental prelude, Eliot's poem speaks of the air: of wind, breath and fog. All these aspects are graphically conjured up in Matthews's instrumentation (the 'Aeolian harp' figurations for viola and basset horn in contrary motion evoke similar formations in Brahms's Clarinet Trio), and his treatment of the voice, including passages of free recitative that include speech, is also very resourceful.

One further example is *Winter Passions* (1999), a setting of three poems by Alexander Pushkin for baritone, clarinet, string trio and piano. (Matthews set the poems in the English translation by D. M. Thomas, but *Winter Passions* was subsequently performed in Pushkin's original Russian at the second St Petersburg Festival of British Music in November 2009.) The three poems

Matthews chose make up, he thinks, 'a short winter narrative'. The opening song, 'Winter Road', in which the poet travels by coach at night over a snow-covered landscape, is a 'troika' – a species of Russian travelling music well-known from, for example, Prokofiev's *Lieutenant Kizhe* suite. The pizzicato strings evoke the strumming of a balalaika. The voice part seems instinct with the spirit of Russian vocal writing, and where the poem refers to the coachman singing, Matthews quotes a Russian folksong: specifically the one that Stravinsky quotes in Parasha's aria in his opera *Mavra* (itself based on a Pushkin story). 'Invocation', beginning with chill trills and harmonics, is inspired by Pushkin's memory of Amalia Riznich, with whom he had an affair in Odessa but who had since died of tuberculosis. Matthews sets this as a deeply-felt and rather spooky elegy: the setting makes Pushkin's appeal to the dead girl to come back to him no mere rhetoric, for the intensity of the string-writing and the desolate clarinet part seem to establish her presence in the ambient air. Clarinet and piano then interpolate a short 'dream-interlude' leading to the third song, 'Winter Morning'. Here we have a joyous C major aubade: Pushkin encourages the girl by his side (not Amalia – Matthews imagines her to be the 'Nina' of the first poem) to enjoy the beauty of the morning with him.

Choral music occupies a relatively small but vital area of Matthews's output – indeed he first attracted widespread attention with the short cantata *Stars* in the early 1970s. Among his choral works none is more important than the 1993-94 *Vespers*, Op. 66 commissioned by the Huddersfield Choral Society, a work at once imposing and intimate, religious and yet resolutely non-denominational. It sets four resonant Latin texts, two of them also set by Monteverdi in his *Vespers* of 1610, juxtaposed with poems from Rilke's *Stundenbuch* (the Book of Hours): poems that seem to Matthews 'profoundly religious' although Rilke's approach to religion was 'highly unorthodox … and completely modern'. Matthews's score is as much choral symphony as proto-oratorio (the setting of 'Alma Redemptoris Mater' incorporates an orchestral scherzo), and, after the ecstatic Amens of the penultimate Magnificat setting, ends with Rilke's 'All will grow great and powerful again', set as a kind of chorale, which Matthews sees as 'a vision of a future free from religious strife'.

One could go on, for Matthews's catalogue of works is a cornucopia of such thoughtful, challenging and yet deeply satisfying pieces that testify both to his respect for tradition and firm grounding in the contemporary world. To a greater or lesser extent they all embody 'moments of vision' – to use the title of the unaccompanied choral work he wrote between 1978 and 1995, whose text draws upon Gerard Manley Hopkins, D. H. Lawrence, Keats, Hardy, Geoffrey Hill and Edward Thomas. It is, in sum, precisely this visionary quality that makes Matthews's music so valuable, and him such an independent creative voice. It is the root of his artistic achievement, which has made him a force to be reckoned with in the music of this country.

2   Enriching the Present:
The Sixth and Seventh Symphonies

Arnold Whittall

In a characteristically bold assertion, the philosopher and composer Roger Scruton once claimed that 'the lingering backward glance towards that which can never be recovered (and which is falsified in the very yearning for it) has been the greatest vice of English music in our century. Like every form of sentimentality, it involves a "turning-away" from the present reality, a desire to lock emotions into a narrow and predetermined world of fantasy, a world which *you yourself* control'.[1]

Scruton's immediate example of such sentimental nostalgia is Vaughan Williams's Housman cycle *On Wenlock Edge* (1908-09), and he contrasts this with a 'fresh, simple, and sincere' vocal work – Janáček's *Diary of One Who Disappeared* (1917-20) – which exemplifies the core attribute of great art: 'Great art […] involves some affirmation, however qualified, of the actual. […] If art ceases to affirm life, then it loses its point: after all, life is all that we have. Even when it turns its thoughts to death, true art seeks a path to affirmation.' Scruton then proceeds to argue that 'such life-affirming works have by no means been rare in late twentieth-century music,' and he instances a trio of British composers – Judith Weir, Robin Holloway and David Matthews – who, following on from the examples set by Michael Tippett and Nicholas Maw, 'have written works which, in the interests of a serious and unsentimental affirmation, have returned to tonal regions, and sought […] for plots in the vast tonal landscape which have not been ploughed into sterility'.[2]

Scruton does not seek to demonstrate that there is 'nothing more' to Vaughan Williams's music than what he finds in *On Wenlock Edge*, or that all Janáček's works are on the exemplary level of the *Diary*. Nevertheless, like all such polemical juxtapositions, the effect is to provoke questions about how fundamental these particular expressive attributes might be, and to raise a host of other troubling aesthetic and analytical issues. If nostalgia and sentimentality are unacceptable in music, how about pathos, or compassion? For that matter, are freshness, simplicity and sincerity totally absent from *On Wenlock Edge*? Exploring how the kind of music Scruton admires can interact with that by composers he likes less is perhaps the best way of keeping his chosen themes in circulation without getting bogged down by the constraining specifics of his dramatically deployed examples. And this strategy suggests itself given the intense and complex results of David Matthews's symphonic responses to – in particular – Bruckner, Mahler, Vaughan Williams and Sibelius.

1   Matthews in Prose

'Renewing the Past' is the part-title of an essay by Matthews that can be seen (whether intentionally or not) as a response to Scruton's claims about the seductiveness of that 'lingering backward glance', and also about how to balance some degree of commitment to living traditions with avoiding that '"turning-away" from the present reality' that Scruton sees as so counter-productive. An earlier version of Matthews's essay had a title – 'The Rehabilitation of the Vernacular' – whose governing concept fixed his critique and rejection of much that is usually regarded as central to post-tonal modernism.[3] For Matthews, a teenager in the 1950s, the 'wildly orgiastic music' of Elvis Presley and Little Richard, 'so different from anything I had encountered in my cosy suburban childhood, was overwhelming': and far from dubbing such pop musicians as unacceptably primitive when compared to Mahler and Britten, Matthews claimed that 'it was by listening to rock music' – rather than by worshipping at the shrine of modern Classicism – that he 'discovered the elemental power of tonality'. Hence his three-pronged credo: 'my principles are: that tonality is not outmoded, but a living force; that the vernacular is an essential part of musical language; and that the great forms of the past, such as the symphony, are still valid.'[4]

Matthews is well aware that, far from having been permanently and decisively banished, 'tonality flourishes again everywhere, and by no means only in the simplistic form adopted by the minimalists': indeed, he notes that even the likes of Boulez and Stockhausen 'have made some accommodation with tonality'. Nevertheless – and here the affinity with the Scruton thesis is manifest – that 'accommodation' is clearly insufficient in itself if the wider ethos of modernism remains unchallenged. 'Modernism in all the arts has often mirrored the isolated, anguished state in which the twentieth-century artist has found himself', and although 'there is a genuine art to be made out of existential despair (such as the early works of Peter Maxwell Davies) [...] composers should beware of the self-indulgent use of an extreme language, which should not be an easy option'.[5]

In his 1980 book about Tippett, Matthews formulated the same idea in a slightly different way:

> despite Schoenberg's assertion to the contrary, the musical language which he formulated and from which most currently fashionable styles are descended, is limited in expressive range. It is an ideal vehicle for the depiction of extreme emotional states. [...] Of those composers

who have used a Schoenbergian language, the most successful have been those who have expressionist things to say: Peter Maxwell Davies, for example. In short, serialism [...] cannot easily evoke states of joy, gaiety, exuberance. If composers still want to express such emotions in their music, they might profitably consider how Tippett's language in its development from orthodox tonality to pantonality has always been a potent vehicle for the widest range of expression.[6]

Matthews's convictions clearly match the earlier Tippett's in identifying the humanistic impulse 'to discover the divine element within us' while remaining free of commitment to religious doctrines requiring belief in God and the established church. The Beethovenian route through 'personal anguish to a profound spirituality' remains the Utopian ideal, and that requires not just 'some accommodation with tonality' but also a truly 'dynamic' use of tonality, involving

> both modulation and the rediscovery of dissonance as a disruptive force. Although one can no longer easily define the difference between consonance and dissonance, it is still possible to conceive of harmony as either stable or unstable. Unless there are real harmonic contrasts in a piece, it cannot have dynamic movement.[7]

This is the main reason why 'modernism', as Matthews understands it, is not to be allowed to return by the back door. Moreover, dynamic tonal harmony is insufficient on its own, since

> the loss of accessible, singable melody in the music of Schoenberg and his successors was a devastating blow to music's comprehensibility. [...] The fact that the majority of the musical public are as likely to miss the deeper, structural level in Beethoven as they are in Boulez is not an argument against the desirability of an accessible surface, for Beethoven's melodies give access to the deeper levels of his music.[8]

These judgements provide the core of Matthews's 'personal thoughts', and his distancing from expressionistic modernism. He pins down and conflates the problematically subjective concepts of 'accessibility' and 'comprehensibility' in terms of a characterisation of musical history that reveals much about his own predispositions and instincts as a composer. Even more directly than his close contemporary Robin Holloway (also born in 1943), Matthews has placed himself in the line of those British and other predecessors who have spent much of their time assembling cycles of symphonies or string quartets. He has even suggested that 'because the Classical style produced nothing of great value in this country and our own symphonic tradition only truly began with Elgar, it may be easier to write symphonies and string quartets today in Britain than in Germany or Austria'. He then notes that 'the symphonies of Vaughan Williams and Tippett, and the string quartets of Tippett and Britten, represent outstanding innovative attitudes towards these forms'. What remains vital, however, is that innovation is not to be sought at the expense of accessibility. As Matthews reiterates, 'music began with song and dance, and however sophisticated it becomes, it must never lose touch with these essential human activities'. 'Dance,' he declares, 'was another of post-war modernism's puritanical exclusions, because of its supposed tainted association with populism.' It follows that 'what is crucial is that dance rhythms must find their way back into contemporary music'.[9]

Matthews evidently does not rule out all ambiguity in the name of accessibility: he has described the various formal strategies – 'confusing' exposition and development, literal and varied restatements – in his Fourth Symphony as 'so subtle I should not be surprised if they are not noticed'.[10] If what is noticed is also memorable – attractive, and in this sense, easily accessible by listeners – then the music will be valued. If one's criterion of memorability extends into something distinctively arresting (hinting at things one has not found in precisely the same way in other compositions) the chances are that the impression will be more penetrating, more intriguing.

Matthews offers ample evidence of music he values and which serves as an example, even of a model to be learned from. As a symphonist, he is aware of a multiplicity of meaningful precedents, including those as immediate as Vaughan Williams and Robert Simpson: and while his attitude to the presence of 'existential despair' in art seems less intolerant than Roger Scruton's, he has faced the challenge of devising an idiom in which the 'conservative' commitment to renewing the past and embracing the 'vernacular' does not result in something that haplessly mirrors the kind of portentous 'hamming-it-up' and effortful straining for epic-heroic effects that afflicts the large-scale works of the American anti-modernist George Rochberg (1918-2005).[11] Matthews's take on affirmation is never more effective than when he seems to turn cherished romantic models inside out: for example, his setting of Pushkin's 'Winter Morning' that ends *Winter Passions* (1999) rejects the Schubertian angst of the solitary, jilted winter traveller and celebrates both companionship and the 'matchless blend' of 'sunlight and frost'.

This rethinking of Romantic conventions goes with the impulse, in symphonic music, to move towards 'a world of Sibelian "purity"' and therefore 'a kind of classicism'. Like Sibelius's own, this is a 'kind of Classicism' deeply implicated with late-Romantic and even post-Romantic initiatives, which in Matthews's case account for affinities with Mahler and Vaughan Williams (the Sixth Symphony, discussed below), as well as with Sibelius himself: Matthews's single-movement Seventh Symphony (2008-9), also considered below, acknowledges the precedent of Sibelius's Seventh and its 'extraordinarily subtle transitions of tempo'.[12] However, this is evidently not a classicism governed entirely by restraint and patent continuities: drama and disruption can be present – and given valid functions – in this music, even if the principal aim is to shun 'the rather cloying, late-Romantic world which I think Schoenberg still represents':[13] and at least some of that 'drama and disruption' might arise because of the different post-Romantic relations between melody and harmony which thinking symphonists at the beginning of the twenty-first century must acknowledge and confront.

2   David Matthews and Ralph Vaughan Williams

Matthews's elegiac *Dark Pastoral* (2010), based on the surviving sketches for Vaughan Williams's unfinished cello concerto from 1943,[14] was preceded by the Sixth Symphony (2002-07), whose generating material is provided by the hymn tune 'Down Ampney' (c. 1905). One does not have to be a Scrutonian sceptic where Vaughan Williams is concerned to feel that this one of his contributions to the *English Hymnal* ('Come down, O Love divine') is an unpromising basis for a structure a good deal more directly and expansively symphonic than his own famous *Fantasia on a Theme by Thomas Tallis*. Nor will sceptics necessarily be reassured by Matthews's comment that as 'a sequence of rising and falling scale fragments', 'Down Ampney' 'seemed very suitable for symphonic working'[15] – although such an unexceptionable technical observation (and how many other found tunes, whether hymns or otherwise, would it not fit?) is surely preferable to assertions about the tune's engagement with spiritual transcendence prompting the further transcendence of a grand symphonic design after Brucknerian and Mahlerian models. As it happens, both these composers have 'roles' in Matthews's design, but little trace is to be found of their more effusive, heaven-storming stylistic propensities.

That Matthews first came to 'Down Ampney' when invited to contribute to a composite set of orchestral variations on the tune for the 2004 Three Choirs Festival, and that his offering was 'a short scherzo', indicates that his instinct was not to 'play up' any sacred solemnity, but rather to acknowledge his affinity, as an agnostic, with Vaughan Williams himself, finding the 'essence' of the material by moving it as far away as possible from its original congregational, text-serving function. It could be argued that one of Vaughan Williams's most productive characteristics as a symphonist was his ability to 'estrange' hymnic material in such a way as to generate effective and original symphonic structures that incorporate it. When he came to compose his Fifth (1938-43), he saw the potential for connection with a dramatic treatment of Bunyan's *The Pilgrim's Progress*; while the desire to suggest the ideal peacefulness of a world without war might have prompted the inclusion of an 'Alleluia'-like theme linked to one of the *English Hymnal* tunes, 'Sine nomine'. It could even be that the main melodic counterpoint to the passacaglia bass in the symphony's finale involves an allusion to the D major contours of 'Down Ampney' itself, with the sublimely serene (or is it nostalgically sentimental?) ending of the symphony acknowledging the hymn-text's intensely Christian vision of souls fulfilled in paradise. 'Down Ampney' and the Fifth Symphony tune can both be shown to involve three stages: an initial arch-like ascent from D to A (Exx. 1(a) and 2 (a)): a descent back to D (Exx. 1 (b) and 2 (b)): then a further, elaborated descent from the upper D through the octave to the original tonic (Exx. 1 (c) and 2 (c)).

Example 1(a)-(c): Ralph Vaughan Williams, 'Down Ampney' hymn tune.

Example 2(a)-(c): Ralph Vaughan Williams, melody from Symphony No. 5 (1938-43, rev. 1951).

Matthews's Sixth Symphony seems to have taken shape as follows: first came the 'short scherzo', begun in September 2003 in response to the Three Choirs Festival Commission: as soon as this was under way, 'I began to think of how it might also find home in a new symphony. In June 2004 I began a first movement, also based on "Down Ampney", and sketched the first 225 bars before I had to interrupt it to compose another piece'. Matthews returned to the work in April 2005, revising and extending the scherzo and surrounding it 'with two 15-minute movements, to make a work that lasts in all around 35 minutes – my largest symphony so far'.[16]

Example 3(a): David Matthews: Symphony No. 6, Op. 100, opening of the second movement.

Example 3(b): Ralph Vaughan Williams, opening of Symphony No. 5.

If this chronology is used to test the hypothesis that the second movement provides a model for a particular way of using 'Down Ampney' that extends across the whole work, it is clear that the beginning of the scherzo – Cs underpinning a D-based statement of the tune (Ex. 3(a)) – is an example of 'questionable rooting' which also embodies a fleeting and probably accidental allusion to the opening sonority of Vaughan Williams's Fifth (Ex. 3(b)). At the beginning of Matthews's first movement (Ex. 4(a)), C is again the bass, but this time the 'Down Ampney' motif starts from F rather than D, making an initial F, G, A♭ progression, whose most obvious Vaughan Williams association is with the opening of his Sixth Symphony (Ex.4 (b)).

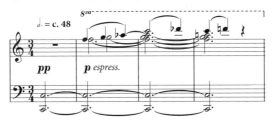

Example 4(a): David Matthews, Symphony No. 6,
Op. 100, opening of the first movement.

Example 4(b): Ralph Vaughan Williams, Symphony No. 6
(1944-47, rev. 1950), opening of the first movement.

Matthews has described the overall form of his first movement in terms of the Brucknerian 'binary' – exposition, expanded counter-exposition, coda: a template he has also linked to the *Concerto in Azzurro* for cello and orchestra

(2000-02) and which might equally be applied to the smaller-scale String Trio No. 2 (2003). In the Sixth Symphony the exposition also embraces its own 'vernacular' dualism, contrasting hymn-derived lyricism with dance-derived dynamism. Matthews builds an evolving dialogue between slower and faster blocks, though in this case the faster blocks are purposefully contrapuntal in ways that suggest more mainstream symphonic models: any overtly dance-like spirit is kept in reserve, and this scheme serves its purpose in fuelling the necessary energy and sense of crisis that make an 'expanded counter-exposition' work – as a combination of development and recapitulation.

At a relatively late stage (Fig. 45, *più allegro ed impetuoso*), stamping rhythms combined with assertion of smoother melodic shapes bring the two modes of expression into a hectic confrontation which, after a preliminary work-out, reasserts itself with even greater force (from Fig. 59). As a powerful demonstration of open-endedness, the movement's final confrontation is between almost mindlessly aggressive patterned 'action' (Fig. 78) – the apotheosis of the anti-lyric – and uneasy hymn-derived phrases set against a dense chord in which the combination of an F minor triad with tritonal counterpoles for two of the notes (F/B, A♭/D) radiates a sense of unfinished business. The tonal association between C and F with which the movement began survives, but has a degree of cloudy instability about it which the rest of the work will need to address.

The next stage is set up by the scherzo's spanning relationship – between an unstable C and a much more decisive F – in a short, ebullient set of variations on 'Down Ampney' that suggests associations with such energetic precedents as Beethoven's Seventh and Bruckner's Ninth, while also managing to blend lyric and dramatic, song-like and dance-like qualities. Since, unlike the first movement, the scherzo seems to find a final convergence (on F) unproblematic, the finale might be expected to return with new determination to the first movement's 'problem': how to explore divergences coherently, a kind of late-modern acknowledgement of Classical symphonism's 'large-scale integration of contrasts'.[17] Matthews has already associated a passage in his first movement (*suddenly still*, Fig. 52, complete with cowbells) with 'the similarly-placed interlude in the first movement of Mahler's Sixth Symphony', and says that his finale begins with an introduction 'which again makes veiled reference to Mahler's Sixth, this time the opening of his finale'. This connection is even more 'veiled' than the Mahlerian echo with which the work ends, and there is little common ground between Matthews's basically slow set of variations and Mahler's turbulent march, with its starkly tragic, even nihilistic outcome. There is nevertheless more than a touch of Mahlerian apocalyptics – Schoenbergian expressionism avoided by a hair's breadth – in what Matthews describes as 'the most violent climax of the Symphony': 'an acutely dissonant version of the chorale [the finale's version of 'Down Ampney'] and a G major/minor chord [rooted on B♭] like a huge question mark' (Fig. 165). The work then moves to a conclusion that does indeed reject Mahler's 'starkly tragic, even nihilistic' coda, as well as the bleakness that concludes Vaughan Williams's Sixth: nor can it embrace the warm D major Elysium that ends Vaughan Williams's Fifth. Instead, a quite different Mahlerian precedent is obliquely invoked.

3   Ending with Mahler?

The suggestion that Matthews's Sixth begins with a minor-mode transformation of 'Down Ampney''s initial scalar ascent to establish a subtle allusion to the start of Vaughan Williams's own Sixth is pure speculation. Rather less speculative is the explicit connection between Matthews's ending, with what the composer describes as 'a glimmer of light' – a 'chord of E, G, A, E on viola harmonics', above a briefly stated bass C – and the final sounds of *Das Lied von der Erde*'s 'Abschied'.

In *The Aesthetics of Music* Roger Scruton fulsomely describes that chord's added sixth as an element 'which wars, however feebly, against the triad – the slight raising of the body for that last glimpse of life'. This image is enough to earn Mahler the accolade of being 'life affirming', and fulfils Scruton's broader requirement that 'life can be affirmed only in the plural – art endorses life only through the "we" of the implied community, which redeems the death and grief of the mere individual'.[18]

By contrast, Matthews's hint of the *Das Lied* chord at the end of his Sixth Symphony stands against Mahler's sustained rootedness: Matthews shuns the resolving stability of Mahler's own context, and as a consequence the element of affirmation, complete with hints of sentimental nostalgia, is even less decisive in Matthews than (if we follow Scruton) it is in Mahler himself. It is also less assertive, less confident than Britten's use of the same basic sonority. In his short biography of Britten, Matthews quotes a letter from 1937 which declares that *Das Lied*'s final chord 'is printed on the atmosphere': the twenty-three-year-old Britten talks extravagantly of basking in the 'heavenly light' of music that 'has the beauty of loneliness and pain, of strength and freedom, of disappointment and never-satisfied love'. Matthews also draws attention to Britten's use of the C-rooted 'Mahler chord' for what Matthews terms the 'ecstatic gestures of acceptance' at climactic moments in two late works, *Owen Wingrave* and *Phaedra*.[19]

The context for Mahler which Matthews creates in his own Sixth Symphony is quite different. He has saved for the later stages of the finale the event that, as he writes, 'I felt must inevitably happen – a presentation of "Down Ampney" in full, in my own rather than VW's harmonisation, but not too far away from the original'. Although Matthews's initial tonal centre is A rather than D, what is most distant from the original is not so much the character of the harmony as the variability of mood: what at first sounds almost like a parody of a musical vision of paradise, with transparently up-beat string arpeggios, reverts to the finale's predominantly dirge-like character for the hymn's central phrases. Then comes the all-important last line of the tune, which, as the composer notes, 'I had not used until this point'. This 'flowers aspiringly into many canonic lines in the strings': but the aspiration is compromised by the way G♮ underpins the A major melody. The canons end with a precariously plain, widespread dominant of A: then there's a brief recall of the first movement's F minor opening before the dominant seventh's deferred resolution onto the fifth A/E – the last ghost, perhaps, of Mahler's Sixth. Then the bass shifts to C, and the final 'Abschied' allusion (E, G, A, E in viola harmonics) throws even that degree of harmonic and tonal stability into doubt (Ex. 5). What for Britten is Mahler's 'ecstatic gesture of acceptance' turns in Matthews (perhaps under Scruton's influence) into something less conclusive: the late-Romantic 'glimmer of light' becomes a late-modernist gesture of ambiguity about closure and connectedness.

Example 5: David Matthews, Symphony No. 6, Op. 100, closing bars.

In deciding how to end his symphony, Matthews will have been aware that, while Mahler reconciled A and C at the end of *Das Lied*, Tippett allowed the same pair of tonal centres to remain estranged at the end of his Third Symphony: Matthews discussed this work in his Tippett study.[20] The use of such inter-textual allusions is a powerful tool for a musical mainstream rooted in a late-modernist aesthetic, even when, as in Matthews's case, that aesthetic is more engaged with modern-classic resistances to disruption than with the explicit fragmentation and stratification of modernism 'proper'. Matthews might even be thought of as refereeing a debate between two very different symphonists who nevertheless share some of the attributes of musical modernism, if only through resisting them. The uneasy play with tension between stability and instability has recently been demonstrated by Daniel Grimley and J. P. E. Harper-Scott in essays on Vaughan Williams's Third and Fourth Symphonies;[21] and this uneasy play turns in Matthews's Sixth into the Mahlerian destabilisation of a Vaughan Williams already destabilised by

Matthews's angle on the way 'Down Ampney' can be transformed through associations with Vaughan William's own symphonic music.

Consistently sceptical, Roger Scruton asks the following question about the Fifth Symphony's opening: 'is the music just a little too banal, too much dependent on worn-out pastoral gestures from which the realities of country life in the modern world have been expurgated?'[22] Matthews's professed admiration for Vaughan Williams's symphonies relates, I would imagine, to that composer's ability to remain in contact with 'the realities of [...] life in the modern world', while at the same time retaining a significant degree of scepticism about what – if anything – artists can honestly affirm: a stance that Tippett also came to adopt in his later years.[23] In place of bleakly dissolving endings – disintegrations – Matthews makes his most personal mark by offering touched-in resolutions, closural strategies that balance pastoral simplicity against technical equivocation. The ending of the Tenth String Quartet (2000-01) as a wisp of song standing next to a sliver of dance is one such high point, with a degree of modal ambiguity echoed, not only in the pacific ending of *Adonis* for Violin and Piano (2008), but also in the concluding melody of the three *Journeying Songs* for solo cello (also 2008) that provided the generative inspiration for the Seventh Symphony. But the ending of the Sixth Symphony is more equivocal than any of these: the stable fifth, A–E, of 'Down Ampney''s final chord loses its major third C♯ and shifts toward more distant, if not exactly unknown, regions of regretful but resigned Mahlerian farewell. It is as if, however improbably, the 'mere individual' that is the connoisseur of contemporary serious music clings to life, part of yet separate from a community that in most cases chooses not to listen.

4   The Seventh Symphony: Continuation or Contradiction?

At first glance, David Matthews's Seventh Symphony, composed in 2008-09, appears neatly complementary to the Sixth: cast as a single twenty-minute movement, it promises Sibelian economy rather than Mahlerian expansiveness, and (as Matthews himself has noted in his Preface to the score) the initial C major tonality suggests an even more explicit tribute to Sibelius's own Seventh. There is nevertheless one very important similarity between the two Matthews symphonies: like the Sixth, the Seventh derives from a pre-existent song-like melody, this time by Matthews himself: 'this [viola] melody was originally the culmination of a solo cello piece that I wrote in May 2008 for Gemma Rosefield.'

On this basis, it is tempting to dub the Seventh 'The Intertextual', after the model of Nielsen's Fourth, 'The Inextinguishable'. Not only does Matthews's symphony relate to the cello piece, but the fact that he has placed that piece as the final section of a three-movement composition called *Journeying Songs* (originally dating from 2004) naturally arouses curiosity about possible links with other works that deal with travel – for example, Mahler's *Songs of a Wayfaring Lad* and Britten's setting of Thomas Hardy's 'Midnight on the Great Western' that is about a 'journeying boy', to name just two composers particularly close to Matthews's heart. Is it conceivable that the turning figure with which Matthews's melody begins embodies a subtle allusion to the opening of Mahler's vocal line, shifted from minor to major, and also less clear-cut in tonal allegiance (Exx. 6a and 6b)? Whether conceivable or not, once noted, such associations reinforce the positive sense of engagement with precedents and models – as materials to 'critique' as much as to celebrate – which has clearly helped to generate both works.

Example 6a: David Matthews, Symphony No. 7, Op. 109, bars 2-8, opening viola melody.

Example 6b: Gustav Mahler, Lieder eines fahrenden Gesellen *(1896), bars 5-8.*

As with 'Down Ampney', turning the *Journeying Songs* melody into symphonic material indicates a problem to be solved, a challenge to be met. In *Journeying Songs*, there is an inherent ambiguity in the way the melody's C major tendencies, reinforced by the punctuating chords, stand against the persistence of a one-sharp key signature, perhaps echoing the kind of 'Lydian' modality that often served Britten as a background for centred yet chromatic writing. But whereas *Journeying Songs* ends with an emphatic assertion of C as G's 'superior' (Ex. 7), cadentially and therefore tonally, the Seventh Symphony, with no key-signatures at any point, sounds uneasy about that central C-ness from the outset. It is as if the search for a suitable chordal and harmonic context for a melody that is, in essence, monodic, generates the momentum of a structure that can only find sufficient clarity and an adequate sense of closure by hoisting the shifting motion between C and G up a further fifth to D and A.

Example 7: David Matthews, Journeying Songs, *Op. 95, third movement, bars 52-9.*

This, of course, is a very un-Sibelian strategy. For all the richness of his harmonic vocabulary, Sibelius (like Vaughan Williams) tended to 'Classical' monotonality as far as ending symphonies in the tonal area where they began is concerned. 'Progressive tonality' is more the province of Mahler, Nielsen, Simpson – or Matthews: and the radical difference between the Seventh Symphony's moderately paced, *cantabile* opening and the *strepitoso* D major ending might suggest a distant memory of the kind of trajectory presented in, say, Mahler's Fifth, were it not for the way in which Matthews makes his arrival in a confirmed D tonality the point of conclusion, and not something to be prolonged or reinforced. The ground traversed is summarised by the contrast between the initial, lyrical outlining of the fifth C to G and the concluding, more dance-like assertion of D to A. And while the symphony's most basic tonal centres can be collapsed into the kind of pentatonic scale or sonority that offers another subliminal connection to the chord that closes *Das Lied von der Erde*, Matthews avoids too obvious a return to either Vaughan Williams-like modality or Mahlerian extended tonality. Rather, he generates a distinctive stand-off between competing tendencies to stabilise and to destabilise, in tandem with the symphony's contested transformation from song into dance, and from reflective, passive moods into hyperactivity.

The most dramatic stand-off in the work is between the melodic aspiration of the opening, with all the associations of refinement and sophistication that accompany it, and the no-less disciplined but alarmingly unmelodic timpani cadenzas that erupt during its central phase. It is, a dramatic scenario might propose, only when the primitive dynamism of this material is confronted and contested that both the lyrical melody and its dance-like complement can emerge from the tensions of the symphony's *tenebroso* core and turn towards the light and joy of the conclusion. Just before the *tenebroso*, at Fig. 57, the main lyric motive is heard against the final projections of the timpani tattoo, estranged but with its identity still intact. When the timpani next emerge with an assertive, purely rhythmic pattern (Fig. 90), it is part of, yet already subordinate to, the evolving thematic process, a turn to conformity that becomes even more marked five bars after Fig. 102, where the (dominant) pedal of A begins to counter the harmonic instability evident up to that point. However, the symphony's skilfully contrived final crisis involves keeping the possible tonal outcome open, not least with respect to the possibility of abandoning D for C after all (see the G-based harmony at Fig. 107).

Despite appearing totally opposite in character from the questingly reticent conclusion of Matthews's Sixth Symphony, the brusque cadence ending the Seventh makes its effect through suggesting that stability remains provisional, even when arrival at a clearly established goal is appropriately euphoric and decisive. In the age of late modernism, composers who wish to retain principles that 'classicise' their modernity cannot ascend convincingly to those grandiose, diatonic, chorale-like affirmations that Mahler made his own. The most explicitly Mahlerian quality of his Seventh that Matthews identifies in his Preface is the 'extensive part' he provides for the baritone saxhorn, saying 'I don't know why Mahler [in his Seventh] didn't allow him at least to join in the jubilation at the end of the finale'. Matthews gives the baritone player a prominent role in his final transformation of the *Journeying Songs* melody into an agent of symphonic dynamism. If the spirit of this ending seems hectic, stressful, as much if not more than joyous, jubilant, after Mahler's well-upholstered consonant fashion, that is surely all to the good.

5   An Open Ending

A century after Mahler's symphonic swansong, eighty years after Sibelius's, and more than fifty after Vaughan Williams's, David Matthews has to confront concepts of community, collectivity and the vernacular that are likely to seem very different to his contemporaries from those that Mahler experienced in early twentieth-century Vienna or New York, Sibelius remained close to in Finland and Vaughan Williams embraced in mid-twentieth-century England. Perhaps what Matthews is really doing here is to suggest that art in his time is not so much endorsing 'life' by turning away from 'the mere individual' – sinking the 'me' entirely in the 'we' – rather, he is accepting that it is the tension, and the ambivalent 'affirmation' that ensues, that is of the essence, even for a composer who is concerned not to lose all contact with the kind of initiatives so prominent in post-1950 popular music. The sense of melodic material searching for sufficient harmonic stability and consistency to ground a viable symphonic process is perhaps even stronger in Matthews's Seventh Symphony, with its up-beat D major ending, than in the Sixth. If so, the road to further symphonic enterprise remains tantalisingly open.

Notes

Source: Revised and extended version of the author's 'The Matthews Mark', in: *Tempo*, No. 257, 2011, pp. 2-10.

1   Roger Scruton, *The Aesthetics of Music*, Oxford, Oxford University Press, 1997, p. 492.
2   Scruton, *op. cit.*, p. 494.
3   David Matthews: 'Renewing the Past: Some Personal Thoughts', in *Reviving the Muse: Essays on Music after Modernism*, ed. Peter Davison, Brinkworth, Claridge Press, 2001, pp. 199-212 (reprinted in Part One of this volume); 'The Rehabilitation of the Vernacular' in *Music and the Politics of Culture*, ed. Christopher Norris, London, Lawrence and Wishart, 1989, pp. 240-51.
4   Matthews, 'Renewing the Past', p. 199. Matthews continued to ponder the challenges of 'learning to use the incredibly complicated language that tonality is' in: Mark

Doran, 'Composer in Interview: David Matthews', *Tempo* No. 223, January 2003, pp. 2-14.

5   Matthews, 'Renewing the Past, p. 201.

6   David Matthews, *Michael Tippett. An Introductory Study*, London, Faber and Faber, 1980, p. 104 (the extract also appears in Chapter 14 (a) of this book).

7   Matthews, 'Renewing the Past', p. 208.

8   *Ibid.*, p. 208.

9   *Ibid.*, p. 210.

10   *Ibid.*

11   See this author's review of: Rochberg's *Five Lines, Four Spaces. The World of My Music*, Urbana and Chicago, 2009, in: *Tempo*, No. 251, January 2010, p. 67.

12   David Matthews, programme note in the score of his Symphony No. 7, Faber Music, 2010.

13   See: Mark Doran, 'Composer in Interview', p. 10.

14   For a detailed discussion of *Dark Pastoral* see: David Matthews, 'My New Music', *Musical Opinion*, No. 478, September-October 2010, pp. 16-17 (reprinted as Chapter 8 of this book).

15   David Matthews, notes on Symphony No. 6, printed as Preface to the score, Faber Music, 2007; and liner notes for Dutton Epoch CDLX 7234.

16   Matthews, notes on Symphony No. 6. Later quotations about the symphony in this essay are from the same source.

17   See Hans Keller, 'The State of the Symphony: not only Maxwell Davies's' (1978), in *Essays on Music*, ed. Christopher Wintle, Cambridge, Cambridge University Press, 1994, pp. 106-10.

18   Roger Scruton, *op. cit.*, p. 495.

19   David Matthews, *Britten*, London, Haus Publishing, 2003, pp. 22, 144 and 152.

20   David Matthews, *Michael Tippett*, London, Faber and Faber, 1980, pp. 91-6.

21   Daniel M. Grimley, 'Landscape and Distance: Vaughan Williams, Modernism and the Symphonic Pastoral', and J. P. E. Harper-Scott, 'Vaughan Williams's Arctic Symphony', in: *British Music and Modernism, 1895-1960*, ed. Matthew Riley, Farnham, Ashgate, 2010, pp. 147-74 and 175-96.

22   Roger Scruton, *op. cit.*, p. 146.

23   See, for example, 'Poets in a Barren Age' in: Michael Tippett, *Moving into Aquarius*, St. Albans, Paladin, 1974, pp. 148-56.

3   Matthews and the
Single-movement Symphony

Edward Venn

The emphatic ending of David Matthews's Seventh Symphony of 2010 prompted the composer to comment that it was 'like a summing up of all the symphonies I have written during the past 35 years'.[1] The claim deserves closer scrutiny: as one of the leading symphonists of our time, Matthews's contributions to the genre are long overdue for extended critical analysis. That, as the familiar excuse goes, remains frustratingly beyond the scope of this chapter. The more modest approach adopted here is to examine one feature of the Seventh Symphony – its single-movement form – alongside the comparable examples of the first three symphonies. Doing so will highlight aspects of the latter work's summative qualities, as well as providing en route the opportunity to explore something of the nature of Matthews's symphonism in general.

Matthews has recounted how the examples of Beethoven and Mahler shaped his first attempts at symphonic writing. More recently, Bruckner and Sibelius have been important influences. His instinctive musical and emotional responses to such models have been given a more secure theoretical footing through the writings of Hans Keller and Robert Simpson. In particular, Matthews is fond of invoking Keller's frequent description of symphonism as the 'large-scale integration of contrasts'[2] alongside Simpson's 'basic observation' that the 'true symphony [...] is active in all possible ways'.[3] Though critically prescriptive, from a creative perspective these theoretical guidelines can be considered sufficiently open-ended to stimulate, rather than constrain, symphonic thought.

The most rigid of Keller and Simpson's ideas concern the dynamic and dramatic function of tonality. Though Keller remains open to the possibility of twelve-note works 'recapturing the secret' of symphonism, 'key used to be, and for some highly imaginative composers still is, the basis of the symphonic act: key provides unity; keys and modulations provide contrast, to which melodic contrasts are, more often than not, secondary, in that harmonic structure dictates their fate'.[4] Simpson would only agree with the second of these quotations: 'the fact that it is tonality that is the deepest current in the river of true symphony, means that the flow of the whole depends on it'.[5]

Matthews has acknowledged the vital role tonality plays within his own symphonic thinking. Defining tonality in general terms is difficult enough, but when faced with Matthews's 'mostly instinctive' feeling for such things,[6] one finds precise explications at best chimerical. One means of approaching local tonal principles in his music is through consideration of contrasts of 'stable and unstable harmony',[7] so long as one understands these states as contextual rather than inherent properties of chords. On a broader scale, the large-scale symphonic properties of Matthews's tonal language are in essence traditional, insofar as they define the 'flow' described by Simpson. Nevertheless, the particular means by which key areas are established, tonal trajectories mapped out, and even notions of what it means to *function* as a tonic, are re-negotiated from one work to the next. To comprehend Matthews's symphonic music one must endeavour to understand better the specific ways in which tonality functions within a work and how it contributes to the overall argument.

The second fundamental characteristic of symphonic writing accepted by Matthews is that of contrasted movement types (sonata allegro, slow movement, scherzo, finale and so on). The integration of these types into a single musical span, as is the case in the four symphonies under examination in this chapter, suggests a number of possible models. Matthews has pointed to the single-movement works of both Schoenberg and Sibelius as backgrounds to his First Symphony.[8] By the time of his Third and Seventh Symphonies, the model of Sibelius's Seventh was to the fore. Uniting these composers is a shared concern to combine aspects of the sonata principle with the cycle of movement types inherited from the symphonic repertoire.

In the case of the Schoenbergian tradition, this concern is generally realised through the mapping of each movement type onto one or more of the regions of the sonata (first subject, second subject, development, recapitulation, coda). Attempts to maintain both multi-movement and sonata principles result in tensions – often musically productive – due to their different tonal and functional demands. Formal ambiguity can arise, too, when such mappings are either unclear or non-existent, as when 'slow movements' or 'developments' are interpolated into the argument.[9] Nevertheless, at least from a thematic perspective, the sonata model remains reasonably close to the surface within this tradition.[10]

Sibelius's Seventh Symphony offers an alternative approach that prioritises sonata *principles* over sonata *form*. The volume of contradictory analyses of the work attests to its lack of formal explicitness. More recent readings that suggest it offers a variant of the Brucknerian formal design of statement-expanded counterstatement-coda serve to confirm its distance from the textbook sonata model.[11] Equally, the multi-movement aspects are rethought. Matthews has spoken approvingly of how Sibelius 'manages to combine the movements of the symphony into one, seamlessly [...] they are not separate movements [...], they are parts of a movement which move almost imperceptibly from one to the other'.[12] It is the way that this formal fluidity is pressed into the service of a compelling symphonic argument, one suspects, that appeals most.

The four works to be examined are fundamentally no different from Matthews's Fourth to Sixth Symphonies in their commitment to rethinking the traditional tonal and formal principles of the symphony. Nevertheless, the single-movement symphony poses particular challenges when considering the dramatic trajectory, tonal dynamism and interrelationship of its parts, since the work by definition incorporates a multi-movement structure within a single overarching design. These challenges will be examined from different perspectives, focusing primarily (but not exclusively) on tonality (First Symphony), expressive shaping (Second Symphony), goal-directedness (Third Symphony), and the creation of 'a wide range of movement [...] within severe and powerfully concentrated limits' (Seventh Symphony).[13] Taken together they hopefully go some way towards understanding better Matthews's unique and compelling range of responses to the symphonic problem.

1   Symphony No. 1, Op. 9

Matthews's most straightforward solution to the formal and tonal demands of the single-movement scheme occurs in his First Symphony, which was composed in 1975, but revised in 1978 and 2007.[14] Broadly speaking, three contrasting movement types – canonic variations on a chorale, a scherzo, and an adagio – are underpinned by a tonal argument that begins and ends in a kind of A minor (see Table 1). A quasi-motto theme plays a significant role in defining and articulating the thematic content and structure (motif *a*; see Ex. 1, p. 164). However, the broad formal and tonal gestures outlined in Table 1 are but landmarks within a far subtler and more sophisticated musical argument that provides indications for Matthews's subsequent symphonic development.

'A kind of A minor': this requires qualification, firstly in terms of what *sort* of A minor it might be, and secondly in the ways in which it might *function* as tonic. That the answer to neither of these questions is straightforward indicates that the tonal centres listed in the various tables of this chapter are to be treated with caution. Nevertheless, the harp solo that opens the symphony (Ex. 1) does suggest A minor, coloured modally perhaps by hints of B major. Though the introduction of the chorale theme upon which the 'first movement' canonic variations are based clarifies the tonal language somewhat, it is not in favour of A minor. The theme opens with a repetition of motif *a*, first heard in the introduction: an arpeggio on C with both major and minor third, rising to the major seventh from the 'root'. The motif thus reproduces melodically a pattern also found harmonically, in which familiar triadic constructions are enriched with semitonal dissonances. The particular choice

I: Canonic Variations on a chorale

Figure	[0]	1	9	11²	11	13²	13	20²	20
Section	Introduction	I: Canonic Variations on a chorale							
Sub-Section				Scherzo interjection (Molto vivace (♩=c.126))		Scherzo interjection (Molto vivace (♩=c.126))		Scherzo interjection (Molto vivace (♩=c.126))	
Tempo	Freely (♩=c.60)	Beginning very still and remote (♩=c.60)	Più mosso (♩=c.84)		As before (♩=c.84)		Energico (♩=c.152)		As before [♩=c.152]
Tonal centre	A minor	Octatonic CIII	CIII	D	unstable	D	CIII and CII	E	CII
Motif *a* (key note)	C; harp	C; violas	F♯; clarinet				F♯; vln 1 / B; vln 2		(at Fig 18: B; hns)

II. Scherzo

Figure	22	34	37	44	47	48	50
Section	II. Scherzo						
Sub-Section	Scherzo	Trio	Scherzo	Trio	Scherzo		
Tempo	Molto vivace (♩=c.126)	L'istesso tempo (♩=♩)	As before [♩=c.126]	Tranquillo e leggiero (♩=♩)	(♩=♩) ma poco più mosso	poco a poco stringendo	Main tempo (♩=c.126)
Tonal centre	D	G	unstable	Diatonic C/ C Lydian	E	unstable	D
Motif *a* (key note)		C; tpt and string harmonics					

III. Lento e sostenuto (Finale)

Figure	57		60	61	64	65	68	70
Section	III. Lento e sostenuto (Finale)							Coda
Sub-Section	Intro	Theme	Scherzo interjection (Molto vivace, come sopra (♩=c.126))	Var 1	Scherzo interjection (Molto vivace (♩=c.126))	Var 2	Coda	
Tempo	Lento e sostenuto (♩=c.46)			Lento [♩=c.46]		Lento [♩=c.46]		poco più mosso
Tonal centre	CIII	towards CII	CIII	increasingly dissonant	CIII	increasingly dissonant	CIII	A minor
Motif *a* (key note)	C; tpt and strings	A♭; hns		a: C; strings		a: G; hns	a: C; hns	a: A; vlns

Table 1: David Matthews, Symphony No. 1, Op. 9, formal outline.

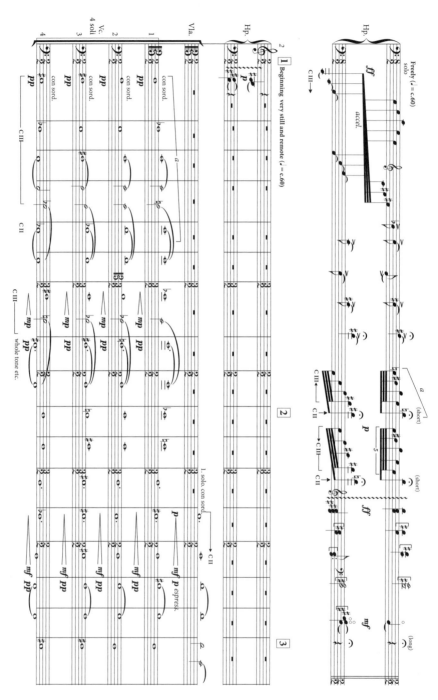

Example 1: David Matthews, Symphony No. 1, Op. 9, opening bars.

of chords is also crucial in determining a sense of harmonic motion (or to put it another way, in defining relative stability and instability). In both the harp introduction and the chorale theme, B is the first note that does not belong to the octatonic collection C-III: in both cases it belongs to chords drawn from a different transposition of the collection.[15] This establishes a principle in which melodically important notes and harmonies are drawn from outside of this referential (or 'tonic') collection C-III (see, for instance, the D two bars before Fig. 2). Such patterns of departure and return are characteristic of the tonal organisation of the symphony as a whole.

The emphasis on octatonicism explains the tonal function of A minor neither within the opening bars nor across the work, for the symmetrical properties of the octatonic collection allow any of its notes, depending on context, to assume the role of tonic. Indeed, the first two appearances of motif *a* in Ex. 1 demonstrate how the same melodic material can, depending on harmonisation, have very different tonal implications: there is little between Figs. 1 and 2 that suggests A as a tonal centre. (It is for this reason that appearances of motif *a* in Table 1 refer to the root of the major/minor triad on which it is based, and not the wider tonal context in which it occurs.) The tonal argument of the symphony can thus in part be considered a series of propositions as to how the referential octatonic collection might be inflected: the harp introduction provides one alternative, the string chorale opening offers another.[16] One of the achievements of the work lies in Matthews's ability to imbue the eventual return to A minor with a sense of finality, if not inevitability. The sense of motion and struggle that carries the listener there provides a thread of continuity that prevents the individual movements from being heard as discrete.

A move towards larger-scale instability is initiated through the superimposition of a countermelody that suggests A minor but is again octatonic (this time C-II; see Ex. 1, four bars before Fig. 3). The accumulation of octatonic fragments from all three collections destabilises matters further; concurrent increases in tempo, intensity and decoration generate considerable momentum. Thus by Fig. 7, overlapping statements of motif *a* lead to the first *tonal* crisis. This in turn precipitates the first *formal* crisis, in which two cryptic references to the forthcoming scherzo interrupt the chorale variations. Significantly, the references are centred around D, one of the four pitches absent from the referential collection C-III.

The middle section of the canonic variations – a series of two-part inventions on motif *a* and its inversion – begins at Fig. 13. The two melodic strands open on F♯ (C-III) and B (C-II), implying some degree of relationship to the opening A minor: we are in a 'related' key area. The contrasted inversion (Fig. 14) revolves around C♯ (C-I) and G♯ (C-II); the tendency is thus to move increasingly away from the 'tonic'. This motion is confirmed in the third and final section (Fig. 18), in which the chorale melody appears as a cantus firmus in the horns, beginning on B and harmonised by C-II. The section concludes with harmonies drawn from C-I over a pedal D in the bass. Thus, despite its climactic quality, the material remains 'tonally' open, as it is centred on pitches drawn from outside of the referential collection C-III. In this way the passage has a dual function analogous to the procedures of the one-movement Schoenbergian tradition: tonally, it postpones closure in the 'tonic' until later in the work (as demanded by the sonata dialectic), but still has sufficient rhetorical weight to be heard as a conclusion to the first 'movement'.

The scherzo offers a similar double perspective. Fulfilling the role of a second movement, it alternates between the quicksilver and the grotesque. Where the canonic variations unfolded slowly, guided by the phrase structure of the chorale, the scherzo is thematically and texturally heterogeneous, with greater variety of phrase length and mood. Pedal points are used to provide local points of harmonic stability, though rapid shifts of focus ensure that the tonal argument, unlike the stately centrifugal motion of the canonic variations, remains largely fluid. Indeed, the two trios are required to give points of tonal repose in contrast to the shifting uncertainties of the scherzo. The first, over a pedal G, includes a spectral version of motif *a*, thereby establishing motivic connections to the first movement; the second is almost exclusively 'white note'. The final scherzo re-introduces D as a point of focus within a variety of harmonic contexts (see Figs. 47, 50 and 56), suggesting some degree of tonal reprise. The closed formal and tonal argument would imply that the scherzo is musically self-sufficient, giving weight to readings that emphasise the multi-movement aspect of the Symphony. Nevertheless, the avoidance of both A as a tonal centre and C-III as a referential collection within the scherzo creates a larger contrast with the first movement, indicating the need for some manner of resolution.

The return of the 'tonic' is heralded by a sudden shift two bars before Fig. 57 from material based on D to that built on A. The reprise of motif *a* at Fig. 57 over a variation of the C-III-derived harmonies of Ex. 1 functions as both the start of the slow finale and as a recapitulation. In terms of a single-movement form, the scherzo is thus retrospectively heard as an extended tonal development. Indeed, the positioning of the tonal and thematic recapitulation approximately two-thirds of the way through the symphony demonstrates the extent to which traditional aspects of sonata form remained central to Matthews's thinking in this work.

The subsequent theme (at Fig. 58, another reworking of motif *a*) adopts a more contemplative character. The contours of motif *a* are reworked in the ensuing variations; what emerges, labelled *a'* in Table 1, is sufficiently distinctive to assert its own identity in the closing pages while nevertheless retaining the characteristic major/minor triad with added seventh of the original motif form. The dramatic tutti of Fig. 57 is recalled in two reminiscences of the scherzo (Figs. 60 and 64). Significantly, these episodes function to demarcate one variation from another, and, by drawing the material from the pitches of C-III, provide a 'tonal' recapitulation as well.

Though the main thematic material has been recapitulated using the C-III collection, the coda effects one final tonal operation, in which motif *a*', substituting for motif *a*, is presented for the first time with A as its root (Fig. 68). This moment is invested with considerable significance, in which the promise of reconciling motif *a* to the sensed background of A minor/major has finally been realised. Two short passages of fanfare-like material for strings lead to the eventual close on a repeated A, coloured by octatonic (C-III!) flurries in the wind.

Although the formal outline of the First Symphony is thus expressed simply, the underlying tonal argument provides a subtle yet powerful means both to intensify and integrate thematic and character contrasts. By achieving this without recourse to traditional tonal functions, Matthews demonstrates the rightness of his convictions about the enduring potential of tonality. Moreover, the procedures explored here point to fruitful ways in which tonality might be harnessed in the later symphonies alongside more complex formal structures.

2   Symphony No. 2, Op. 17

The composition of the Second Symphony (1976-79) overlapped with the first set of revisions to the First. Its thematic material derives from an extended melody that was initially composed for another work: a similar procedure was to be employed also in the Third and the Seventh Symphonies.[17] In contrast to the relatively compact and expressively ambiguous motto of the First Symphony, its opening bassoon solo offers both a fund of diverse motivic material as well as a clearly defined emotional state that functions as a point of departure.

Matthews had originally conceived of the work programmatically, moving from innocence to experience via a 'fall', and culminating in a rebirth.[18] The reworking throughout the symphony of melodic fragments from the opening, and in particular motifs of overlapping fourths and a rising and falling shape, provides a degree of stability amidst the contrasting states encountered on the journey. Yet even if the programme is unknown to the listener, the catastrophic character of the explosive percussion-and-brass-dominated passage beginning at Fig. 9 (the 'fall') sets up formal, tonal and emotional shockwaves that can only be worked through on the largest of scales. The result is one of Matthews's most compelling symphonic structures.

The journey is intimately and inseparably bound up with a symphonic handling of tonality and form, with the main expressive stages of the work corresponding respectively to a slow movement, a sonata allegro and a scherzo; these are framed by an introduction and epilogue and punctuated by the percussive interludes (see Table 2). Notably, the sonata allegro employs the Brucknerian statement-expanded counterstatement model in order to generate continual intensification; the positioning of the scherzo at the climax of this process allows for the contrasting Trio to have its revelatory function. Few single-movement symphonies offer such a cumulative, innovative and effective rethinking of the traditional formal design.

The tonal argument emerges from the harmonic tensions and contradictions within the opening section. There, the background is based on diatonic clusters that gradually clarify into superimposed G and A major chords; prior to that, emphasis is given to E in the bass (suggesting E minor) and B minor in the melody. The interaction between chords and melody establishes a broader harmonic field, incorporating pitches drawn from G Lydian (with F and C♯s) and G Mixolydian (with F and C♮s); five bars after Fig. 1, an E♭ is added. Together, the pitches and centres described above shape the tonal identity of the symphony as a whole. If E minor (coloured by its relative major G, often Lydian) is viewed as a point of departure, then E♭ and F (with C acting at times as a dominant) form significant regions on either side of it; B (with F♯ as dominant) is important in the sonata allegro movement as the key of the second subject group.

The way in which these tonal possibilities are realised in the symphony can be interpreted as a continual attempt to recapture and reassert the 'innocence' of the opening. The careful use of timbre and mood aids the apprehension of this tonal experience. Thus the early stages of the symphony – the catastrophic 'fall' and its aftermath – explore the flat key areas of F Dorian, and more poignantly E Phrygian, associated primarily with percussion/brass and strings respectively. E minor and string sonorities serve as the point of departure for the slow movement. From here, a sharpwards motion eventually returns to G Lydian territory and from there to E minor. The increase of energy at Fig. 28 coincides with a short-lived and ultimately fruitless attempt to settle in E minor; tensions between sharp and flat key material find a balance of sorts in the melody and accompaniment respectively of the passage beginning at Fig. 29.

The second phase of struggle – beginning with the sonata allegro (Fig. 34) – begins in the flat key area a semitone beneath the tonic, counterbalancing the tendencies towards F heard at Figs. 9 and 29. An E minor of sorts recurs in the coda of the sonata allegro, rendered unstable by both harmonic context and the use of brass (which has been associated with the 'fall' and the turbulence of the sonata allegro). In this light, the second percussion interlude, centred around G Lydian, acts as a stabilising force. Nevertheless, its rhythmic momentum and tonal ambiguity – pedal points turn out to be fifths of chords

Introduction / Interlude I / Slow Movement

Figure	[0]	9	13	14	15	16	17	21	22	24	25	27	29	33
Section	Introduction	Interlude I					Slow Movement							
Sub-Section			Interjection: Moderato (♩ = c.60)		Interjection: Moderato (♩ = c.60)		A	Interjection: Risoluto (♩ = c.84)	B	Interjection: Moderato (♩ = c.60)	C			Interjection: (♩ = c.84)
Tempo	Lento e calmo (♩ = c.48)	Risoluto (♩ = c.84)		Risoluto, come sopra [♩. = c.84]		Risoluto [♩ = c.84]	Molto Adagio (♩ = c.42)		Calmo (♩ = c.48)		Adagio (♩ = c.54)	Incalzando (♩ = c.60)	Molto calmo (♩ = c.54)	
Tonal centre	E minor / G Lydian	F Dorian	(E Phrygian)	F Dorian	(E Phrygian)	F Dorian	E minor (with motion 'sharp-wards')	F Dorian	C Lydian	[unstable]	[unstable]	Leading towards G Lydian/ Mixolydian	F	F

Sonata-allegro / Interlude II / Scherzo

Figure	34	48	72	75	98	117	135	136	149
Section	Sonata-allegro			Interlude II	Scherzo				
Sub-Section	Statement	Expanded Counter Statement	Coda		Scherzo	Trio (beginning Figure 126)	Interjection: Lento (♩ = c.60)	Scherzo	Trio
Tempo	Allegro energico (♩ = c.66)			Più mosso (♩ = c.144)	Presto veloce (♩ = c.192)	Un poco meno mosso (♩ = c.144)		Presto veloce, come sopra (♩ = c.192)	poco meno mosso (♩ = c.144)
Tonal centre	E♭			G Lydian / Mixolydian	C♯	towards B♭	E minor	C♯	C♯

Epilogue

Figure	151
Section	Epilogue
Sub-Section	
Tempo	Lento, come prima (♩ = c.48) Calmo e mesto
Tonal centre	E minor/ G Lydian

Table 2: David Matthews, Symphony No. 2, Op. 17, formal outline.

Figure	Section	Sub-Section	Tempo	Tonal Centre
[0]	Introduction	String Fugato	Allegro Moderato (♩= c.92)	D Dorian / G mixolydian
[4]		Wind/Brass Chords		
[5]		Codetta		Towards F
[7]	Slow Movement	Contrapuntal Material for Strings	Molto sostenuto (♩= c.42)	D/F (CII)
[9]		Wind Chords		CII
[10]		Clt/Cello duet	poco più mosso	CII-CI
[12]		Continuation of duets	a tempo (♩= c.84)	CIII
[15]		Melody in upper registers	(♩=♩)Andante (♩.= c.126)	CII, leading towards Em
[20]		Codetta	Molto sostenuto (♩= c.42)	Em with octatonic inflections
[21]	Sonata-allegro (Paragraph 1)	First subject group	Vivacissimo (♩= c.60)	A minor
[23]		Second subject group		Unstable,
[27]		Codetta		D minor/B♭

Figure	Section	Sub-Section	Tempo	Tonal Centre
[29]	Episode (recollection of Introduction)	Introduction	Allegro Moderato, come prima (♩= c.92)	A/C♯
[30]	Sonata-allegro (Paragraph 2)	Development of material	Vivacissimo (♩= c.60)	unstable
[43]		Codetta		A

Figure	Section	Sub-Section	Tempo	Tonal Centre
[45]	Episode 2 (Minuet and Trio)	Introduction	(♩=♪) Allegro moderato, come prima	G minor – B minor
[46]		Minuet	poco più mosso, come prima, scherzando	G lydian
[50]		Trio	a tempo (♩= c.92)	Diminished harmonies over pedal B
[53]		Minuet	Minuet	A minor – C
[56]	Sonata-allegro (Paragraph 3)	Recapitulation (climax at Fig. 69)	Vivacissimo (♩= c.60)	G minor – E♭ –
[70]		Coda / Transition	Poco meno mosso	D
[73]	Finale (Coda)		Molto tranquillo (♩= c.72)	C

Table 3: David Matthews, Symphony No. 3, Op. 37, formal outline.

as often as roots – prevents any sense of tonal closure. G, strongly coloured if not opposed by Lydian C♯s, becomes the point of departure of the final movement, in which E minor appears as a dream-like interlude for strings shortly before the reprise of the scherzo material. The return of the opening harmony at the start of the epilogue highlights the distance covered in its journey: the coruscating ostinato of bells, recalling the instrumentation of the second percussion interlude, heightens the ambiguity of the underlying harmony (is it E minor or G major? Or both?). As a result, it is no longer heard in the same way as in the Introduction, for its expressive riches have been made increasingly explicit over the course of the symphony.

In comparison to the First Symphony, the Second appears to offer a radically different solution to the one-movement problem. The emphasis is accordingly on projecting a single-movement structure by means of the introduction-epilogue frame and the inexorable increase in tempo across the movement types. Tonally, too, the notion of departure and return from a home key that informs the First Symphony is reworked in the Second Symphony: the effect is akin to the inverse of Heraclitus's river in which the water remains the same (E minor/G Lydian) but has carried us to an entirely different environment so that it appears to us transfigured. The innovative rethinking of the traditional precepts of the genre as a result of the urgent expressive demands of the Second Symphony would be startling enough in and of itself, but when considered alongside the First, the breadth of Matthews's symphonic thought becomes apparent.

3   Symphony No. 3, Op. 37

Writing eight years after its completion, Matthews suggested that the Third Symphony was his 'most successful attempt so far, and the closest to the Sibelius Seventh model of an organic whole'.[19] Such concerns clearly informed the decision during the composition to integrate a two-movement (fast and slow) structure into one. But although passages of fast and slow tempi can be identified in the final version, the emerging structure, while owing something of the Second Symphony's use of increasingly fast tempi, has a greater propensity for, and sophisticated use of, interpenetration of movement types. The fragmentation of the 'sonata allegro' equivalent into three separate sections embodies this principle (see Table 3).

Sibelius's music – this time the third movement of his Fourth Symphony – was also the model for the 'discovery of its principal theme at the very end of the piece'.[20] The revelation of the closing theme of Matthews's Third thus differs from the overarching patterns of departure and (transfigured) return that shape the thematic and tonal plans of the first two symphonies. It is surprising to discover, therefore, that the 'principal theme' to which the symphony is directed is so seemingly undramatic (the opening of this theme is given in Ex. 2). The entire melody calmly unfolds over a sustained C–D pedal, with the prevailing white-note diatonicism ruffled only occasionally by chromatic intrusions.[21] Slow, valedictory finales are common enough in Matthews's music, but normally in works in which 'the highest energy [is] near the beginning, and there will be a gradual dissipation after that point.'[22] The requirement for such a finale to be simultaneously a dramatic revelation *and* a calm counterbalance to the energetics of the preceding sonata allegro has consequences for its function. Instead of a 'return', the finale becomes a 'goal'; freed from the demands of tonal recapitulation, the Symphony is also Matthews's first that ends in a different key. In short, the Third Symphony reformulates the one-movement symphonic problem anew.

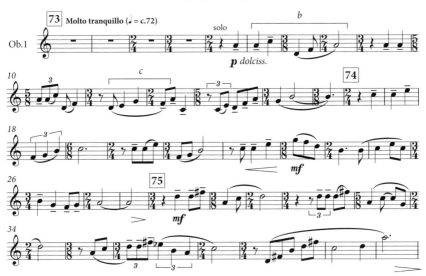

Example 2: David Matthews, Symphony No. 3, Op. 37, Figs. 73-6 (oboe melody only).

Three of the most important tendencies of the material in the Third Symphony, and their presentation within the principal theme, are as follows. First, there exists a basic contrast between diatonicism and chromaticism (and in particular octatonicism). Second, the interval of a third is melodically and harmonically important. This can be observed with the minor third A–C in Ex. 2. These pitches are the head notes of the thematic statements beginning at Figs. 73 and 74 respectively, are the first two heard in motif *b*, and form the gently ambiguous tonal centres underpinning the entire passage. Third, the theme tends to present a statement followed by a varied repetition. As with the Second Symphony, much of the musical argument results from the exploration of symphonic potential within such material. The difference between the Second and Third Symphonies is that in the latter, the closing theme ultimately functions (for the listener, rather than the composer) as a clarification and confirmation of tendencies heard earlier in the work, rather than being perceived as the source of them.

Such tendencies are apparent from the opening string fugato. The subject begins with a retrograde of motif *b* in a pure D Dorian; the answer transposes the same motif, no longer in retrograde, so as to open on a B. All of this is underpinned by a pedal D in the timpani. The passage continues with the addition of F and C♯s, establishing a D major/B minor ambiguity analogous to that of C major/A minor in the finale. Though this provides one hint of the nature of the eventual destination of the work (even if the listener is not aware that this is the case), the presentation of the motif in both prime form and retrograde leaves open the question of its final form. A varied repetition follows immediately; the timpani pedal falls a fifth to shift the tonal centre towards G Lydian. This move is supported by a chordal interjection from wind and brass at Fig. 4, harmonising a glittering three-note scale filling out the melodic major third G–B. This too is repeated, after which a bassoon calmly reiterates the fugato theme in D minor. A deflection to F balances the otherwise sharp-wards leanings of the opening paragraph; the use of oboe and strings anticipates the end of the symphony.

Emphasising the introductory function of the string fugato, Matthews has nevertheless noted that it 'sounds like the start of a sonata allegro'.[23] In fact, this impression is only gradually eroded, for the slow movement opens with the character of a second subject group. Accordingly, much of its material links back to the melodic shapes of the fugato. The use of ascending notes in the introduction to the section, at Fig. 9, and in the contrapuntal fabric throughout, recalls the melodic thirds of Fig. 4, but transforms them from diatonic to chromatic. Further tonal contrast is derived from the use of superimposed octatonic collections, beginning from an ambiguous D major/F major. Traditional 'second subject' features can also be found in the slow movement's comparatively looser formal construction and in its emphasis on lyricism, not least in the use of duets between wind instruments (predominantly clarinet) and cello. It is only once the listener has noticed the apparent proportional imbalance – the 'second subject' is three times the length of the 'first' – that the formal functions of the sections become clearer. Such retrospective mobility of functional meaning and the *need* for continuous reappraisal reflects the influence of Sibelius's later symphonies.

The sonata allegro follows the slow movement (Fig. 21). The choice of movement order is not necessarily based on the increase of tempo, as in the Second Symphony. Rather, it is likely that the sonata dialectic alluded to at the outset of the work could be withheld no longer. The rising three-note figure heard at Fig. 4 thus recurs in a diatonic form to initiate the argument, now filling in the same A–C minor third found in motif *b*. Subsequent thematic material includes a scherzo-like passage for horns and an extended dotted figure rising from the bass.

The three paragraphs of the sonata allegro are divided by episodes (see Table 3). These episodes are in turn a short recollection of the introduction (Fig. 29) and an extended minuet and trio. The minuet finds new expressive resources in both the dotted rhythms of the sonata and the three-note scale; the trio reworks motifs *c* and *b*. Both minuet and trio alike employ the statement-plus-(varied) repetition phrase structure that characterises the coda.

Though Matthews claims that three paragraphs of the sonata allegro correspond respectively to an exposition, development and recapitulation,[24] the tonal and functional properties of the second and third paragraphs deviate from traditional norms. The second paragraph begins at Fig. 30 as if it were a development of, or extended counterstatement to, the first. It closes, however, with an extended passage of 'nocturnal scene painting', beginning at Fig. 43, on the local tonic of A.[25] Doing so pre-empts the return of the tonic in the recapitulation, and undermines the traditional tonal function of the development. In terms of the symphony as a whole, both key and structural function can be understood in the way that the version of motif *b* over the sustained A major chord intoned softly in the cor anglais provides a premonition of the finale.

Just as the second paragraph ends 'incorrectly', the third opens 'off-key', in G minor. This initiates a further developmental phase which arrives at a sustained E♭ pedal, a tritone away from the notional local tonic. Tonal closure, as in the slow movement before it, is ultimately evaded. The climax of the sonata allegro emerges, via a rising scale between B and D, into a passage centred on D. The B–D third recalls the tonal properties of the introduction as well as the (transposed) three-note motif at Fig. 4; D was also prominent (along with F) at the opening of the slow movement. All the indications are that the symphony is heading towards a close in this key.

There is, however, a twist in the tale. The D is held over from the climax not as a tonic, but as a pedal within the otherwise C-centred harmonic field of the finale. The motion to C demands explanation. The diatonic C collection could be considered the next stage on from the D–G motion in falling fifths initiated in the introduction; equally, C major establishes the same minor-third relationship with the key centre of the sonata allegro (A major) that can be found in motif *b*; and the more local tonal motion from D to C replicates the same melodic interval heard in the opening bars of the work. Nor is D altogether lost as a tonal centre in the finale: it becomes a point of local contrast within the melody (see Fig. 75). Yet none of these accounts entirely convince, for they rely on associative relationships between keys rather than Matthews's more organic tonal processes. The undoubted 'rightness' of this conclusion is perhaps something that the analyst ought to defer to Matthews's 'intuitive' feeling for tonality.

Nevertheless, by the time the finale appears, its motivic, harmonic and phrase structures have become familiar. Its character and distinctive timbre, too, have already been essayed (at Fig. 43, and more obliquely at Fig. 5), and form a satisfying contrast to the preceding climax. What imbues it with the quality of a close, however, is the fact that its symphonic potential has already been thoroughly explored, if not exhausted. All that remains is to present the material one last time, freed from the damn braces of symphonic tension, blessed from the relaxation that results. And in this, the finale fulfils its function as the dramatic and musical goal of the work, and achieves a structural weight that could barely be expected from such seemingly simple material.

4   Symphony No. 7, Op. 109

Formally, the Seventh Symphony most closely resembles the First, insofar as the various movement types are presented more or less in the expected order, with a 'recapitulation' approximately two-thirds of the way through. In its use of a single melody as the basis of all the thematic material, it recalls the Second and Third Symphonies; the percussion interludes of the Second form a distant background to a timpani cadenza in the Seventh. Tonally, its progression from C to D reverses the trajectory of the Third Symphony.[26]

These are, however, ultimately superficial resemblances: the sophisticated blurring of formal boundaries in the Seventh, an emulation of those to be found in Sibelius's Seventh, has no precedent in the earlier single-movement symphonies. In this sense, Matthews's Seventh is a summation of tendencies to be found in the first three. Indeed, by virtue of the ubiquity of the generative melody, the Seventh Symphony assumes something of the character of a monothematic sonata: the recapitulation of the opening at Fig. 80, albeit a tone higher, strengthens such associations. The overall impression is of a line being taken for a walk, passing through a variety of landscapes, both stable and unstable. In doing so, the Symphony belongs to the tradition of works such as Debussy's '... Des Pas sur la neige', which Arnold Whittall has noted is concerned with the '"journey" of a melodic line and its dialogue with accompanying material'.[27] It is the extent to which this journey enables the presentation and integration of contrasts that partly determines its symphonic character. This is facilitated by a control of motion on various hierarchic levels that affords the work a sense of scale and grandeur that belies its modest duration.

Whittall has drawn attention to the 'uneasy' quality of the opening C major.[28] Certainly, on the one hand, the presence of Lydian F♯s indicate the potential for motion away from C as a tonal centre. But equally, and on the other hand, the Mixolydian tendencies in the accompaniment embodied by numerous B♭s provide a tonal counterbalance to this sharp-wards pull; the resulting Brittenesque mixed modality creates a tensile balance that infuses this 'C major' with a dynamic potential. Crucially, this dynamism is controlled by radiant C major chords that articulate phrase boundaries. Such 'pillars' provide a larger-scale harmonic framework within which local activity takes place, contributing to the sense of different rates of motion that characterises the symphony. One is reminded of Matthews's comment that 'tonality hasn't been exhausted. But if you're going to use these resources, then you've got to use them in a different way from ninteenth-century tonality, say'.[29] The result – at least in the Seventh – is something that both draws from and deviates from traditional practice. Thus with the caveat that the C major of the opening isn't necessarily the same sort of C major that one would find in, say, a Haydn symphony, the theme has the same sort of key-defining role that one would expect in a traditional symphony. The leaps that initiate each of the phrases of the theme trace the pitches, and intervals within, a C major triad.

The opening perfect fifth of the theme is particularly important in this respect. It does not always recur when the theme is reprised. When it is employed, the fifth often clarifies the tonal activity, either confirming arrival or providing a point of departure. On the occasions when the fifth is omitted, or when it is diminished (such as at Figs. 22, 56 and 62) the local tonal environment is unstable, dramatic. Transplanted from the melody into the bass, the perfect fifth frequently functions as a traditional dominant, and thus again as key-defining: instances can be found at Figs. 34 and 51 (G), 43 (A), and with the perfect cadence in D that closes the work. Such points of articulation control motion on the largest scale.

The tonal processes described above have a clarity and explicitness largely absent from the first three symphonies. Yet it should not be presumed that the tonal logic of the Seventh Symphony is the same as that of traditional practice. As with the earlier symphonies, the tonal 'journey' emerges from the properties of the musical material. Two procedures are of particular importance. The first of these is the way in which the Lydian leanings of the theme serve to destabilise the opening C major, by deflecting it towards E minor (two bars after Fig. 2). E minor also closes the first section (at Fig. 14). Doing so explores ambiguities within the opening theme, for the G–E leap belongs to the tonic triads of both C major and E minor. When transplanted to E minor, the opening C–G takes on a modal colouring. A certain ambiguity between harmonic regions a third apart thus colours the symphony as a whole.

The second tonal procedure that emerges from the opening concerns the interaction between the key-defining fifths and the modal tensions of the harmony. Put simply, the Lydian implications of the melody tend to pull the fifths sharpwards (C–G), generating the second melodic fifths of the work

(D–A; Fig. 4) and confirming D major as a contrasting tonal region to – as well as eventual goal from – C. Yet the Mixolydian B♭s in the harmony also instigate an opposite motion flatwards, first explored around Fig. 10, and most prominently leading into the recapitulation (Fig. 75).

The evolution of this tonal argument is crucial for the perception of how the various movement-types function. Unlike the relatively 'closed' tonal arguments of the various movements within the first three symphonies, those of the Seventh remain mobile (see Table 4, overleaf). Contributing to this effect is the ongoing development of tempo and metre: though one perceives the generative theme in a series of contrasting situations, it is always as part of a larger motion. Even the *tenebroso* 'slow movement', in which the expressive weight is such that it aspires to the condition of a separate movement, is ultimately part of the ongoing process. In essence, this is a consequence of the multiple rates of change that can be detected in the work. Writ large, one senses in the Seventh Symphony a Sibelius-like hierarchy of movements from the level of the bar through to the level of the 'movement' and ultimately the work as a whole.

~

The rethinking, and mastery, of the interrelationships between motion, movement types and tonal processes in the Seventh Symphony imbue it with the summative quality identified by Matthews. Its jubilatory close is earned not just by virtue of the trials (tonal and otherwise) undergone by the melodic theme, but also as a result of the ongoing acceptance and grappling with the symphonic challenge that characterises all seven of Matthews's symphonies so far.

In treating tradition as a source of inspiration rather than prescription, Matthews demonstrates the willingness to rethink the basic tonal and formal characteristics of the genre from the bottom up. A more extended survey of the symphonies would not only pursue with greater rigour the tonal and formal arguments made above, but link these to other processes such as Matthews's consistently vital rhythmic development and his motivic working, which similarly fashion themselves anew according to the material in question. Such an inquiry would doubtless confirm that, in Simpson's words, 'the music has grown by the interpenetrative activity of *all* its constituent elements'.[30] In short, it would corroborate the experience, readily gained through listening to the works themselves, that Matthews is a symphonist of the highest order.

Figure	[0]	15^{-2}	19	20	22	31	33^{-4}	33	34	51
Section	First movement/ Exposition	Transition			Scherzo I	Transition			Scherzo II	Cadenza
Tempo	Allegro Moderato (♩=c.100)	poco più mosso	Tempo I	Subito più mosso (♩=c.100); accel.	Allegro Moderato (♩=c.80)	accel. poco a poco	(♩=c.132)	(♩.=♩)	Molto vivace (♩.=♩)	
Tonal centre	C	Modulatory	B♭	E♭	Modulatory; unstable	A minor	D	unstable	G Lydian (NB dominant pedal, Fig. 47^2 to Fig. 51)	Increasingly unstable

Figure	58	62^4	66	67	70	72	75	80	90
Section	Slow movement				Transition		Scherzo II (reminiscence)	Finale/ Recapitulation	Coda
	Introduction	A	B	A'					
Tempo	Tenebroso (♩=c.72)	Più mosso (♩=c.84)	poco più animato	a tempo (♩=c.84)	Più mosso (♩=c.100)	Ancora più mosso (♩=c.108)	Molto vivace (♩=c.132)	Allegro Moderato (♩=c.100)	Allegro strepitoso (♩=c.138)

Table 4: David Matthews, Symphony No. 7, Op. 109, formal outline.

Notes

1   David Matthews, programme note to the Seventh Symphony.

2   This description appears in a number of Keller's writings; see for instance 'Wolfgang Amadeus Mozart' in: *The Symphony: Volume One. Haydn to Dvořák*, ed. Robert Simpson, Harmondsworth, Penguin Books, 1966, p. 52; and 'Frankel and the Symphony' in: *The Musical Times*, Vol. 111, No. 1524, February 1970, p. 146.

3   Robert Simpson, 'Introduction', in: *The Symphony*, p. 14.

4   Hans Keller, 'Frankel and the Symphony', p. 147.

5   Robert Simpson, 'Introduction: Stravinsky, Hindemith, and Others', in: *The Symphony: Volume Two. Elgar to the Present Day*, ed. Robert Simpson, Harmondsworth, Penguin Books, 1967, p. 11.

6   Mark Doran, 'Composer in Interview: David Matthews' in: *Tempo*, Vol. 57, No. 223, January 2003, p. 4.

7   David Matthews, CD liner notes to *Symphony Nos. 2 and 6*, Dutton Epoch CDLX 7234.

8   The influence of Sibelius is discussed at length in 'Living Traditions', *The Musical Times*, Vol. 134, No. 1802, April 1993, p. 190 (reprinted in Part One of this volume). In response to Mark Doran's suggestion that Schoenberg was an influence on, amongst other things, the use of a 'three-in-one' scheme in his music, the composer responded 'Well, he's a classic case of the father figure whom you must ... kill, I suppose. In the Freudian way.' See: 'Composer in Interview', p. 10.

9   My account here has been informed by Steven Vande Moortele's *Two-dimensional Sonata Form*, Leuven, University of Leuven Press, 2009.

10   See, for instance, Berg's (admittedly controversial) analysis of *Pelleas und Melisande*, or Schoenberg's own analysis of his First Chamber Symphony. Alban Berg, 'A. Schönberg, *Pelleas und Melisande*, Op. 5: Kurze thematische Analyse' in: *Alban Berg: Analysen musikalischer Werke von Arnold Schönberg*, eds. Rudolf Stefan and Regina Busch, Vol. 3, Vienna, Universal Edition, 1994, pp. 97-111; and Arnold Schoenberg, 'Analyse der Kammersymphonie' in: *Stil und Gedanke: Aufsätze zur Musik* ed. Ivan Vojtěch, *Gesammelte Schriften* 1 (1949), Frankfurt, Fischer, 1976, pp. 440-05.

11   See: Tim Howells, *Jean Sibelius: Progressive Techniques in the Symphonies and Tone-Poems*, PhD diss. (University of Southampton), New York, Garland Press, 1989, p. 66.

12   Interview broadcast by BBC Radio 3, 17 May 2010.

13   Robert Simpson, 1967, 'Introduction', p. 13.

14   All score references are to the 2007 revision of the First Symphony.

15   The three different transpositions of the octatonic set are often classified as C-I, C-II and C-III. Although the sequence of alternating semitones and tones can begin on any pitch, these transpositions conventionally begin on C♯, D or E♭. Thus C-III consists of E♭–E–F♯–G–A–B♭–C–C♯, and thus includes (amongst others) the triads of A major and A minor.

16   Arnold Whittall makes a similar observation about the theme of the Seventh Symphony (see 'Enriching the Present' above).

17   In the case of the Second Symphony, the melody dates from May 1971. See the CD liner notes for Dutton Epoch CDLX 7234.

18   *Ibid.*

19   David Matthews, 'Living Traditions', p. 190.

20   *Ibid.*, pp. 190-91.

21   The melody is a transcription of Matthews's setting of Kathleen Raine's 'Spell of Sleep' from his song cycle *The Golden Kingdom* (1983).

22   'Composer in Interview', p. 7. Matthews was speaking of his *Concerto in Azzurro*, of which he also noted that 'it didn't have an allegro finale. But that's always been a problem anyway: I've always tended to avoid that. [...] It would be nice to do something different one day – to write a real allegro finale, which I've hardly ever done.'

23   David Matthews, CD liner notes to *Symphony Nos. 1, 3 and 5*, Dutton Epoch CDLX 7222.

24   *Ibid.*

25   *Ibid.*

26   This tonal progression is also the reverse of Mahler's Seventh Symphony, for which Matthews's Seventh was commissioned as a companion piece in the BBC Philharmonic's 2010 Mahler cycle.

27   Arnold Whittall, *Musical Composition in the Twentieth Century*, Oxford and London, Oxford University Press, 1999, p. 47.

28   See Arnold Whittall's contribution to this volume.

29   Mark Doran, 'Composer in Interview', p. 5.

30   Robert Simpson, 'Introduction: Stravinsky, Hindemith, and Others', p. 10.

4   Symphonic Poems and Some Concertos

Geraint Lewis

The times they are a-changin'! A BBC Prom at the Royal Albert Hall on 16 August 2012 was eloquently encapsulated by Fiona Maddocks in *The Observer*: 'The fabulous BBC Scottish Symphony Orchestra, conducted by Andrew Manze, played three Vaughan Williams symphonies. Once, the very idea would have emptied the place faster than a fire alarm. On Thursday the hall was packed'. What had happened? Vaughan Williams's Fourth, Fifth and Sixth Symphonies all remain unchanged as scores – but something else had altered. The treacherous quicksands of cultural evaluation and critical perception are, to my mind, generally best left to the mysterious practitioners of *Rezeptionsgeschichte*; music itself is often the last thing on their agenda. However, I believe that a powerful message was contained in the fiftieth anniversary celebrations of Vaughan Williams's death in 2008 that also says much about a painful awareness of 'The Matter of Britain' and our troubled national psyche.

A similar moment had occurred in 2007 when David Matthews seemed suddenly to be heard by different ears with the premiere at the Proms of his Sixth Symphony, which happened to be an unashamed tribute to Vaughan Williams. Emerging from the shadow of his younger brother Colin's more fashionably progressive position, a modern symphonic master was enthusiastically hailed. After lonely decades of championing the symphony and string quartet as valid abstract forms, it was as if he had come in from the cold at last.

In the recent past, of course, it was dangerous to present critics with titles such as 'symphony', 'string quartet' or 'concerto'. At a pre-concert talk at the 1993 Cheltenham Festival, the first question invited from the floor amounted to a verbal assault on Matthews by a famously pretentious newspaper writer: "How on earth in this day and age can you justify calling a piece 'Oboe Concerto, Op. 57'? - you might as well pretend to be Vivaldi". The poor composer looked pained and surprised. Feeling that Matthews should be robustly defended, I retorted that as the work *was* in fact an Oboe Concerto and happened to be his Opus 57, the title was exactly right. A burst of applause moved things on and the journalist retired. Those last-gasp days of spindly compositions for ensemble and tape, with titles like *Mobile-orgasm 3:12*, whose programme notes took longer to read than the pieces did to play, seem now mercifully to be behind us. It would be unfortunate, however, if Matthews's belated acceptance as a major symphonist and *Quartettmeister* were to distract attention from his equally rich harvest of orchestral and chamber music with very clear and explicit extra-musical sources of inspiration in painting, literature and landscape.

Vaughan Williams himself found, to his great annoyance, that critics and audiences were often reluctant to take his music at face value. In response to some particularly silly speculation about the 'meaning' of his Sixth Symphony in 1948, he is supposed to have said, "It never seems to occur to people that a man might just want to write a piece of music!" Matthews has always been the most open and helpful guide to his own music and compositional processes: on occasion, we can almost see how his mind has pursued a thread through its gradual elaboration and evolution to create a map of the music for us. He is the most lucid exponent of the verbal articulation of musical form and his very manner provides clues to the essence of his approach to composition. Forms or structures are more often than not rooted in Classical types, which he then loves to manipulate and re-work within a wider framework, and his delineation of material is tonal in its local detail as well as in relation to the broader conception. Such concerns are as pertinent to the pithy one-movement, twenty-minute First Symphony as to the grander scale of the three-movement, forty-minute Sixth composed some thirty years later. But these attitudes to the essential integrity of melodic formulation within a coherent harmonic structure also imbue those works inspired by programmatic or colouristic subjects.

My own first encounter with David Matthews's music in the 1980s was with just such a juxtaposition of pieces, and so it may be pertinent to try to recapture my initial reactions before attempting a more considered response. The Second Symphony, though composed hard on the heels of the First in 1976-79, was not performed until 1982, when it was given a high-profile premiere by the Philharmonia and Simon Rattle. It immediately impressed as a large-scale canvas in which the traditional symphonic movements were integrated within a single-movement design, seemingly closely related to Michael Tippett's recent Fourth Symphony (1976-77), but lacking, at first hearing, the concision and inevitability of that score. At nearly 37 minutes (but to be fair it *feels* shorter), it is intriguing now to read the composer's note of 2010, in which he bravely shows his initial structural working-plan of seven linked sections adding up to a proposed 30 minutes. This is, after all, a young man's music and all its exuberance of spirit and profusion of content are there to be embraced. In colour too, the first thing to register was unabashed boldness and an uninhibited love of percussion – although the pitched variety seemed to have bounced in a little too obviously from the children's beach-games in Venice as hypnotically conjured by Britten a few years earlier. At around the same time, however, I was equally captivated by a much smaller piece by Matthews called simply *Introit*, first performed by the English Chamber Orchestra in 1981. This was written for strings and two trumpets and lasts a mere six minutes; but it casts a potent spell and seems, in this case, to last a lot longer than its actual span. Even without the composer's later guidance that it was written with Gloucester and Lincoln cathedrals in mind (and eventually premiered in St George's Chapel, Windsor) this ravishing work breathes distance and atmosphere and seems instinctively to invoke an English musical Eden. Here is an innocent pre-lapsarian Vaughan Williams seeping out of tall Gothic pillars and nature radiantly imbued with the birdsong of *The Midsummer Marriage* as transmuted by Tippett in his Triple Concerto (1979-80). 'Angel' trumpets at the end add a glowing halo to the sound.

Two works then – the one suggesting nothing extra-musical, sufficient within its own musical procedures, the other inhabiting an imagined narrative and exploring a particular 'world' from first bar to last. My next pair of encounters worked this same alchemy in reverse. The two works – the Third Symphony, Op. 37 and the 'symphonic poem' *In the Dark Time*, Op. 38 – were completed together in April 1985, though the symphony was started a year before the symphonic poem. Hearing *In the Dark Time* first, as a broadcast premiere in December 1985, what came across immediately (compared to the Second Symphony) was an enormous advance in structural coherence and cumulative power. Knowing too the *Introit*, it seemed that here was a natural development and elaboration of the atmospheric sense of colour and narrative evolution. And it now seemed entirely natural to feed the imagination with judiciously selected quotations from T. S. Eliot's 'Little Gidding', last of the *Four Quartets*, and to allow such potent sentences as 'Midwinter spring is its own season' and 'no wind, but Pentecostal fire / in the dark time of the year' to guide the mind when listening. Allusions to favoured influences (whether deliberate or not) seemed more deftly assimilated here, the control of orchestral forces entirely geared to the unfolding of material. Oddly enough, the only momentary lapse, to my mind, came at the very end, when Tippettian gestures and sounds of regeneration suggest the emergence of spring and light from winter darkness. But at the same time, these pages glow with a tensile energy, and form a memorably moving open-ended coda on a structural upbeat. With hindsight, the cogent half-hour journey can be extended backwards (in our ears) to an initial downbeat, since the work has its thematic origins in the earlier chamber orchestra piece *September Music* (1979).

This concentrated power is even more potent in the Third Symphony, where the urge (almost obsession) of the earlier two symphonies to integrate the four contrasted movements within one unbroken symphonic span is finally achieved with impressive mastery of rhythmic momentum in a series of diverse but ultimately unified panels. The process of conceiving and completing the symphony in such close proximity to *September Music* and *In the Dark Time* must have profited from the greater structural freedom possible within a symphonic poem, even allowing the symphony to close with the reworking of a song.

With that major symphonic objective now so satisfyingly conquered for the time being, Matthews seems to have moved on with renewed power and intensity to further exploration of the possibilities offered by the symphonic template. *Chaconne* (1986-87) is the dryly formal title of a meticulously constructed musical span, which quickly reveals itself as a visceral 'landscape of the mind'. The work is inspired by some pungent passages in Geoffrey Hill's magnificent poem 'Funeral Music' from the collection *King Log* (1968). One cannot but feel instantly attuned to Matthews's vision here of attempting to translate poetry into music. Like T. S. Eliot, Geoffrey Hill is a writer who uses musical imagery to create resonance; even a cursory reading can evoke an inner response. Yet, again as with Eliot, daring to set Hill's words seems rash, so saturated are they with their own musicality and layers of meanings. *Chaconne*, then, is perhaps a 'symphony without words' in suggesting the very smell and sensation of the English landscape – now not as a vision of earthly paradise but of the hell of battle and human slaughter. The 'dark time' or 'the very dead of winter' in the seasonal cycle always comes round to natural renewal. But, on the snow-clad battlefield of Towton on Palm Sunday 1461, the eventual melting of the Easter ice released the blood of twenty-six thousand men and it flowed as an unbroken stream for two to three miles. Matthews's music is perhaps the deeper for his innate understanding of the obverse in pastoral terms: this now is literally a 'dark pastoral'.

After such profound concentration on darkness, there is, nonetheless, catharsis in the musical outcome. It is perhaps no coincidence that so soon after the composition of *Chaconne* came *Cantiga* (1988) in which the truly macabre scenario of Doña Inês de Castro's posthumously-encorpsed coronation is brought vividly yet economically to life in a 25-minute *scena* for soprano and small orchestra. Whole operas on the same subject, for vast forces, have said much less, and much less potently. Here is surely evidence of what a Matthews opera could lead to were one of our major companies (or lesser, for that matter) to show sufficient foresight to commission him.

Orchestral music has been commissioned regularly. Before another symphony was attempted, the symphonic poem was revisited in *The Music of Dawn* (1989-90). The inspiration here was a remarkably vivid and sonorous painting of the same name by Cecil Collins. Collins had died in 1989 just after the opening of a Tate Gallery retrospective where the composer first saw this painting. The predominant colour is a golden yellow – many-hued and intricately-textured – yet in terms of its figuration the work is oddly simplistic, even crude. Nothing in Matthews's music can be described as simplistic, but this bold evocation of a primarily visual sensation as triggered by a painting (and a related, radiant altarpiece by Collins in Chichester Cathedral) seems to unlock a new freedom of approach. The ground-plan is as skilfully detailed as ever in its incorporation of symphonic types within the structure, yet the colour in the score emerges now entirely from within the texture; the virtuosic deployment of the orchestra is part-and-parcel of the whole conception. *The Music of Dawn* seems to form a natural structural and emotional climax to what might be thought of as Matthews's 'first period'.

The Fourth Symphony, composed concurrently with *The Music of Dawn* between October 1989 and December 1990, seems to embark on a new path: it embraces a symphonic structure comprising a sequence of discrete and distinctive movements. It is almost as if the culmination of one particular orchestral trajectory simultaneously released a new lease of structural life in a different direction. The Fourth Symphony has five movements in all, with a jauntily interloping tango as the fourth.

When it came to composing the Oboe Concerto, Op. 57 between August 1991 and March 1992, Matthews used the five-movement template of the recent symphony to solve the textural problems of balancing the solo oboe with large orchestral forces. The distinctively-contrasted characters of each movement allow changes of orchestral colour to set off the wide-ranging and varied timbres of the soloist, Nicholas Daniel. Something else which spills over from the Fourth Symphony is a new, neoclassical crispness that counterbalances the 'first-period' tendency towards long-breathed structures and elongated melodic ideas. With the acceptance of self-contained movements in sequence, and a sharper focus on shorter-term thematic material, Matthews was able to engage with a greater range of distinctively chiselled material.

And so one arrives at that memorable Cheltenham concert in July 1993. What seems so bizarre at a twenty-year distance is not so much that the music now seems as fresh-minted as it did then (and fortunately we now have a performance by Nicholas Daniel committed to disc), but rather that its most striking feature at the time remains equally striking today, and yet is something very rare in the composer's output. After three well-balanced short movements – fast, faster and slow, as in the Fourth Symphony – comes the totally unexpected sound of an orchestral piano introducing a 'Moderate Blues'. This is taken up by an immaculate jazz-band of clarinets, saxophone and brass, out of which the oboe sings a heart-rending lament, unerringly blending with its idiomatic background – while also seeming to be Matthews's own commentary upon it. There is a natural Tippettian innocence and strange integrity in this invocation of a vernacular idiom within a classical context. The tiny two-bar germ from the obscure Blues pianist Arthur 'Montana' Taylor (1903-54) had haunted Matthews ever since he had heard it accidentally on the radio. His inspired 'Homage to Montana Taylor' draws an astonishingly open-hearted emotional response from a composer whose music can often seem more reticent, suggesting perhaps that this exotic camouflage enabled him to sing his own Blues without restraint.

But in retrospect, the most surprising thing about this 'Blues' movement is just how unusual such a deliberate change of tone is for Matthews. It has, therefore, the effect of throwing into sharper relief the distinctive profile of his own musical voice, whilst at the same time showing how his natural refinement is brought to bear on the crafting of a seemingly alien sound into his personal landscape. The Montana Taylor quote may only be two bars, but Matthews turns it into a potent yet unobtrusive kind of ground bass, and cunningly exploits the fact that each of the two bars is (deceptively) the same! The gently reiterative harmonic circuit, with melancholy descending semitones, is contained within a single frame, and its hypnotically repetitive dotted rhythm immediately lulls the listener like a lullaby. The composer's own magical touch now is to conjure a further blurring of the underlying unit by introducing the oboe (in bar 10) singing a high descant which itself extends for an unbroken ten bars. These cumulative extensions create a breadth of line that turns the music into a continuous lyrical span, enabling Matthews to pull away from the constraints of the repetitive foundation. The two eventual returns to the original are thus all the more poignant, and the movement as a whole is made gloriously cathartic in its effect. The fast finale then seems lifted 'out' of the Blues by the act of their having been sung, and the sense of well-being drives the music, transformed, to a positive conclusion.

The symphonic poem *A Vision and a Journey* that followed in 1992-93 drew from Matthews a specific reference to Sibelius as the most obvious predecessor to have oscillated productively between symphony and symphonic poem. In this work there is no specific source of inspiration other than the suggestion of a journey whose direction is redirected by 'moments of vision'. *Night Ride and Sunrise* might seemingly be evoked as a model, though the designation 'symphonic fantasy' recalls the more integrated *Pohjola's Daughter*. Meanwhile, the invocation of a seventeenth-century fantasia in an extended string passage after the first 'vision' points once more at Tippett's Fourth Symphony and its use of Orlando Gibbons. Matthews appears to have identified flaws in *A Vision and a Journey*, since a later and substantial revision of the score between 1996 and 1999 proceeded alongside the completion of the Fifth Symphony (1998-99). This symphony takes on the separation of four movements, making of them two well-balanced pairs: the return to the earlier 'symphonic fantasia' enabled a seamless unity to emerge with apparent ease. Here now is a composer who can handle the complementary demands of symphony and symphonic poem with confidence and command.

This synthesis was then put to highly effective use in the cello concerto composed for Steven Isserlis and completed in 2002. Remarkably, this shows

Matthews's most brilliantly integrated attempt to date at a single movement form that encompasses all the other movements. It may well be the greater 'freedom' suggested by the concerto form and the presence of a lyrical soloist that led to this rapprochement. There is also here the added dimension of a stimulus in landscape resulting in the evocative title *Concerto in Azzurro*. The 'blue' here is not that of the alcohol-fuelled Blues or jazz, but rather the radiantly-occluded blue of sea and sky as seen from the magical island of Lundy in the Bristol Channel. Matthews had never previously struck me as a composer steeped in synaesthesia, but he professes here to having heard 'blue' as B♭: this casts an intriguing light over the earlier works, each of which is thoroughly bathed in multifariously-related tonalities.

What makes the unfolding of the tonal landscape so rewarding in this cello concerto is the way in which the music succeeds in inhabiting so naturally the different keys which counterbalance the B♭ insisted upon by the solo cello at the outset. A scurrying orchestral undergrowth of E minor pitted against this B♭ will, by the centre of the score, reveal a thematic, rhythmic *and* colouristic affinity with Elgar's E minor Cello Concerto (its own slow movement in B♭). Swathes of A, G, A♭ and E♭ provide a kind of polychromatic canvas reminiscent of the seascapes of Donald McIntyre in their intertwining of related blues and greens, to create several new and infinitely resonant colours. The very end of the concerto even avoids an overt B♭ by letting it emerge as a heightened dominant within an E♭ texture. The horizon now seems to stretch far into the distance as sea and sky together transform the mutable sands of tonality into a realm of sheer sonority.

5   David Matthews's String Quartets: Some Reflections

Hugh Wood

The string quartet is the great survivor. Two or three generations ago we were continually being told that the symphony – and the opera too – were dead. Now this sort of half-baked prophesying is dead itself, and so are most of those who mouthed such silliness. But nobody has ever proclaimed the demise of the string quartet. Sir George Dyson came close when, discussing Stravinsky's *Three Pieces* (1914), he dolefully wrote: 'Now if this type of passage has any proper place in the art of the string quartet, then the end is near.'[1] It was a false alarm. More recently, Paul Griffiths has written, accurately and eloquently: 'More than any other sort of music in the western tradition, the string quartet has enjoyed the stability yet also the capacity for constant renewal'.[2]

How has such a renewal been brought about? The answer partly lies in the delicate balance which the quartet has preserved between public and private existence, professional and amateur practice. When the unbelievably distinguished team of Haydn, Dittersdorf, Mozart and Vanhal played quartets, they were four professional musicians playing for their own pleasure, and in private surroundings. Very soon a change in social conditions caused the quartet's migration from the aristocratic salon to the public venue of the concert hall. Haydn saw the beginning of the virtuoso leader; then Beethoven came, and in his late quartets altered the consciousness of a whole century and a whole culture.

So the quartet became a medium that welcomed, even required, an audience. But its practitioners would continue to maintain that its true nature lay in practical mutual participation; briefly, that it was better to be a player than a listener if you wished to approach the heart of the string quartet. Hans Keller held this view. He went further in suggesting that quartets were best written by composers who were also string players. But what about Bartók, Debussy, Ravel, Janáček? (Then one notices that all these names lie outside the Viennese charmed circle.) And we have to deal with another complication: over the last century valid advances in the art have meant that many works have appeared whose technical difficulties as well as their field of expression have put them beyond the reach of all but the very best of amateurs.

It is time to re-assert that writing string quartets remains an entirely customary and natural activity for composers. And that some composers should write the sort of music whose difficulty could be surmounted by the best of amateurs, played or listened to with pleasure and intelligent appreciation the first time round. Neither the giggles nor the frowns of contemporary fashion should be able to destroy that. The string quartet always has been and remains a broad church, and it is that which ensures, not only its 'capacity for constant renewal', but also its survival.

It is with this perhaps too expansive *tour d'horizon* that one introduces the quartets of David Matthews, discovery of whose work brought many of these thoughts to mind. He is living proof that the string quartet is alive and well.

Matthews has been concerned with writing quartets since the beginning of his career. In the liner notes to the Toccata Classsics disc of his Fifth and Twelfth Quartets, he writes that his attempts to compose quartets go back almost half a century to when he was a student reading Classics at Nottingham University; and that an early quartet was accepted by the BBC and subsequently broadcast by the Dartington Quartet. Two further quartets were then discarded, and his official First Quartet was written in 1970. He cites the early influence of Beethoven – particularly through recordings by the Busch Quartet – and then of Bartók – as played by the Végh Quartet. Later came the Second and Third Quartets of Tippett, Berg's *Lyric Suite* and Schoenberg's First Quartet. He adds, 'I am not a string-player, but have learned a good deal about string technique from the many players I have worked with over the years'. All these influences are apparent in his music, and all have been put to good creative use. And the truth of his statement should be abundantly clear from the first moment of hearing any of his writing for string quartet, which is expert, imaginative and intuitive.

Matthews has now completed twelve quartets, and a voyage of discovery for the present writer began with the two most recent: the Eleventh Quartet of 2008 and the Twelfth of 2011. Both are rare examples in the music of our times in that they make an immediate positive impact: just for once one does not need to work hard in order to scrape even a mere acquaintance with them. Two factors assist both listener and player – the apparent familiarity of the musical language and the use of pre-existing forms. The language largely depends on a structure determined by a sense of key. In other words it is tonal. But the use of this word – so often hurled *pro* and *contra* like a small hand grenade – inevitably leads to banal dismissal or equally glib acceptance of the piece in question. It is not a category, much less a value judgement. Matthews's own considered views on tonality can be found elsewhere.

And he comes to similar conclusions over matters of form. Wagner's comment on the youthful Brahms's *Handel Variations* comes immediately to mind: "It shows what can still be done with the old forms by someone who knows how to handle them." Typical of the old monster to pay so double-edged a compliment! But discount that, and you have a perfect epigraph to place above Matthews's Eleventh Quartet. It is simply a set of variations (and this is a musical form that underwent rigorous transformation at the hands of some twentieth-century composers). Matthews returns to old ways and methods, and the result is clear and immediate. What are these? The ability to recognise a fruitful theme, to extract from its analytical dissection its nearest and, step by step, furthest consequences, to preserve the prevailing momentum set up by bar-length and tempo, to know when to destroy it to build a macro-structure that will give the piece a large architecture, and to provide a culmination with a conclusive ending. Bach in the *Goldberg*, Beethoven in the *Diabelli*, Brahms in the Fourth Symphony finale – all achieve these necessary aims. It is good to find that Matthews has mastered them all.

The theme itself is taken from Beethoven's Op. 119 Bagatelles – No. 8 in C major. But what sort of C major? One in which treble and bass are both chromatic from the start. After a conventional modulation to the dominant after 8 bars, the second half (8 + 4) begins by leaping to B♭, introduces a new motif and later brings in a third idea taken up by each voice in turn. The last four bars are purely in the tonic, the parts presented in pairs.

Matthews uses every aspect of all this. In the first variation, the chromaticism largely disappears and the harmony is dissolved into broken chords. In the second variation chromaticism is back with a vengeance: it has spread to all four parts, and now falls rather than rises in the bass. Much of the third variation is monadic in triple octaves, and the chromaticism is everywhere, later on in canon. The dramatically faster tempo (*presto*) serves to offset the longer bar-lengths. With the 23 bars of the fourth variation, the original dimensions of the theme are left behind and its opening motif transformed by additive rhythms into an amalgam of Bartók and Tippett. Its character dominates the next two variations: Variation 5 (*tempo di tango feroce*) features an ostinato on the viola, which in Variation 6 takes over the figure of Variation 4 against a thrumming background (quadruple *pizzicati* on the other instruments, sounding like tuned castanets, an amazing effect). This sort of working is heard on a much grander scale in Variation 9; on either side of it, in Variations 8 and 10, there is something of a return to the original character of the theme, presented with peremptory, almost military tapping rhythms.

But by now we are at our furthest point in this orbit round the theme. The *misterioso* harmonics and *pizzicati* of Variation 7 serve as an avatar of the *quieto* of Variation 11. This is a skeletal variation in which the upper strings have a murmuring line in semiquavers against sporadic *pizzicati* from the cello. For the analyst and the listener alike (they are often quite different people) this is really *ultima Thule* – the remotest point from the theme.

It is expertly timed to introduce the most symphonic part of the work and its expressive core – a centre for the macro-structure. The cryptic vacancy of Variation 11 is the ideal preparation for the *Cavatina* of Variation 12. Marked *adagio*, this places the head motif in a solemn E♭ minor, and goes on to present greatly enhanced versions of much we first encountered in the theme itself, notably the new motif after the double bar in B♭, here at its original pitch but completely re-harmonised. The music rises to a majestic climax of commanding sonority. But we are only half way through this transfiguration of the theme. From a new beginning marked *ppp* the music rises steadily to *ff*, before gradually subsiding – or rather it floats away into the heights over a pedal E♮.

But the best of the piece is yet to come. The E♮ pedal falls to E♭; then the composer cannot resist a brief hint of the birdsong-inspired passages that have already appeared in some of his earlier quartets (for instance, in the Tenth) and will play a more prominent role in his Twelfth. But this is only a whisper, and suddenly we are plunged into the finale. What better to follow a cavatina than a cabaletta? Even better, a great fugue. Over a pedal (it has now sunk to D) the viola quietly produces a jig-like theme in 6/8 taken up enthusiastically, and soon exuberantly, by the other instruments except for the first violin, which produces a counter-theme. The joyous polyphony is prolonged. As this finale has now taken on symphonic proportions we find that the original B♭ theme after the double bar provides a more relaxed *andante tranquillo* middle section. But soon the cello comes rushing up *tempo primo* with the fugue theme. The magnificent outburst of the beginning is to be more than matched by its return, lasting for over 120 bars, and culminating in the variation theme riding high above the general commotion like a chorale tune used as a *cantus firmus*. It is as successful a gesture as the triumphant return of the Purcell tune in Britten's *Young Person's Guide to the Orchestra*. The ending is punctual: it leaves the listener in the highest spirits.

The fugue is such a splendid form (or procedure, or texture, or whatever) – protean in the many characters it can take on. Its capacity for generating immense energy is to be found in the greatest works, like the finale of Beethoven's *Hammerklavier* Sonata or the 'Par lui tout a été fait' of Messiaen's *Vingt regards*. Such works bring to mind Blake's 'Energy is Eternal Delight' – and so does this movement.

However, such cataloguing of detail inevitably results in a heavy read; but it is deserved by a composer here working at his very best. Nevertheless, one reflects that such a description takes longer to write down than the music takes to be played, and for the hundredth time one is reminded that Mendelssohn said:

> The thoughts which are expressed to me by music that I love are not too indefinite to be put into words, but on the contrary too definite.[3]

One can only hope that such spontaneity of utterance as this piece possesses may in turn produce a similar spontaneity of response.

The Twelfth Quartet is a more ambitious piece, laid out on more ample a scale, having some things even better than the Eleventh, others less successful. The Preface that Matthews wrote for it gives a useful insight into his working methods in general. *A Little Serenade* for quartet was written to commemorate Michael Berkeley's years as Director of the Cheltenham Festival, and Matthews thought 'eventually it might form part of a larger work'. This readiness to re-use pre-existing material is characteristic of him. Two other pieces came into his mind: a tango from a concerto for piano and strings; and a re-working – for John McCabe's seventieth birthday – of a minuet from one of Haydn's piano sonatas. But the decisive moment in the creation of a new quartet came with hearing the Kreutzer Quartet play Beethoven's Op. 130 with the *Grosse Fuge* finale.

Now the main outlines of the new work were set: it should consist of 'two big movements at either end and a number of divertimento-like movements in the middle'. But there was also a slow movement to be written, and various other shorter and slimmer movements attached themselves in the course of writing. It is necessary to give a list:

I	Prelude and Fugue	
II	Tango	followed by Cadenza I
III	*Menuetto scherzando*	followed by Cadenza II
IV	Serenade	followed by Cadenza III
V	*Canto mesto* (slow movement)	
VI	*Menuetto grazioso*	
VII	Finale	

The three cadenzas act, to a certain extent, as commentaries on the movements immediately preceding them: they are, respectively, for first violin, cello, and second violin and viola. The *Menuetto grazioso*, like the original version of the Serenade, started life as a dedicated piece, this time for the Australian composer Peter Sculthorpe. But by this time the Beethovenian modelling had been left behind: for the finale in no way aims to compete with the *Grosse Fuge*, but in fact is closer to Beethoven's alternative finale for Op. 130 – a splendid and sometimes unjustly despised movement. In any case, a large-scale fugue would have been too much after the fugue at the end of the Eleventh Quartet.

The modelling on Op. 130 is at its closest and finest in the opening movement, though the title Prelude and Fugue gives yet another way of interpreting its form. As so often with Matthews, the simplicity and straightforwardness of the material is a virtue everywhere in the piece. The initial scalic motif in crotchets, which pervades the work, could almost – but not quite! – have been conceived by Haydn: the semiquaver counterpoint against which it is shortly to be played off is almost entirely diatonic, and for most of the time deals entirely in white notes. Yet the music is in no way pale, nor is it thumpingly in C major. Nor do occasional F♯s and C♯s suggest a modulation to G or D major. The tonality remains suspended, like a great bird in flight.

Crotchet scales and semiquaver polyphony alternate freely – the ghost of Op. 130 is there. The first three sections of crotchet movement last for 17 bars each: is it too much to see in this attraction towards prime numbers a nice Messiaenic touch? From bar 80, the two elements combine. In the second half of the movement, from bar 119, after a presentation of the crotchet material as a duet between the two violins, the *allegro energico* resumes. This time the semiquaver counterpoint points downwards rather than upwards – but with no diminution of vigour.

But meanwhile, at bar 108, there has been a most un-Beethovenian surprise (*pace* the *Pastoral* Symphony, admittedly). Suddenly the polyphony is interrupted by another kind of polyphony, a flurry of birdsong – already a feature of Matthews's previous quartets, as has been mentioned in connection with the Eleventh Quartet. In this quartet it is to play a more extensive part; for it appears in the fourth movement (the Serenade), and briefly in the Finale, just before the end of the piece.

With the resumption of the *allegro energico* at bar 136, the exhilaration is, if anything, greater than before, and the two elements more thoroughly mixed together. The crotchets appear on their own for eight bars at bar 191; there is a final outburst of polyphony; then, at bar 216, a prolonged and triumphant return of the crotchet figure for some 45 bars, before wisps of scales float off into the distant sky. The whole movement has been a marvellous re-creation of the Beethoven original in the age of Tippett, and lacks nothing of Tippett's dancing gaiety and blithe exuberance of spirit, possessing as it does wonderfully sustained bounding vigorous energy.

Matthews was intent on going further with his modelling on Op. 130. Beethoven's middle movements comprised three very different kinds of scherzo, followed by that embodiment of *Innigkeit*, the cavatina. To replace such predominantly dance forms with some approximation to their modern equivalent seems all right in theory. The Tango (to be compared with the *tempo di tango feroce* of Variation 5 in the Eleventh Quartet) is not only very spirited, in fact *strepitoso*, but already has a motivic connection (D–C–E–B) with the opening of the whole work at bar 11 (A–G–E–B) and there is the transformation of this motif still to come in the fifth movement. So it could be said to be organically justifiable. A less strong case in this respect can be made out for the subsequent *Menuetto scherzando*, though the rising scale does appear in it. Such prolonged Haydn pastiche perhaps reminds us that only Haydn is able to make really good Haydnesque jokes.

The Serenade, forerunner of the whole quartet, together with its evocation of nightingale, song thrush and quail halfway through its recapitulation, has been successfully integrated into the rest of the work – or should it be the other way round? The three cadenzas occupy themselves with free reminiscence of certain aspects of their preceding movements. Matthews has described the following *Canto mesto* as 'probably my most ambitious attempt to revive Classical tonality, with extensive use of modulation'. Its main theme is another transformation of the scalic *Urmotif*, and the key is B♭ minor. The first move is to A minor (bar 18) and then to a sort of G minor (bar 32) before returning to B♭ minor. The next departure is to G major/minor, then to G♭ minor and then back to an unfulfilled G minor. The movement's most effective moment is when at bar 52 we slip quite magically into D♭ minor – a Mahlerian gesture of great expressiveness, matched only by the *ppp* pedal in E major/minor at bar 65. When the *tempo primo* is regained, together with the B♭ minor tonic, it is only with hindsight that you could realise that the movement is less than halfway through. It is simply far too long, and in particular the working of the accompanying rhythmic motif soon becomes too invariable and monotonous. Bach's Chromatic Fantasy is more highly organised, and shorter; so is Haydn's *Fantasia* movement in his late quartet in E♭ major, Op. 76, No. 6, which makes an even crazier anabasis through remotely related keys. The *Menuetto grazioso* for Peter Sculthorpe has more than a touch of birdsong, but is otherwise rather slight.

With the Finale we first go back to the beginning of the whole work, with the scalic crotchets being given to the cello in an ample reminiscence lasting 36 bars. A thudding B♭ on the cello breaks in *allegro molto* – and there is an impetuous rhythmic version of the *Urmotif* on the first violin. We are soon involved in a passage of pulsing, bounding energy, double-stopping pounding away on the cello giving a particularly solid basis for this. The second subject, *meno mosso e cantabile*, is a lyrical burst of clear D major; when the first theme returns, it undergoes some development, first of all in close canon, latterly broadening out and ending with a vigorous fugato and ever more excited polyphony. The second subject appears again, this time in a Mixolydian G slipping into F minor, followed by much development of the second theme, mostly in inversion. The air of breathless expectation that has so informed this movement gradually disperses until the second theme appears, *tranquillo*, in unambiguous D major. One final glimpse of the Australian magpie and the red wattlebird, and then a transfigured version of the scalic *Urmotif* and the work comes to a calm end.

These two outer movements of the Twelfth Quartet represent two of the most outstanding achievements of Matthews's quartet writing. Their open-air quality, untroubled lyricism and above all their vitality make them irresistible.

Now for a surprise.

The twentieth century witnessed a new phenomenon in music history – indeed in all the arts. It is that of the artist who finds it necessary to break violently with his own artistic past, who disavows it, proclaims and takes up radically new ideals and techniques. This is not always suspect; over the course of time one can eventually trace the organic growth that leads from one stage to another. There is very often a Damascus Road moment in most artists' lives, but sometimes, more mildly, it is merely a path they choose not to take.

There has never been a place for any such violent drama in David Matthews's artistic life. But these reflections came about after discovering his Third Quartet Op. 18, written thirty-five years ago. It was composed, in response to a BBC commission, between June 1977 and July 1978, revised in September 1981 and first performed by the Fitzwilliam Quartet; later it was recorded by the Brindisi Quartet. In its 19 minutes of continuous playing time, a sequence of four movement-types can clearly be delineated. An *Allegro animato* is followed by an *Andante tranquillo*. The latter has an extended middle section marked *prestissimo, spettrale* – which turns out to be an anticipation of the one-in-a-bar scherzo that follows *prestissimo, molto intenso*. By way of two sudden irruptions from the upper instruments and two aggressive solos on the cello, the link is made to a *Largo sostenuto* – a long and periodically troubled finale, elegiac in character.

This is a brilliant, deeply accomplished and altogether enviable work. It is also markedly different from the two works already discussed. From the opening major ninth thrusting upwards on all instruments (a figure which will recur in many different characters throughout the work) and the chordal passage which immediately succeeds it, the music is urgent, compelling, passionate and virile, with highly dissonant tough harmony to drive it along. A high degree of thematic integration reveals itself throughout. The opening ninth continues in double octaves: D–E–F#–A–C – a Mixolydian but entirely diatonic fragment. It is soon to return in its original character and pitch, seven bars after Fig. 2. But it also returns in varied forms throughout the first movement – at Fig. 14 richly harmonised, at Fig. 16 at another pitch and treated in canon, and elsewhere.

But when the magical *misterioso* passage at Fig. 17 has run its course and the slow movement begins, this rising ninth and the rest of the five-note figure associated with it, is to be heard in an entirely different character – a whispering *dolce espressivo con sord*. It is to dominate the whole of the Andante – coming back, for instance, at Fig. 24. Then in the long period of harmonic stasis from Fig. 46 onwards (over 5ths, C#–G# on the cello) the viola struggles to establish a new version of this *Urmotif*, now spelt D–F#–E. And after a passage of cadenza-like confusion with many trills after Fig. 50, the *Largo* at Fig. 55 works its way towards this latter version just quoted. But in the end, it is given to the viola to reveal the original sequence of pitches in slow motion, two bars before Fig. 60.

Matthews's high degree of creative control over his material must be further emphasised. The continuation of the opening theme at the upbeat to bar 6 after Fig. 1 (a consequent to an antecedent) then appears a tone lower at Fig. 3, in varied form at Fig. 5, on the viola at Fig. 6 and back on first violin at Fig. 7. So far we are only narrating the normal but skilful working of a figure. But when the scherzo character first appears we recognise the very similar contours of the theme whistled high up on the first violin at Fig. 27, then on the high cello at Fig. 28. More remotely, its characteristic four-note pattern is scrunched up into semiquavers at the 'irruption' of Fig. 43.

Words can never become an ideal way of describing, explaining or evaluating music. It is much better just to listen to it. But it is nevertheless necessary and desirable to salute good composition with the aid of factual detail rather than a display of one's finer feelings, which after all get us nowhere. The reappearance of transformed material (i.e. its development) does not, in Classical music, require exactness of interval, but rather its variation. Serial thought, on the other hand, requires the absolute integrity of its pitch pool at least – whether it be of twelve or any smaller number of pitches. Matthews shows in this piece that he is fully aware of, and sympathetic to both methods of musical thought, and can write naturally in an amalgam of both, and make superb, tough and passionate music in doing so.

This work, however, seems to stand alone among its successors. Yet it did not mark a turning of the ways – why should it? We should all pay good composers the respect of recognising and accepting that they know best what they are doing.

In 1980 – shortly after writing the Third Quartet – David Matthews published what he modestly called an 'introductory study' to the music of Michael Tippett. What he said in his Preface could well be applied, thirty years down the road, to himself:

> He has gone his own way, without regard to what has been considered fashionable, writing only those works he felt compelled to write. He has forged his own highly distinctive language out of what he loves best. A composer today has to create a personal tradition for himself if his work is to have anything more than ephemeral value. Tippett has, by his own example, shown us how necessary this is and how it may be done. He has also shown, at a time when much contemporary music seems weighed down by an Oblomov-like inertia, that it is still possible to compose music of irrepressible energy and exuberance.[4]

Notes

1   George Dyson, *The New Music*, Oxford, Oxford University Press, 1924, p. 129.

2   Paul Griffiths, *The String Quartet: A History*, London, Thames and Hudson, 1983, p. 7.

3   Felix Mendelssohn, letter to Marc-André Souchay, Berlin, 5 October 1842, quoted in: Deryck Cooke, *The Language of Music*, Oxford, Oxford University Press, 1959, p. 12.

4   Preface to: David Matthews, *Michael Tippett. An Introductory Study*, London, Faber and Faber, 1980.

6   David Matthews,
Melody and a Sense of Place

Thomas Hyde

How does one write about a body of music that presents the listener with such apparent *naturalness*? All good music speaks for itself, but there is in David Matthews's music a clarity of thought, realised through technique, that seems to require little explanation or comment. One can question, even dismiss, the music's frame of reference, or the validity of the compositional aims Matthews explicitly pursues. But, once accepted on its own terms, this music apparently invites few questions outside of itself. In the short overture *From Sea to Sky*, four minutes of superbly crafted music for small orchestra captures the exhilaration of a great expanse of sea through bustling semiquavers, and an open sky through a long-breathed melody. The piece follows a ternary (a-b-a) form and the English string tradition is audible as a nourishing background. But such things are obvious. What can remain to be *said* that is not said eloquently by the music itself?

Analysis may reveal how the wheels of any given piece go round; how the notes fit (or not), the harmony moves and the sections balance with each other. And cogent analysis, as demonstrated by the essays in this volume, will make the listener want to return to the music to listen again, to hear anew, and thereby love it more. But as a composer who has learned a great deal from Matthews's example, I want in this essay to stay near the surface of the music in order to consider how the sounds coalesce into a musical voice. What has this musical voice to say in expressive terms, and how does it project itself? In exploring these questions I shall discuss the nature of Matthews's approach to musical material, his melodic writing and his depiction of the natural world.

In an age when stylistic self-consciousness and questioning have become the norm, music that does not exhibit these traits may arouse the suspicion that such a composer has either retreated into a world of cosy naiveté, or else has uncritically accepted a set of musical parameters and happily scribbled away. Such suspicions may be compounded when it becomes clear from Matthews's output – and it is a large output now – that he has remained constant to the compositional beliefs with which he began: in the validity of tonality, in traditional structural principles, in the musical vernacular and melody.[1] In short, he has felt no need to change direction. There are no Damascene conversions, no major stylistic shifts: instead we are presented with a body of work that has evolved through experience to greater heights of expressive power and subtlety.

What then are the expressive possibilities and limitations of this kind of musical voice? Is the naturalness I perceive really a polite term for mildness or playing it safe? Or is it rather evidence that compositional aim, technique and realisation are in healthy alignment? A fundamental point to recognise is that throughout Matthews's work one senses an absence of tension between the composer and his material that is rare today. This is not to suggest that the actual 'stuff' of his music lacks tension: harmonically, there are some moments of powerful dissonance. Nor does it indicate that his musical structures are predictable. And it is not a judgement on his compositional process: Matthews does not find composing easy. Rather, this 'absence' of tension is an aspect of the way the finished pieces 'speak' to the listener.

One might think that such an absence amounts to a deficiency, and in many composers' music it would be. Writing about his exact contemporary Robin Holloway, Matthews identified how the tension between composer and material could produce the expressive power of a musical voice:

> Holloway is by temperament himself a Romantic, sharing many of the Romantics' ideals, tastes and aspirations; but he can also look on their world with scholarly detachment, and it is in the tension between identification and detachment that much of the fascination of his music lies.[2]

Matthews's music also betrays a huge debt to the Romantics in many ways. But the tension that Matthews identifies as a source of 'fascination' in Holloway's music is palpably not a feature of his own work. Or, to be more precise, when such a tension between 'identification and detachment' *does* arise in Matthews's music, notably in several early works, it 'speaks' not so much as a mode of expression, but as a weakness; an indication that the work's personal voice is in some way compromised. Matthews's approach is different from Holloway's, and if his music fascinates us, it must be for different reasons.

At first, one finds it easier to identify what Matthews's musical voice excludes than what it includes. Matthews has never treated musical material as a 'found object' with which he must self-consciously construct a relationship by examining, manipulating or 'getting inside' it (the use of birdsong in his recent works may suggest otherwise, but I will take this up later). This excludes from his expressive orbit the kind of irony found in composers such as David Del Tredici or even Mahler. Similarly, there is never a sense of the composer adopting a 'mask', as Rochberg does in his Third Quartet, or of the thrill of stripping away inhibitions and picking what had once been considered forbidden fruits, as Holloway does in *Scenes from Schumann*. Nor do we find the dramatic confrontation of opposing musical worlds (and values) as in Maxwell Davies's *St Thomas Wake* or *Resurrection*. On the rare occasions when Matthews bases a work on pre-existing music, he makes every effort to remove the quotation marks and absorb it into his own language.[3] In the Sixth Symphony, based on a Vaughan Williams hymn tune, he finds inspiration in the tune itself, breaking it down into raw melodic figures 'very suitable for symphonic working'[4] before building them up again in his own voice. Matthews was originally wary of quoting the original hymn tune at the end of the Symphony precisely because he wished to avoid presenting it as an *objet trouvé*. His solution is a subtle balancing act: the hymn tune is revealed as the symphony's goal, but in a new harmonisation, and is then developed in the final bars to bring the musical argument of the entire work to a conclusion.

When Matthews has looked outside Europe to other cultures and folk traditions for inspiration, he has been attracted to structural devices and formal shapes rather than melodic or harmonic idioms. In this respect, he is a very different composer from Judith Weir (whom he admires enormously), who has found her voice through the treatment of 'found things' both formally and melodically. In *The Bagpiper's String Trio* (1988) Weir uses techniques of melodic ornamentation of Scottish bagpipe music, even though no actual quotations are used. In contrast, Matthews's String Trio No. 2, Op. 89 (2003), takes its formal model from North Indian classical music: a slow quasi-improvisatory first movement is followed by a joyful dance based upon a drone. At no point does the *sound* of North Indian classical music rise obviously to the surface: this is not the musical equivalent of a picture postcard. A formal idea has been completely re-imagined in Matthews's own musical voice. At the end of the trio, the long drone on G♮, which has been the basic tonality of the work, 'resolves' onto a C tonality. But any sense of arrival is quickly undermined and the music ends on a high B♮ poised precariously between the two tonalities.

Matthews's relationship to the past, essential for a composer wishing to uphold the symphony and string quartet as viable forms, is therefore to a living tradition of which he himself is part, rather than something to be engaged with from a distance. This is crucial to his expressive world. What he loves from the past can never be treated as 'found objects', for the simple reason that they were never lost. Respect for tradition also demands a respect for the historical flow and sequence that provides the context for all music, including his own. What he loves and wishes to emulate from the past he knows he must remake, rather than steal.

It is the finished music's lack of self-consciousness that is intriguing. The Fourth Symphony allows us to observe how the aspiration towards renewal plays out. Unlike its three predecessors, each of which attempted to fuse the constituent parts of a symphony into a single movement, the Fourth is, in the composer's own words 'in many ways closer to the classical archetype',[5] being in separate movements and scored for a classical orchestra of two flutes, two oboes, two bassoons, two horns and strings. Consider how the odds are stacked against success: a Haydnesque symphony written in 1989 for a Classical orchestra (complete with horn calls and other Classical tropes) without even the (ironic?) detachment of neoclassicism for cover! Yet it is one of Matthews's greatest achievements: music that is recognisable both as continuing a tradition while also containing a freshness that few composers – himself included – have captured before or since. Certain decidedly un-Haydnesque elements also feed into the Symphony; for example a scherzo that nods towards both American minimalism and also 'the pure excitement produced by simple repetition of a tonic chord' that Matthews found in rock music of his youth.[6] And there is also the wonderfully eccentric formal plan of the first movement, in which a series of embellished monodies flower into 'harmony' only as the movement comes to an end. This movement was inspired by hearing a performance of Machaut's *Messe de Notre Dame* in which the Mass movements 'appeared as islands of polyphony surrounded by plainsong'.[7]

It is, however, two other movements in this Fourth Symphony whose triumphs over the many risks inherent in the whole enterprise bring Matthews's achievement into the sharpest focus. The finale is a sonata allegro with slow introduction. Finales have long been problematic for the composer and were avoided in the earlier symphonies through the adoption of a single-movement form. Different solutions were attempted in two earlier four-movement chamber pieces. In the Fourth String Quartet, Op. 27 (1981), all the structural weight is thrown onto a finale that is almost as long as the preceding three movements combined; while the finale of the Piano Trio No. 1, Op. 34 (1983), is more explicit in avoiding any attempt at 'summing up' by opting for utter simplicity through an aria-like accompanied melody repeated twice. In the Fourth Symphony, Matthews raises the stakes by attempting a finale that is definitely conclusive in character, opening with a slow introduction that returns to the material that ended the first movement. The sonata form includes a triple-bluff at the repeat of the exposition that is worthy of Haydn: the listener is first convinced that a repeat has been embarked on, then that a development has started, only to discover that in fact it *is* a repeat – though modified! So much for the formal design; but what none of this makes clear, of course, is how fresh this music sounds. It joyfully and wholeheartedly inhabits a world that has evolved from the symphonies of the past without recourse to pastiche or nostalgia. It has nothing of the neoclassical displacement and self-consciousness that one finds in, say, Prokofiev's *Classical Symphony*. What it takes from the past is also what liberates it.

Another aspect of renewal can be heard in the movement before the finale: a tango that Matthews treats as a 'replacement' for the Classical minuet. Here too, the tango is treated, not as a 'found object', but rather as a rhythmic dance-form that can provide a mood of lightness and grace between a slow movement and a weightier sonata-allegro finale. The extra beats that appear throughout the movement are not so much a disruption of the essential dance rhythm as a means of maintaining an unstable, 'slightly manic' mood, as the tempo mark has it. To my ears, these irregular bars and the subtle and inventive orchestration are not distancing devices: there is no sense of the music being placed in quotation marks.

Given Matthews's belief in music's foundation in song and dance ('what music has always been about'),[8] it is easy to understand the appeal of the tango, a dance to which he has returned in several works since the Fourth Symphony. Formally the tango is open to limitless manipulation while also carrying a set of musical expectations that the composer can meet, or challenge, in the spirit of Hans Keller's definition of the richest musical experiences as 'the meaningful contradiction of expectation.'[9] However, the real attraction for Matthews, I suspect, is that like other dance forms he has used (which include the minuet, the blues, and the waltz), the tango has demanded from him a new approach to melodic writing. If the tango in the Twelfth String Quartet, Op. 114 is less successful than that in the Fourth Symphony, it is precisely because its melodic material is less striking, veering too closely to a sort of anonymous pastiche, unmarked by the full stamp of its composer's personality.

Melody is also central to the naturalness that Matthews's musical voice communicates. The composer has commented that his initial starting point in the birth of a new work is nearly always melodic: 'it is true that I often base pieces on a chord [but] it can often be the "verticalisation" of a melody ... I do usually start with melodies rather than chords.'[10] The result is that, however dissonant or texturally intricate the music becomes, it always seems to be yearning to return to a state where it might be sung by the human voice. Matthews may well endorse Ned Rorem's remark that "whatever my music is written for – tuba, tambourine, tubular bells – it is always the singer in me crying to get out".

Melody in Matthews's early music is often the kind of freely-evolving line that he inherited from Nicholas Maw, with its roots in the Romantics (Strauss and Mahler) as well as in the Tippett of *The Midsummer Marriage*. It is abundant and open-ended, in that it rarely cadences. And it flowers through loosely manipulating a small melodic figure, while adopting wider leaps for heightened expressive effect, as in this extract from *September Music*, Op. 24 (1979):

Example 1: David Matthews, September Music, bars 148-54.

Some thirty years later, however, the Seventh Symphony is built almost entirely on a melody that is very different. More triadic in character, this melody has inflexions that are more modal than chromatic. It moves in shorter phrases, but the changes of metre and irregular phrase-lengths convey a deeper implied balancing of question and answer. Unlike the melodies in *September Music*, it now has cadences.

Example 2: David Matthews, Symphony No. 7, Op. 109, bars 1-16.

Matthews has used birdsong in several pieces in recent years. A lifelong birdwatcher, he has been primarily attracted by the melodic quality of birdsong, which has provided him with 'simple and striking motifs [that] are in contrast to the elaborate songs that Messiaen notated and included in his music – too complex and pedantic for my taste. I prefer Beethoven's stylised nightingale, or Mahler's cuckoo call in his First Symphony which he used motivically'.[11] Listen to the opening of the orchestral piece *Aubade*, Op. 83 (2001), based on the song of an Australian magpie that Matthews wrote down while staying with friends near Canberra in September 2000. Here too, the aim has been to absorb these melodies into his own language (even at the point of initial notation they are conditioned to equal temperament tuning). Although he always acknowledges the names of the birds in his programme notes, Matthews is able to allow birdsong material to arise naturally and recognisably in the surface of the music, paradoxically sounding at one with the wider musical context in which it is placed. This gives a special, almost magical, quality to his music.

The depiction of the natural world in his work provides my final example of the naturalness of Matthews's musical voice. The inclusion of the melodies of birdsong in his work is a feature of the music that, whatever journey it follows, and whatever turmoil it passes through, ultimately affirms, and reaffirms, a sense of the human being at one with nature. This is achieved, I think, in part through the use of a structural device that has become increasingly important in his work. Throughout the music there are what one might call 'moments of stasis': harmonically static and frequently using ostinati, these non-directional passages are nearly always built upon a pedal note. In the early music such moments were often problematic, creating tension by anchoring against a pedal melodic material that cried out to be allowed to *move* harmonically. The expressive effect could often be that of 'treading water', resulting in a stasis that disrupted the flow of a work. *September Music*, Op. 24 suffers from this problem, notably in the central section where a beautifully elaborate 'composing-out' of a series of chords is at odds with the goal-orientated harmony of the material either side. Similarly, the Second Symphony's first 'interlude', a series of percussion patterns over a long-held F pedal, is placed too near the start of the work to be convincing. Following an opening that is melodically rich and pregnant with one of Matthews's best melodies, the static quality of this 'interlude' holds up the flow of the symphonic argument, no matter how neatly it fits into the symmetrical formal plan of the whole symphony.

In contrast, consider the naturalness of another early work built on pedal notes, *Introit*, Op. 28 for two trumpets and strings. This piece is as convincing as it is ravishing: material and technique are perfectly matched. The work's expressive character, a response to the Gothic architecture of Gloucester Cathedral, is that of a huge elaboration and ornamentation of a single glowing chord: not moving, but shimmering.

Matthews has acknowledged that his earlier works 'tended to shift from one pedal to the next. And I have consciously worked on that.'[12] A more obviously functional bass line led to tighter harmonic structures in works like *Chaconne* and the Third Symphony. But there was still expressive potential in these 'moments of stasis'. It was when Matthews came to use them to express the natural world that he found a way to bring form, technique and content together with new purpose. In the chamber orchestral *Burnham Wick*, Op. 73 (1997), Matthews wrote what he called a 'modern pastoral':

> [The] earlier pastoral tradition in British music belonged to a more innocent age which is gone for ever, and there is now an almost universally held feeling that nature is fighting a losing battle with man. In the face of our profound melancholy about the future, it is hard

> to celebrate the beauty of nature without lapsing into nostalgia and
> sentimentality. Nature, however, is not yet spent, nor are we obliged to
> deconstruct the delight we may feel on a country walk. [13]

To deconstruct is potentially to allow a level of awareness to separate us from
unselfconscious, natural feelings of delight: as with a country walk, so with
music. The one-movement *Burnham Wick* adopts a mosaic form in which
slowly evolving melodic material is contrasted with more active and dance-
like music. Then, before the final *giocoso* section (Fig. 61) comes a 'moment
of stasis' in which a solo violin cadenza representing a skylark is projected
against a static chord on strings. Furthermore, the string players are instructed
to hold small caxixis in their bowing hand, so that 'when playing the tremolos
between figures 54 and 55 the shakers will make a soft continuous sound, like
the buzzing of insects'. Meanwhile the five wind players move from the stage
to play their short melodic fragments from a distance. The striking expressive
effect of this moment emerges organically out of the flow of the music; one
does not get a sense of dislocation, or of music that has self-consciously
stepped outside its own argument. Such moments in Matthews's recent work
have increasingly spoken as powerful musical expressions of a sense of 'home':
of a place, real or imagined, that is settled, rooted and sacred.

Matthews quickly went on to explore this new territory further. As already
described, *Aubade* opens with the song of a magpie, but other birdsongs are
also added to create a 68-bar 'dawn chorus' projected over a B♮ pedal note.
Another 'dawn chorus' appears towards the end of the Sixth Symphony. In
the third movement, after a climax of ferocious violence, the music comes
to rest on major-second pedal notes (D and E). Above this, a sequence of
Australian birdsongs and other melodic fragments is heard, along with ostinati
and percussion tappings. This static harmonic moment conveys the feeling of
nature opening up, of rebirth and renewal after a great storm. We feel we have
arrived home, and soon this settled place reveals the A major hymn-tune coda.

To write about a living composer is always to be aware that a perspective
on his or her music must be provisional: future works may alter our view. The
recent Twelfth String Quartet (2011) has suggested a new avenue in Matthews's
work. The interrupting *canto d'uccelli* in the first movement is a true disruption
that creates a more fragmented surface in the music. Partly this is because the
birdsong interrupts a rigorously worked Prelude and Fugue, and its appearance
is too brief to sound as if it has arisen naturally. As a result, the music's tone
of voice is brought into question. Here is a sense of contradiction – indeed
perhaps even irony – quite new in Matthews's music: it will be exciting to see
whether future works take this new direction further.

I will end this celebration of the composer's seventieth birthday by turning
to a vocal work that not only conveys in a different way a profound sense of

home, but also a faith and hope in future creativity. *The Sleeping Lord*, Op. 58 (1992), is a setting of words by David Jones for soprano and an ensemble of flute, clarinet, harp and string quartet. In his book *Landscape and Memory*, Simon Schama describes how the contours of our landscape everywhere reveal the influence of man, and evokes the 'veins of myth and memory' that lie beneath the surface of things, awaiting rediscovery.[14] *The Sleeping Lord* is a gentle and understated work that only gradually reveals its secrets. Its strength lies in a deceptive subtlety that can, on a first hearing, appear to be a shortcoming. Even in the faster music there is a curious lack of 'lift', a frustrating sense of material never being let off the leash, never allowed to blossom fully. But it is precisely this quality of 'held-back' potential that makes *The Sleeping Lord* special. The work opens with three dense chords that convey the weight of earth and foliage. As in *Introit*, melodic lines elaborate slow-moving chords – a musical response, the composer says, to Jones's paintings and poetry. The faster music only hints at a future joy and rebirth; in the haunting final moments of the work, a distant wordless soprano sings against gently repeated strummed harp chords, suggesting a mood of tentative hope. A phrase for flute and clarinet, vividly evoking the powerful sense of expectation in Jones's verse, brings the work to a close with an atmosphere that is curious and questioning:

> Does the land wait the sleeping lord
> or is the wasted land
> That very lord who sleeps?

Notes

1   David Matthews, 'Renewing the Past: Some Personal Thoughts', in: *Reviving the Muse: Essays on Music after Modernism*, ed. Peter Davison, Brinkworth, Claridge Press, 2001, pp. 199-212 (reproduced in Part One of this volume).

2   David Matthews, 'The Rehabilitation of the Vernacular' in: *Music and the Politics of Culture*, ed. Christopher Norris, London, Lawrence and Wishart, 1989, p. 246.

3   An obvious exception is to be found when pre-existing music is used as the basis for a set of variations, as in the String Quartet No. 11, Op. 108 (2007-08), which takes a bagatelle by Beethoven as its theme (this described in Hugh Wood's essay, above).

4   David Matthews, programme note in the score of his Symphony No. 6, Faber Music, 2007.

5   David Matthews, programme note in the score of his Symphony No. 4, Faber Music, 1990.

6   Ivan Hewett, 'The English Romantic', *BBC Music Magazine*, March 1993, p. 45.

7   David Matthews, programme note in the score of his Symphony No. 4, Faber Music, 1990.

8   Matthews discusses the importance of song and dance at length in 'Renewing the Past'.

9   A favourite quotation of Keller's regularly used by Matthews, as in 'Renewing the Past'.

10   Thomas Hyde, 'Visions of Reality', *The Musical Times*, Vol. 144, No. 1882, Spring 2003, p. 34.

11   David Matthews, programme note in the score of his *Aubade*, Faber Music, 2001.

12   Hyde, 'Visions of Reality', p. 38.

13   David Matthews, programme note in the score of his *Burnham Wick*, Faber Music, 2002.

14   Quoted in: David Matthews, programme note in *Burnham Wick*, 2002.

Envoi:
Seven Wines for Seven Symphonies

Frank Ward

Wine, according to Robert Louis Stevenson, is 'bottled poetry'. He could equally well have called it bottled music. Wine and music dovetail beautifully. Most oenophiles love music, and hosts of musicians, composers not least, love wine. Beethoven's very last words, uttered on his deathbed ("Pity, pity, too late!"), expressed his anguish at the fact that his favourite wine had not arrived in time. Both music and wine exist in time, in the fourth dimension, and *need* time in which to divulge their full complexities, opening up as the seconds tick away, revealing fresh nuances at every moment, with full disclosure not occurring until the very end.

In both cases, start and finish are inextricably linked. Daniel Barenboim makes the cogent point that 'the last sound is not the end of the music … the last note must be related to the silence that follows it.' The aftertaste of a fine wine performs a comparable function.

My friendship with David Matthews began some years ago, and it was precisely music and wine that brought us together. By chance, he and I were buying fish at Jenkins's excellent fishmonger's shop in Deal. Impulsively, I introduced myself, thanking David for the many superb concerts he'd organised while director of the annual Deal Music Festival. It seemed only natural to invite him back to taste a couple of wines in my eighteenth-century cellar, and that turned out to be the start of a rewarding friendship in which both music and wine have played a big role.

I can't read a note or play any musical instrument but music has flowed through me like, well, wine ever since I can remember. And many a wine tasted in the course of the week calls to mind a particular piece of music. The comparisons I make below are half playful and half serious, but as I start to think about which wines best match David's symphonies I cannot suppress the notion that we should one day try to prevail on him to write a symphony to match a wine.

Symphony No. 1 – Champagne (Krug or Pol Roger)

Of his debut symphony, David writes that it is made up of three movements in one. Trios and trinities manifest themselves throughout nature and art and, not infrequently, in wine. Some champagnes are fashioned from each of three permitted grapes. Each contributes something unique, but all three meld into a seamless whole – as do the three components of this first symphony. Champagne seems like an ideal choice here, being the liveliest and most effervescent of wines and also the most aural (think of the pop of the cork and the tantalising susurration in the glass). It's also the perfect aperitif, and can now perform that function by launching the first of the seven symphonies, which also seems to be infused with freshness and youthful vitality. Just as the various groups of instruments in the orchestra bring different but complementary qualities to David's symphony, so do the different grapes confer their separate but harmonising traits on the wine. Chardonnay – vitality, delicacy, incisiveness (strings, flutes, harp); Pinot Meunier – roundness, a kind of unifying warmth (cellos, French horns); Pinot Noir – structure, depth, volume (double bass, bassoon, timpani, etc.). The scherzo, David writes, 'bursts out energetically' – as when the glass of champagne is replenished, causing the wine to seethe and bubble with still greater vitality, sending almost invisible columns of microscopic bubbles to ascend with ever-increasing vigour. A heady wine for a heady symphony.

Symphony No. 2 – Châteauneuf-du-Pape (Beaucastel, Mont-Redon)

This symphony is on a larger scale and strikes a more serious note – an expansive, purposeful work that shows great sweep and focus. All of the instruments are given great play, but also perform together too, to great effect, with the whole adding up to very much more than the sum of its parts. Châteauneuf-du-Pape fits the bill perfectly, being voluminous, assertive, but also able to show delicacy and subtlety. A maximum of thirteen different grapes may be used – pretty well an entire vinous orchestra – with some of them used in tiny quantities, yet each still discernible in the finished wine (as with some instruments). A Châteauneuf producer, more than any of his colleagues, really has to act like a conductor, making sure that each grape comes into its own without drowning out any other. David's Second is a Châteauneuf-du-Pape of a work: dramatic, forceful, heady, full of purpose.

Symphony No. 3 – Corton, a Grand Cru of Burgundy

Only truly great wines have both power *and* finesse. In some it is power that has the upper hand, in others, finesse. Music is like that too: think of Wagner and Bruckner on the one hand and Mozart and Schubert on the other. In this symphony, both qualities are present but in varying strengths at varying times. To me, the Third's beginning is full of finesse, even if the power is seldom far away. Of all the red grapes in the world none can rival Burgundy's Pinot Noir when it comes to sheer finesse. I choose a Grand Cru, Corton, because, while exhibiting all the finesse one could wish for, it also shows an almost daunting, slightly savage, power: like this symphony. A silky, subtle wine when mature, it never quite loses that firm, ferruginous backbone that reminds one of the forces of nature. Again, like the symphony.

Symphony No. 4 – 1978 Château Lafite

David describes this work as a 'classical archetype' in five movements. The most classical of all wines, surely, is claret, and the most classical of clarets is Château Lafite. It too has four movements (or four grapes at least), the fifth component being the moment when as a quartet they fuse together to create a unified whole.

The essential nature of claret was brought home to me as never before when a bottle of '78 Lafite was sent to our table at the Parisian restaurant Le Taillevent by its owner, the late Jean-Claude Vrinat, surely the greatest restaurateur who ever lived. The Fourth Symphony's 'light and flowing' opening calls to mind the initial bouquet of that lovely wine, which to start with was dominated by the lightest and most delicate of the four grapes, the Cabernet-Franc, the other four being subdued at this early stage (as with the symphony's movements, the grapes in this particular wine presented themselves in sequence). Soon the round, voluptuous Merlot took over, exhaling its round, sensuous aromas. Then came the intense, structured Cabernet Sauvignon, which stayed in the ascendant for quite some time. Finally, the densest variety of all, the Petit-Verdot, brought its fascinating truffle-and-liquorice flavour to the ensemble. I'm sure that any musician could suggest one or other instrument that plays such parts in the orchestra. Last of all, the quintessential character of the wine asserted itself, a fusion of all four grapes, ennobled by the unique Lafite vineyard, melded into a seamless whole, expressed in a long aftertaste which, like David's Fourth, concludes on a note of 'lusher harmonic textures'.

Neither wine nor symphony is a blockbuster, but both show superb harmony and great tensile strength. They are the very soul of classicism.

Symphony No. 5 – Hermitage 'Les Bessards'

This work, in David's own words, has a 'dark and restless mood' and its 'energy hardly relaxes'. This makes me think of that powerhouse of a wine, Hermitage, and of the choicest part of that fabled vineyard, 'Les Bessards', where the granitic subsoil supplies a massive backbone to the wine. Hermitage has been famously called the manliest of French wines. I enjoy the thought that it is in fact made from one of the few French grapes that is of the feminine gender: *La Syrah*. In the symphony, too, power and subtlety are intertwined.

The music is complex and structured; so too is the wine from the Bessards section, that unique plot covering just a few precious hectares. I relish the notion that the vineyard, because of its steepness, is divided into many terraces, a visual parallel to the many-layered structure of David's work. But Hermitage, like the Fifth, is not about power alone. The wine can be elegiac, just as in the third movement violas provide a gentler theme. There are no violas in an Hermitage, but it often carries a whiff of violets. The mood of the symphony's finale is 'brightly energetic'. When the glass of Hermitage is replenished, the wine is reanimated and a whole range of redoubled scents and flavours emanate from the glass. The finish of both music and wine is full of energy, and both reverberate long after the last note, and drop, has faded away.

Symphony No. 6 – Riesling Smaragd (Prager) from the Wachau, Austria

The rousing, tinglingly fresh opening and the use of Austrian cowbells, not to mention David's allusion to Mahler's evocation of the Austrian Alps, turn my thoughts instantly to the great bone-dry, cracklingly alive Rieslings of that country. A glass of fine Riesling is almost like an electrical charge, so full of energy is it. Its scent brings thoughts of birdsong and wild flowers. But classic Riesling is about more than bouquet and freshness of flavour. The grape, more than most, extracts all manner of minerals from the subsoil, which gives added texture almost in the way the multiple subsidiary themes of David's piece do to the music. When David writes 'the timpani hammers out the first notes of the opening', I have an image of the Riesling hammering out its complex, mineral aftertaste, which is given additional intensity by its bracing fruity acidity, comparable in its way to that blast of brass and timpani in the symphony. Some passages, indeed, deliver a kind of delicious shock, comparable to the moment when the Riesling releases its manifold subsidiary flavours, forming part of a rolling finish which is dry yet contains a kind of honeyed sweetness at its core. Both wine and music have a finale that's both an aftertaste and an aftershock.

Symphony No. 7 – Chambolle-Musigny 1er Cru 'Les Amoureuses'

One leading critic has written that this single-movement piece 'rings endless changes on a rapturous viola melody, heard ... over the tremulous violins'. This rare Burgundy red is a single-grape wine that rings endless changes on the Pinot Noir, producing rapturous sensations. It, too, has a tremulous quality, the wine village of Chambolle-Musigny giving the most delicate and subtle of all Burgundies (you can almost feel the wine tremble as you taste it). This apparent fragility does not prevent the wine from being one of the most structured and long-lived of the whole region. This one-movement symphony has many parts – as does this one-grape wine, whose delectable ripe-grape sweetness is given backbone and structure by the iron-rich subsoil and the complex mix of minerals and metals therein. Acidity and tannin – which function a bit like timpani and brass in a symphony – give rigour, while lightly-toasted oak in the barrels, in interaction with the Pinot Noir grape, provides a slightly exotic touch of spice. The finishes of both wine and symphony are very long.

6. Menuetto grazioso

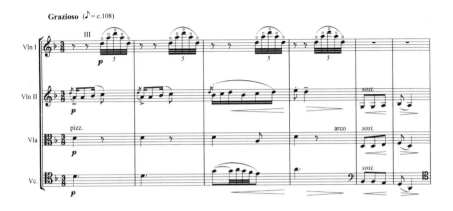

David Matthews, Menuetto grazioso *from the String Quartet No. 12 (2011), Op. 114.*

Selected Works, Discography
and Bibliography

David Matthews, Chaconne *for orchestra, Op. 43: the conclusion.*

Selected Works

Year	Opus	Title
1968	–	*Christ is Born of Maiden Fair*, for choir
1968-71	1	Three Songs, for soprano and orchestra
1969-70	4	String Quartet No. 1 (revised 1980)
1970	3	*Stars*, for choir and orchestra
1974-76	16	String Quartet No. 2
1975-78	9	Symphony No. 1 (revised 2007)
1975	10	*The Book of Hours*, for soprano and piano (revised 1999)
1976	13	*Toccatas and Pastorals*, for oboe, bassoon and harpsichord
1976-79	17	Symphony No. 2
1977-78	18	String Quartet No. 3
1979-80	24	*September Music*, for small orchestra
1980	25	*The Company of Lovers*, for choir
	26	*White Nights*, for violin and small orchestra (revised 2012)
1981	27	String Quartet No. 4
	28	*Introit*, for two trumpets and strings
1982	29	*Serenade*, for small orchestra
	30	*Duet Variations*, for flute (or violin) and piano
1982-83	31	Violin Concerto No. 1
	32	*Winter Journey*, for violin (or viola, arranged 1993)
1983	33	*The Golden Kingdom*, for high voice and piano
	34	Piano Trio No. 1
1983-85	37	Symphony No. 3
1984	35	Clarinet Quartet
1984-85	36	String Quartet No. 5
	38	*In the Dark Time*, for orchestra
1985	39	Three Studies, for violin
1986	40	Variations, for string orchestra
	41	Aria, for violin and piano

1986-87	42	*The Flaying of Marsyas*, for oboe and string quartet (also arranged for oboe, violin and string orchestra, 2013)
	43	Chaconne, for orchestra
1987-88	45	*Cantiga*, for soprano and chamber orchestra
1988	44	*Marina*, for baritone, basset horn, viola and piano
1988-89	46	*The Ship of Death*, for choir
1989	47	Piano Sonata
	48	String Trio No. 1
1989-90	50	*The Music of Dawn*, for orchestra
	51	Symphony No. 4, for chamber orchestra
1990	49	Romanza, for cello and small orchestra
	52	*Scherzo capriccioso*, for orchestra
	56a	Adagio, for string quartet (or string orchestra)
1990-91	53	*From Coastal Stations*, for voice and piano
	56	String Quartet No. 6
1991	54	Capriccio, for 2 horns and string orchestra
1991-92	57	Oboe Concerto
1991-93	55	*Long Lion Days*, for cello and piano
1992	58	*The Sleeping Lord*, for soprano and seven players
	59	*From Sea to Sky*, for small orchestra
1992-93	60	*A Vision and a Journey*, for orchestra (revised 1996-97)
1993	62	*A Little Threnody*, for cor anglais
1993-94	61	Piano Trio No. 2
	63	*A Congress of Passions*, for counter-tenor, oboe and piano
1993-96	66	*Vespers*, for mezzo-soprano, tenor, choir and orchestra
1994	64	String Quartet No. 7: *Skies now are skies,* for tenor and string quartet (or string orchestra, 2013)
1995	65	*A Song and Dance Sketchbook*, for piano quartet
	68	*Moments of Vision*, for choir
1995-96	67	Sinfonia, for chamber orchestra
1996	69	*Three Housman Songs*, for soprano and string quartet
1996-2000	70	Two Pieces, for string orchestra
1997	71	*Hurrahing in Harvest*, for six voices
	72	Variations, for piano
	73	*Burnham Wick*, for chamber orchestra

1997-98	74	Violin Concerto No. 2, for violin and ensemble
1998	–	*Y Deryn Du*, for violin, viola, cello and piano
	75	String Quartet No. 8
1998-99	78	Symphony No. 5
1999	76	*The Doorway of the Dawn*, for choir
	77	*Winter Passions*, for baritone, clarinet, viola, cello and piano
1999-2001	79	Eight Duos, for two violins
2000	80	String Quartet No. 9
	80a	*Total Tango*, for string orchestra (arranged 2003)
	81	*Three Roman Miniatures*, for clarinet
	–	*Sarabande*, for flute and piano
2000-01	82	*After Sunrise*, for chamber orchestra
	83	*Aubade*, for chamber orchestra
	84	String Quartet No. 10
2000-02	87	*Concerto in Azzurro*, for cello and orchestra
2000-04	84a	*Four Australian Birds*, for violin
2001	85	*Band of Angels*, for organ
	86	*Winter Remembered*, for viola and string orchestra
2002	88	Fifteen Fugues, for violin
2003	89	String Trio No. 2
	90	*Psalm 23: The Lord is My Shepherd*, for choir and organ (or string orchestra)
2003-04	91	*Aequam memento*, for choir
	96	*Voyages*, for medium voice, violin, viola and cello
2003-05	98	*Movement of Autumn*, for soprano and chamber orchestra
	98a	*For a Wine Festival*, for soprano and piano (2003)
2003-07	100	Symphony No. 6
2004	–	*The Two Cuckoos*, for recorder
	92	Piano Quintet
	93	Little Serenade, for string quartet
2004-07	94	*Two Dionysus Dithyrambs*, for piano
2004-08	95	*Journeying Songs*, for cello
2005	97	Piano Trio No. 3
	102	*Darkness Draws In*, for viola

	102a	*Goodnight Song*, for string orchestra
2005-06	103	*Fanfares and Flowers*, for wind band
2006-07	104	*Terrible Beauty*, for soprano and seven players
2007	105	*Adonis*, for violin and piano
2007-08	108	String Quartet No. 11
2007-09	110	*Happiness*, for soprano and recorder
2008	107	*One Foot in Eden*, for tenor and piano quintet
2008-09	109	Symphony No. 7
2009-10	113	*Actaeon*, for narrator and ensemble
2010	111	Piano Concerto, for piano and string orchestra
	112	*Dark Pastoral*, for cello and chamber orchestra
	114	String Quartet No. 12
	115	Horn Quintet
2011	117	*Toward the Sun*, for orchestra
	118	*Three Birds and a Farewell*, for string orchestra
2011-12	119	Romanza, for violin and string orchestra (or piano)
	120	*Fortune's Wheel*, for chorus, percussion and string orchestra
	121	*A Blackbird Sang*, for flute and string trio
	122	Double Concerto, for violin, viola and string orchestra
2012	123	Duo Sonata, for violin and cello
	124	*Four Portraits*, for piano
2012-13	125	*A Vision of the Sea*, for orchestra
2013	126	*Three Dunwich Songs*, for high voice and piano
	127	*Two Poems of John Clare*, for unison children's voices and piano

Discography

Actaeon
Eleanor Bron (narrator), Counterpoise
Deux-Elles: DXL 1151 [2013]

Adagio for String Quartet
Brodsky Quartet
Silva Classics: SILKD 6001 [1994]

Adagio for String Quartet, String Quartet Nos. 4, 6, 10
Kreutzer Quartet
Toccata Classics: TOCC 0058 [2010]

After Sunrise, Oboe Concerto, Violin Concerto Nos. 1 and 2
Philippe Graffin (violin), Nicholas Daniel (oboe), Bournemouth Symphony
Orchestra, Orchestra Nova, George Vass (conductor)
Dutton Epoch: CDLX 7261 [2010]

Aubade, A Congress of Passions, From Sea to Sky, Goodnight Song,
Movement of Autumn, The Sleeping Lord, Total Tango
Orchestra Nova, George Vass (conductor)
Dutton Epoch: CDLX 7189 [2007]

Cantiga, Introit, September Music;
Gustav Mahler: Seven Early Songs (arr. Colin and David Matthews)
Jill Gomez (soprano), Bournemouth Sinfonietta, John Carewe (conductor)
Unicorn Kanchana: DKP 9120 [1991, deleted:
Matthews works reissued on NMC D084]

Cantiga, Introit, September Music, Symphony No. 4
Jill Gomez (soprano), Bournemouth Sinfonietta, John Carewe (conductor),
East of England Orchestra, Malcolm Nabarro (conductor)
NMC Recordings: NMC D084 [2003]

Capriccio
Richard Watkins (horn), RAM Orchestra, Michael Thompson (conductor),
Royal Academy of Music
Royal Academy of Music: RAM 016 [2002]

Chaconne, In the Dark Time
BBC Symphony Orchestra, Jac van Steen (conductor)
NMC Recordings: NMC D067 [2001]

Christ is Born of Maiden Fair, Hurrahing in Harvest, Moments of Vision, Psalm 23, The Ship of Death
Colmore Consort, Charles Janz (conductor), Colmore Consort
Colmore Consort: CC CD1 [2006]

Clarinet Quartet, Marina, String Trio Nos. 1 & 2, Terrible Beauty, Winter Passions
Susan Bickley (mezzo-soprano), Stephen Loges (baritone),
The Nash Ensemble, Lionel Friend (conductor)
NMC Recordings: NMC D152 [2010]

Concerto in Azzurro, The Music of Dawn, A Vision and a Journey
Guy Johnston (cello), BBC Philharmonic Orchestra, Rumon Gamba (conductor)
Chandos: CHAN 10487 [2008]

Dark Pastoral
Guy Johnston (cello), Royal Scottish National Orchestra,
Martin Yates (conductor)
Dutton Epoch: CDLX 7289 [2012]

The Doorway of the Dawn
The Joyful Company of Singers, Peter Broadbent (conductor)
EMI Classics: CDC 5 56961 2 [2000]

Duet Variations
Jeffret Khaner (flute), Charles Abramovic (piano)
Avie: AV 0016 [2002]

Eight Duos for Two Violins
Retorica: Harriet Mackenzie (violin), Philippa Mo (violin)
NMC Recordings: D182 [2012]

Fifteen Fugues, Three Studies, Winter Journey
Peter Sheppard Skærved (violin)
Toccata Classics: TOC 0152 [2013]

The Flaying of Marsyas, A Little Threnody, String Quartet Nos. 3 and 6
Nicholas Daniel (oboe), Brindisi String Quartet
Metronome: MET CD 1005-0 [1994]

For a Wine Festival
Gillian Keith (soprano), Simon Lepper (piano)
Metronome: MET CD 1065 [2004]

Fuga (from Fifteen Fugues), Three Studies for Violin
Peter Sheppard Skaerved (violin)
Metier Sound & Vision: MSV CD92028 [2000]

The Golden Kingdom
Margaret Field (soprano), Andrew Ball (piano)
Redcliffe Recordings: RR 009 [1995]

A Little Pastoral
John Turner (recorder)
Divine Art: DDA21217 [2011]

One to Tango, Piano Concerto, Piano Sonata, Two Dionysus Dithyrambs, Variations for Piano
Laura Mikkola (piano), Orchestra Nova, George Vass (conductor)
Toccata Classics: TOCC 0166 [2013]

Piano Sonata
William Howard (piano)
NMC Recordings: D012S [1994]

Piano Trio No. 1
English Piano Trio
Kingdom Records: KCLCD 2029 [1992]

Piano Trio No. 2 (slow movement), Three to Tango
Triptych
Dunelm Records: DRD 0094 [2000]

Plover's Peak (from Three Dunwich Songs)
Benjamin Hulett (tenor), Andrew Ball (piano)
NMC Recordings: D150 [4 disc box, NMC Songbook, 2009]

Romanza
Mstislav Rostropovich (cello), English Chamber Orchesta,
Raymond Leppard (conductor)
EMI Classics: CDC 7 54164 2 [1990]

Sarabande
Sally Walker (flute), Philip Mayers (piano)
Chartreuse: 318420130203 [2012]

String Quartet Nos. 5 and 12
Kreutzer Quartet
Toccata Classics: TOCC 0059 [2012]

Symphony Nos. 1, 3 and 5
BBC National Orchestra of Wales, Martyn Brabbins (conductor)
Dutton Epoch: CDLX 7222 [2009]

Symphony Nos. 2 and 6
BBC National Orchestra of Wales, Jac van Steen (conductor)
Dutton Epoch: CDLX 7234 [2010]

Symphony No. 4
East of England Orchestra, Malcolm Nabarro (conductor)
Collins Classics: 20082 [1994, deleted: reissued on NMC D084]

Symphony No. 7, Vespers
Bournemouth Symphony Orchestra, The Bach Choir,
John Carewe (conductor); David Hill (conductor)
Dutton Epoch: CDLX 7305 [2013]

Toccatas and Pastorals
The Sheba Sound
Oboe Classics: CC 2014 [2006]

Winter Journey
Peter Sheppard (violin)
Fish Ear Communications: FECD 621 [1995]

Winter Remembered
Sarah-Jane Bradley (viola), Orchestra Nova,
George Vass (conductor)
Dutton Epoch: CDLX 7186 [2007]

Y Deryn Du (The Blackbird)
The Schubert Ensemble
NMC Recordings: NMC D075 [2001]

Bibliography

Items marked '❯' appear in the main text.

1 Books

Michael Tippett. An Introductory Study, London, Faber and Faber, 1980.

Landscape into Sound (expanded version of Peter Fuller Memorial Lecture), St Albans, Claridge Press, 1992.

Britten, London, Haus Publishing, 2003; new edition with new author's foreword, 2013.

2 Articles

'Messiaen and Large-scale Form', *The Listener*, 9 December 1965, p. 972.

'Shostakovich's Eleventh Symphony', *The Listener*, 24 March 1966, p. 448.

'Copland and Stravinsky', *Tempo* No. 95, Winter 1970-71, pp. 10-14.

'1912: Zvezdoliki', *Tempo* No. 97 (Stravinsky memorial issue), 1971, p. 9-14.

'Britten's Third Quartet', *Tempo* No. 125, June 1978, pp. 21-4.

'Music for Chamber Ensemble (and "Scenes from Schumann")' (on Robin Holloway), *Tempo* No. 129, June 1979, pp. 20-6.

'Holloway's "Aria"', *Tempo* No. 136, March 1981, pp. 47-8.

'Editorial Preface' to: Deryck Cooke, *Vindications. Essays on Romantic Music*, London, Faber & Faber, 1982, pp. 7-8.

'Act II Scene 1: An Examination of the Music' in: *Peter Grimes: Cambridge Opera Handbooks*, ed. Philip Brett, Cambridge, Cambridge University Press, 1983, pp. 121-47.

'Berthold Goldschmidt: A Biographical Sketch', *Tempo* No. 144, March 1983, pp. 2-6.

'Berthold Goldschmidt: The Chamber and Instrumental Music', *Tempo* No. 145, June 1983, pp. 20-5.

'The String Quartets and Some Other Chamber Works' in: *The Britten Companion*, ed. Christopher Palmer, London, Faber and Faber, 1984, pp. 383-92.

'Mirror Upon Mirror Mirrored' in: *Michael Tippett OM: A Celebration*, ed. Geraint Lewis, Tunbridge Wells, The Baton Press Ltd., 1985, pp. 35-42.

'On the Mahler Phenomenon', *The Listener*, 10 July 1986, p. 35.

➤ '*Death in Venice* and the Third String Quartet' in: *Death in Venice: Cambridge Opera Handbooks*, ed. Donald Mitchell, Cambridge, Cambridge University Press, 1987, pp. 154-61.

'Czech Music from 1900 to the Present Day' in: *Czechoslovakia: The Unofficial Culture*, ed. Roger Scruton, London, Claridge Press in association with the Jan Hus Educational Foundation, 1987, pp. 170-81.

'The Rehabilitation of the Vernacular' in: *Music and the Politics of Culture*, ed. Christopher Norris, London, Lawrence and Wishart, 1989, pp. 240-51.

'Whistle While you Work', *The Independent*, 19 August 1989.

'Peter Sculthorpe at 60', *Tempo* No. 170, September 1989, pp. 12-17.

➤ 'Deryck Cooke's Performing Version of Mahler's Tenth Symphony: my own involvement, some notes on the evolution of the score, and some ethical problems' in: *Fragment or Completion?: Proceedings of the Mahler X Symposium, Utrecht 1986*, ed. Paul Op de Coul, The Hague, Universitaire Pers Rotterdam, 1991, pp. 60-73.

'David Matthews' in: *Contemporary Composers*, ed. Brian Morton and Pamela Collins, Chicago and London, St James Press, 1992, p. 632.

➤ 'Living Traditions', *The Musical Times*, Vol. 134, No. 1802, April 1993, pp. 189-91.

'Landscape in British Music' in: *Towards a New Landscape*, ed. Bernard Jacobson, Bernard Jacobson Limited, 1993, pp. 70-6.

'The Flaying of Marsyas', *Salisbury Review*, Vol. 12, No. 3, March 1994, pp. 12-14.

➤ 'In Search of Mahler's Childhood' in: *On Mahler and Britten: Essays in Honour of Donald Mitchell on His Seventieth Birthday*, Woodbridge, Suffolk, The Boydell Press, 1995, pp. 89-93.

'Mahler and *Parsifal*', *Muziek & Wetenschap*, Vol. V, No. 3, 1995/96, pp. 385-404.

'Berthold Goldschmidt 1903-1996', *Professional Composer*, No. 39, Summer 1997, p. 6.

'The Music of the English Pastoral' in: *Town and Country*, ed. Anthony Barnett and Roger Scruton, London, Jonathan Cape, 1998, pp. 81-90.

'Tippett Symphony No. 4', *BBC Music Magazine*, March 1998.

'The Sixth Symphony' in: *The Mahler Companion*, ed. Donald Mitchell and Andrew Nicholson, Oxford, Oxford University Press, 1999, pp. 366-75.

'Wagner, Lipiner, and the "Purgatorio"' in: *The Mahler Companion*, ed. Donald Mitchell and Andrew Nicholson, Oxford, Oxford University Press, 1999, pp. 508-16.

▸ 'The Middle Way' (on Berthold Goldschmidt), *Salisbury Review*, Vol. 17, No. 3, Spring 1999, pp. 12-15.

▸ 'Renewing the Past, Some Personal Thoughts' in: *Reviving the Muse: Essays on Music after Modernism*, ed. Peter Davison, Brinkworth, Claridge Press, 2001, pp. 199-212.

'Berthold Goldschmidt', *BBC Music Magazine*, March 2003, pp. 42-5.

'Foreword' to: *The Selected Letters of Michael Tippett*, ed. Thomas Schuttenhelm, London, Faber & Faber, 2005, p. xi-xiv.

'The Music of Dawn' in: *In Celebration of Cecil Collins*, London, Foolscap, 2008, p. 269.

'David Drew: Tributes and Memories (I)', *Tempo*, No. 252, April 2010, p. 18.

▸ 'My New Music', *Musical Opinion*, Vol. 133, No. 478, September-October 2010, pp. 16-17.

'Music to My Ears', *BBC Music Magazine*, July 2010, pp. 18-19.

'Gustav Mahler – Life and Death', *Musical Opinion*, Vol. 134, No. 140, January-February 2011, pp. 20-1.

'Thoughts on the Second Symphony' (on Malcolm Arnold) in: *Composers on the 9*, Buckingham, Queen's Temple Publications, 2011, p. 121.

'Robin Walker at 60', *Tempo*, No. 265, July 2013, pp. 50-6.

~

There is also a series of short columns in the *Radio Times* between 1966 and 1968.

3 Book Reviews

'Affirmations and Ambiguities', review of Arnold Whittall, *The Music of Britten and Tippett: Studies in Themes and Techniques*, in: *Times Literary Supplement*, 27 August 1982.

Review of Ronald Duncan, *Working with Britten: A Personal Memoir*, in: *Tempo* No. 143, December 1982, pp. 34-5.

'Gothic Monumentality', review of Gerald Abraham, *The Age of Beethoven 1970-1830, Volume VIII, The New Oxford History of Music*, in: *Times Literary Supplement*, 31 December 1982.

'Purest of Romantics', review of David Brown, *Tchaikovsky: A Biographical and Critical Study. Volume II: The Crisis Years (1874-1878)*, in: *The Times Educational Supplement*, 22 April 1983.

'Focus on Perception', review of David Pryce-Jones, *Cyril Connolly: Journal and Memoir*, in: *The Times Educational Supplement*, 29 July 1983.

'Exception', review of Joan Chissell, *Clara Schumann: A Dedicated Spirit*, in: *The Times Educational Supplement*, 21 October 1983.

Review of *Boult on Music*, in: *Tempo* No. 148, March 1984, pp. 48-9.

'Serious and Popular', review of Denis Arnold, ed., *The New Oxford Companion to Music*, in: *Times Education Supplement*, 18 May 1984.

'A Note of Loneliness', review of Paul Griffiths, *Bartók*, in: *Times Literary Supplement*, 10 August 1984.

'Strings Attached', review of Paul Griffiths, *The String Quartet*, in: *The Times Educational Supplement*, 17 December 1984.

Review of Herta Blaukopf, *Gustav Mahler, Richard Strauss: Correspondence 1888-1911*, in: *Tempo* No. 152, March 1985, pp. 41-2.

'Intermezzo', review of David Brown, *Tchaikovsky. Volume III: The Years of Wandering, 1878-1885*, in: *The Times Educational Supplement*, 19 September 1986.

'Pulpit Thunder', review of Pierre Boulez, *Orientations*, in: *The Times Educational Supplement*, 16 January 1987.

'From Romance to Ritual', review of Jann Pasler, ed., *Confronting Stravinsky: Man, Musician and Modernist*, in: *Times Literary Supplement*, 13 February 1987.

'Reorientation', review of Pierre Boulez, *Orientations*, in: *Salisbury Review*, Vol. 5, No. 3, April 1987, pp. 39-42.

'Composing Themselves', review of various composers' writings, in: *The Times Educational Supplement*, 24 April 1987.

'Splendid Inconsistency', review of Tim Page, ed., *The Glenn Gould Reader*, in: *The Times Educational Supplement*, 3 July 1987.

'Drafting the Resurrection', review of Gustav Mahler, *Symphony No. 2 in C minor ('Resurrection') Facsimile*, in: *Times Literary Supplement*, 17 July 1987.

'Ambivalent Requiem', review of David Fanning, *The Breath of the Symphonist: Shostakovich's Tenth*, in: *Times Literary Supplement*, 19 August 1988.

Review of Wilfrid Mellers, *Vaughan Williams and the Vision of Albion*, in: *Tempo* No. 171, December 1989, pp. 39-40.

'The Secret Programme', review of Douglas Jarman, ed., *The Berg Companion*, in: *Times Literary Supplement*, 13 April 1990.

'Romanticism in Unlikely Corners', review of Douglas Jarman, *Alban Berg: Lulu*, in: *Times Literary Supplement*, 26 April 1991.

'Ambiguous Utterances', review of Anthony Pople, *Berg: Violin Concerto*, in: *Times Literary Supplement*, 23 August 1991.

'Looking Forward to the Millennium', review of Michael Tippett, *Those Twentieth Century Blues*, in: *The Musical Times*, Vol. 132, No. 1784, October 1991, pp. 511-12.

'That Carefree Feeling', review of Peter Franklin, *Mahler: Symphony No. 3*, in: *Times Literary Supplement*, 10 April 1992.

'The World, the Universe, and Everything', review of Boris Ford, ed., *The Cambridge Cultural History*, in: *Modern Painters*, Vol. 5 No. 3, Autumn 1992, pp. 110-11.

➤ Review of Humphrey Carpenter, *Benjamin Britten. A Biography*, in: *BBC Music Magazine*, September 1992.

'Perverse Genius', review of William Thomson, *Schoenberg's Error*, in: *Salisbury Review*, September 1992, p. 69.

'Love Song for Alma', review of Gustav Mahler, *Adagietto*, in: *Times Literary Supplement*, 13 November 1992.

'Symphonic Voices', review of Robert Layton, ed., *A Companion to the Symphony*, in: *BBC Music Magazine*, May 1993, p. 94.

Review of Jean-Jacques Nattiez, ed., *The Boulez-Cage Correspondence*, in: *BBC Music Magazine*, February 1994, pp. 43.

> 'This What You Call Music?', review of Andrew Ford, *Composer to Composer*, in: *Times Literary Supplement*, 27 May 1994, p. 17.

'Radical Angst', review of John C. Crawford and Dorothy L. Crawford, *Expressionism in Twentieth Century Music*, in: *Times Literary Supplement*, 19 August 1994.

Review of Constantin Floros, *Gustav Mahler: The Symphonies*, in: *BBC Music Magazine*, October 1994, pp. 53.

Review of Boris Ford, ed., *Benjamin Britten's Poets*, in: *BBC Music Magazine*, November 1994, p. 55.

Review of Deborah Hayes, *Peter Sculthorpe: A Bio-bibliography*, in: *Tempo* No. 191, December 1994, pp. 45-6.

'One From the Heart', review of Donald Mitchell, *Cradles of the New*, in: *BBC Music Magazine*, May 1995, p. 53.

Review of Boris Ford, ed., *Benjamin Britten's Poets*, in: *Times Literary Supplement*, 22 September 1995.

'The Cycle of Seasons', review of Dorothy Lamb Crawford, *Evenings On and Off the Roof: Concerts in Los Angeles*, in: *Times Literary Supplement*, 19 July 1996.

'All Art is a Diary?', review of Ned Rorem, *Other Entertainment*, in: *Times Literary Supplement*, 17 January 1997, p. 9.

'Mind-boggling Mahler', review of Jonathan Carr, *The Real Mahler*, in: *BBC Music Magazine*, October 1997, p. 19.

> 'To the Point of Chaos', review of Jan Swafford, *Charles Ives. A Life with Music*, and Philip Lambert, *The Music of Charles Ives*, in: *Times Literary Supplement*, 28 November 1997.

'Nothing of the Circus', review of Erik W. Tawaststjerna, *Sibelius. Volume Three: 1914-1957*, in: *Times Literary Supplement*, 3 April 1998.

Review of Hans Werner Henze, *Bohemian Fifths*, in: *BBC Music Magazine*, January 1999, p. 86.

> 'His Relationship with Time', review of David Clarke, *Tippett Studies*, in: *Times Literary Supplement*, 21 May 1999.

'That Intimate, Familiar Sense', review of John Caldwell, *The Oxford History of English Music*, in: *Times Literary Supplement*, 19 November 1999.

'No, No, Adorno', review of Jonathan Cross, *The Stravinsky Legacy*, in: *The Musical Times*, Vol. 140, No. 1869, Winter 1999, pp. 68-9.

➤ 'Debts and Credits', review of Stephen Walsh, *Stravinsky: A Creative Spring*, in: *The Musical Times*, Vol. 141, No. 1871, Summer 2000, p. 72-3.

'Symphony of a Thousand', review of Henry-Louis de La Grange, *Gustav Mahler, Vol. 3: Vienna: Triumph and Disillusion (1904-1907)*, in: *BBC Music Magazine*, July 2000, p. 96.

'Kristallnachtmusic', review of Michael H. Kater, *Composers of the Nazi Era*, in: *Times Literary Supplement*, 17 November 2000.

'Art – Books in Brief', review of Paul Allen, ed., *Art, Not Change*, in: *Times Literary Supplement*, 10 August 2001.

'Enriching Influence', review of Christina Bashford and Leanne Langley, eds., *Music and British Culture, 1785-1914. Essays in Honour of Cyril Ehrlich*, in: *Times Literary Supplement*, 24 August 2001.

Review of Philip Rupprecht, *Britten's Musical Language*, in: *BBC Music Magazine*, May 2002, p. 107.

'Music', review of Richard Osborne, *Till I End My Song*, in: *Times Literary Supplement*, 4 October 2002.

'The Village Inn with the Blues', review of Suzanne Robinson, ed., *Michael Tippett, Music and Literature*, in: *Times Literary Supplement*, 25 April 2003.

'The Unperformed', review of James Fenton, *The Love Bomb and Other Musical Pieces*, in: *Times Literary Supplement*, 16 January 2004.

'A Wistful Sophisticate', review of Daniel M. Grimley and Julian Rushton, eds., *The Cambridge Companion to Elgar*, and Jerrold Northrop Moore, *Elgar*, in: *Times Literary Supplement*, 11 March 2005.

➤ 'Pieces in Our Time', review of Patricia Hall and Friedemann Sallis, eds., *A Handbook to Twentieth-Century Musical Sketches*, in: *Times Literary Supplement*, 12 August 2005, p. 26.

➤ 'Form-Compelling', review of Joseph Kerman, *The Art of Fugue: Bach Fugues for Keyboard 1715-50*, in: *London Review of Books*, 21 September 2006, p. 27-9.

➤ 'Lucky Thirteen', review of John Bridcut, *Britten's Children*, in: *Times Literary Supplement*, 10 November 2006, p. 6.

'Key Figures', review of Edward W. Said, *Music at the Limits*, and Catherine Parsons Smith, *Making Music in Los Angeles*, in: *Times Literary Supplement*, 25 July 2008.

> Review of Alex Ross, *The Rest is Noise: Listening to the Twentieth Century*, in: *Musical Opinion*, Vol. 132, No. 1471, July-August 2009, pp. 12-14.

'Tennis with Gershwin', review of Dorothy Lamb Crawford, *A Windfall of Musicians*, in: *Times Literary Supplement*, 9 July 2010.

Review of Robert Riggs, *Leon Kirchner: Composer, Performer and Teacher*, in: *Tempo* No. 258, October 2011, pp. 60-1.

'Refuge in the Forest', review of Daniel M. Grimley, ed., *Jean Sibelius and His World*, in: *Times Literary Supplement*, 27 January 2012.

4   Concert and Recording Reviews

'Copland Folk Opera', review of Aaron Copland, *The Tender Land*, Chelsea Town Hall, in: *The Daily Telegraph*, 30 November 1965.

'Fervour Lacking', review of F. J. Haydn, *Tobias*, Handel Opera Society, St Pancras Town Hall, in: *The Daily Telegraph*, 2 December 1965.

'Many Things to Admire in *Il trovatore*', review of Figaro Opera Group, Hawkey Hall, Woodford Green, in: *Walthamstow Guardian*, 1 April 1966.

'Britten's *Prodigal Son*', in: *Tempo* No. 85, Summer 1968, pp. 28-30.

'Henze's *El Cimarrón*', in: *Tempo* No. 94, Autumn 1970, pp. 24-6. (See also: 'Hans Werner Henze: An Apology', *Tempo* No. 96, Spring 1971, p. 24.)

LP review of Peter Maxwell Davies, *Hymn to St Magnus*; *Psalm 124*; *Renaissance Scottish Dances*, in: *Tempo* No. 121, June 1977, pp. 42-3.

LP review of Michael Tippett, Orchestral Works, in: *Tempo* No. 121, June 1977, pp. 43-4.

LP review of Bohuslav Martinů, Violin Concerto Nos. 1 and 2, in: *Tempo* No. 124, March 1978, pp. 48-9.

LP review of Nicholas Maw, *The Voice of Love*; *La Vita Nuova*, in: *Tempo* No. 140, March 1982, pp. 40-1.

'Busily Bacchic', review of Richard Strauss, *Ariadne on Naxos*, London Coliseum, in: *Times Literary Supplement*, 7 October 1983.

LP review of Benjamin Britten, *Temporal Variations*, etc., in: *Tempo* No. 147, December 1983, pp. 41-2.

LP review of Anthony Milner, Orchestral Works, in: *Tempo* No. 156, March 1986, pp. 24-5.

'The Flourishing Tradition of Janacek [*sic*] and Bear Steaks', review of the Brno Music Festival, in: *The Independent*, 21 October 1986.

'Breakfasting with Mahler', in: *The Independent*, 21 November 1986.

'Trial and Transcendence', review of Benjamin Britten, *Billy Budd*, London Coliseum, in: *Times Literary Supplement*, 4 March 1988.

'Surface Sensations', review of Tony Palmer's film *Testimony*, in: *Times Literary Supplement*, 20 May 1988.

'A Master of Endings', review of Benjamin Britten, *Death in Venice*, Glyndebourne Touring Opera, in: *Times Literary Supplement*, 3 November 1989, p. 1213.

'Forest Folk', review of Leoš Janáček, *The Cunning Little Vixen*, Royal Opera House, in: *Times Literary Supplement*, 22 June 1990.

CD review of Berthold Goldschmidt, Chamber Music, in: *Tempo* No. 178, September 1991, pp. 46-7.

'Royal Splendours', review of Michael Tippett, *King Priam*, London Coliseum, in: *Times Literary Supplement*, 17 February 1995.

Review of 'Deal Festival: Pavel Novák', in: *Tempo* No. 227, January 2004, pp. 59-60.

Review of Benjamin Britten: *Plymouth Town*, Royal College of Music, London, in: *Tempo* No. 230, October 2004, pp. 57-8.

Review of Pavel Novák concert, St Giles, Cripplegate, London, in: *Tempo* No. 244, April 2008, pp. 34-5.

Review of LPO/Vladimir Jurowski/Barnabás Kelemen, in: *Musical Opinion*, Vol. 134, No. 1482, May-June 2011, p. 50-1.

Review of LPO/Jurowski/Jansen, in: *Musical Opinion*, Vol. 134, No. 1484, September-October 2011, p. 56.

~

There are also contributions to the 'Last Week's Broadcast Music' column in *The Listener* between 1970 and 1971.

5   Editions

Deryck Cooke, *Gustav Mahler: An Introduction to His Music*, manuscript prepared and updated by Colin and David Matthews, London, Faber, 1988.

Michael Tippett, *A Child of Our Time*, with editorial preface, London, Eulenburg, 2007.

Michael Tippett, *Piano Concerto*, with editorial preface, London, Eulenburg, 2007.

Michael Tippett, *Ritual Dances from 'The Midsummer Marriage'*, with editorial preface, London, Eulenburg, 2007.

Ralph Vaughan Williams, *Concerto for Bass Tuba and Orchestra*, with editorial preface and textual notes, Oxford, Oxford University Press, 2012.

Ralph Vaughan Williams, *Sinfonia Antartica*, with editorial preface and textual notes, Oxford, Oxford University Press, 2012.

$\sim$

There are also several CD liner notes for commercial recordings, including music by Britten, Mahler, Schumann and David Matthews himself.

Index

Above: Colin and David Matthews in 1988 (Jane Bown)
*Below: Sally Cavender, Jenifer Wakelyn, David Matthews and
John Carewe at the Presteigne Festival in 2012* (Jolita Vadopalaite)

Index